Ben Lopez was born in New York and spent part of his childhood in Venezuela, where he witnessed first hand the devastating effects of Kidnap for Ransom (K&R). His work has taken him across the globe, from Mexico to Colombia to the Middle East. In more than twenty years in the K&R field he has never lost a hostage. Ben Lopez isn't his real name. If he told you it, it would be too dangerous for him to travel to many countries ever again. He lives in London.

THE NEGOTIATOR

MY LIFE AT THE HEART OF
THE HOSTAGE TRADE

Ben Lopez

sphere

SPHERE

First published in Great Britain in 2011 by Sphere
Reprinted 2011
This paperback edition published in 2012 by Sphere

A CIP catalogue record for this book
is available from the British Library.

ISBN 978-0-7515-4766-5

Typeset in Bembo by M Rules
Printed and bound in Great Britain by
Clays Ltd, St Ives plc

Papers used by Sphere are from well-managed forests
and other responsible sources.

MIX
Paper from
responsible sources
FSC® C104740

Sphere
An imprint of
Little, Brown Book Group
100 Victoria Embankment
London EC4Y 0DY

An Hachette UK Company
www.hachette.co.uk

www.littlebrown.co.uk

This book is dedicated to my dear D for your love,
gentle patience and unflagging faith.
Without those, I could never have finished it.

This book is also dedicated to my G and my L.
You make me so proud I could burst.

Author's Note

We live in dangerous times.

Terrorism, recession, the proliferation of cheap weapons and the globalisation of organised crime have made kidnapping one of the most lucrative growth markets in the criminal underworld. It's an industry that is now worth more than $1 billion a year and that's just the cases we know about. It's the tip of the iceberg.

The business of ensuring the safe return of hostages falls to the hands of a trusted few: hostage negotiators. These men and women work tirelessly to bring a peaceful end to hostile and potentially deadly crises. Their work is carried out in the shadows: away from the media glare, in situation rooms and negotiator cells in some of the most desperate and desolate places on earth.

None of us seek out the limelight. But I believe it's important the world knows the work we do and the sacrifices we make. The names of all the people and organisations have been changed, as have the locations. Dialogues are not verbatim and should not be treated as such.

Everything in this book, however, is based on actual events.

May you be safe, well and happy.

Ben Lopez
London, June 2011

'**Kidnapping**.
The deliberate **creation** and **marketing** of human **grief**,
anguish and **despair**.'

Tom Hargrove, FARC Hostage
Day 325 of 334, 1994
Somewhere in the jungles of Colombia

'He who saves **one** life,
saves the world **entire**.'

Talmud

'**Knowledge** dispels **fear**.'

Motto of the Parachute Training School,
Australian Army

Contents

PART FIVE: BAD BLOOD

PART SIX: PIRATES

Acknowledgements

You wouldn't be holding this book in your hand if it weren't for another man named Ben. Not long ago he changed my life for ever by suggesting it be written.

It was his idea and he guided it masterfully from conception to fruition. For this and many other reasons, he is the World's Greatest Agent. I look forward to more adventures with him.

Special thanks go to Tim, for his astonishing talent, patience and friendship. Special thanks also go to Adam, for taking the risk on this book and me.

I'd also like to acknowledge Iain, Maddie and everyone else at Sphere who made this book happen.

My most sincere and humble thanks go to the many other people who for security and other reasons I can't name. These include former hostages and their families, clients past and present, fellow response consultants, law-enforcement professionals and others who've given generously of their time and experience. Your experience, dedication and generosity have given me so much that I can never repay it. I'll keep trying anyway.

Any mistakes or liberties taken are entirely mine.

Kidnap For Ransom: A Snapshot

- More than 20,000 kidnappings are reported each year.

- Only 1 in 10 of these is reported to the authorities.

- The number of kidnappings around the world has increased by 100 per cent in the past twelve months.

- Over 50 per cent of all kidnappings take place in Latin America.

- 70 per cent of kidnappings result in a ransom payment; only 10 per cent of hostages are rescued by force.

- 78 per cent of abductions occur within 200 metres of the victim's home or workplace.

- Most kidnaps happen on weekday mornings.

- Ransom demands range from $5000 to $100 million.

- Mexico experiences 7000 reported kidnappings each year. The real figure is much higher.

- In Colombia there are ten kidnappings per day, with only 3 per cent of kidnappers prosecuted. By contrast, 95 per cent of kidnappings in the USA result in prosecution.

- 90 per cent of kidnappings globally are of locals, not expats or tourists.

- In London, insurance premiums for K&R (kidnap for ransom) bring in over $130 million per annum.

- 21: the percentage of hostages in Latin America who survive rescue attempts.

Abduction – Captivity – Proof of Life –
Negotiation – Ransom Drop – Release

Part One

END GAME

'Play any trics and I will mutilate the package.'

Zeze

1

THE PACKAGE

'I have the money.'

'Good.'

'I have it here to the last cent.'

The voice on the other end of the line was tense. 'Divide the money into two. Put half in a black bin bag and the other in an identical bag.'

'Okay.'

'No false or marked notes.'

The communicator said, 'I guarantee the money isn't marked.'

'And I want you to buy a pre-paid cell phone.' The kidnapper was barking orders in staccato bursts, anxious not to make the call last a second longer than necessary.

The communicator said, 'Okay.'

'The package has a chauffeur. His name is Henrique. You are to use him to deliver the money. Give him the cell phone then wait for my call. Try playing any tricks and I will mutilate the package.'

'You have my—'

Click.

The communicator, Luis Feola, breathed out like he was coming up for air. He stared blankly at the screen of his BlackBerry Bold. The guy on the other end of the line was known only as 'Zeze'. He was a professional kidnapper whose gang of toughs had abducted Luis's brother, Diego, seven days previously, snatching him at gunpoint from his silver BMW E90 as he was clocking off work. Zeze was no fool. He'd played the kidnapping game for longer than a little while. But he was uneducated and greedy. And something about Zeze's demands just did not seem right.

Luis lifted his eyes to meet mine. I removed the headphones and said, 'We're in the end game now. But this is very important. Next time he calls, you have to be absolutely clear and immovable on that point.'

Luis nodded at his shoes. He had been a cycling champion in a past life. Not that you could tell it by looking at him. The Luis of today sported a jowly face, pasty complexion, portly frame and a belly that betrayed a sedentary lifestyle of too many caipirinhas and tapas lunches. Luis had quit the road in his early thirties to go into business with his brother. They ran a shipping firm that exported luxury goods to Europe. Luis did the day-to-day stuff, younger brother Diego brokered the deals and ran the shipping. Now Luis was having to play the role of communicator in securing the release of his little brother.

They say the two most dangerous parts of any kidnap are the abduction and the exchange. I don't own a gun and I can't predict the future, so there's not much I can do about somebody being abducted. But I'm plenty good at influencing the exchange. That was where I came in to help the Feola family.

'When will he call?'

'Soon,' I said. 'A couple of hours.' I made for the meeting room door. 'Hang by the phone. I'm going to brief the family. If he calls, you come get me.'

We were conducting negotiations from the brothers' offices in the Campo Grande district of the West Zone, an hour's drive from Copacabana beach and the famous Rio de Janeiro nightlife. Not that I'd seen any of it. Campo Grande had a bunch of modern offices and the Church of Our Lady of the Exile and a view overlooking the surfers' beaches at Barra da Tijuca. It wasn't a buzzing place, but then again, I wasn't here for the sightseeing.

Brazil has the third highest number of kidnaps per year anywhere in the world. Rio de Janeiro and Sao Paulo are the hotbeds. In recent years there has been a marked shift away from the overtly wealthy as the gangs instead target the middle classes, with ransom demands lowered so that they can secure a quick payday. In 2005 a new trend emerged: targeting the families of footballers.

'Where are you going?' Luis asked as I grabbed my coat.

'The family home,' I said. 'I need to brief the committee.'

Diego Feola lived in a palatial mansion located inside a gated community half a mile from Copacabana beach, the kind of place where wealth has insulated itself against the extreme poverty encircling it on all sides. In this case, the slum favelas and shanty towns that crawled up Rio's hillside, where the drug gangs were engaged in a constant running battle with the police. In a country like Brazil, where the gap between rich and poor is more like a yawning gulf, there are dozens of such gated communities.

I drove my rented Chevrolet Corsa sedan straight to the house. Traffic was light; the drive took a little over thirty minutes. Flashing my identification papers at the guard stationed at the bronze gates, I pointed the Chevrolet up the smooth blacktop flanked by manicured lawns and parked at the front of the Feola place. I was greeted at the door by a maid. She led me down the marble-floored hallway to the living room, where I found Diego's wife, Lara, and his father, Humberto.

Lara was classically beautiful. She had long dark hair, an hourglass figure shrinkwrapped inside a black knee-length dress with a plunging neckline, and alluring green eyes. I had never met the family before Diego's abduction, but I guessed Humberto had looked a lot healthier a month ago. He was gaunt and pale, as if the colour had drained from his face into his feet. He was sitting up straight on the edge of the sofa alternately wringing his hands or running them through his cobweb-coloured hair. Lara paced up and down, wearing a groove into the floor. The clicking of her high heels echoed around the whitewashed room.

'It's almost time,' I said, searching their eyes. Reading their body language. They were both anxious. Very anxious. But both were struggling to keep a lid on it.

Humberto asked, 'How much?'

'Half a million.'

'That's a lot of money,' he grumbled. Half a million reals was equivalent to a touch under $400,000 US.

'But a lot less than we might have paid,' Lara said. She smiled a kind of tired, weary smile at me. I'd seen the same on the faces of dozens of hostages' relatives.

'You're doing a great job,' she said.

'We're not out of the woods yet. There's an issue with the driver.'

Lara reached for a pack of Marlboro Reds on the coffee table. Humberto said, 'What issue?'

'The kidnappers are demanding that Diego's chauffeur be the one to make the exchange. Name of Henrique?' I raised my eyebrows at Lara. She appeared distracted. 'I need to know we can trust this guy.'

'What if we tell him no, someone else will deliver the money?' Humberto asked, looking from me to Lara and back again.

I shook my head. 'Won't work. The kidnappers might see you as another target.'

'So let Henrique do it.'

I said to Lara, 'How well do you know this guy?'

She jerked her shoulders and lit her cigarette. 'He's a driver. What else can I say?'

'You can give me a reason to trust him or not,' I said.

Lara took a long pull on her cigarette and blew smoke at the ceiling. The ornamental fan sliced and diced the smoke. 'I was in Porto Alegre when I heard that my husband had been kidnapped. It was Henrique who called to tell me. He told me I should get on the next plane. You know that same day he personally came to pick up my car and drive it back all the way here.' She looked away and added, 'I trust him.'

'Call him,' I said, giving my back to Humberto and Lara and preparing to return to Campo Grande. I hadn't slept in more than twenty-four hours. My bed at the Hilton Hotel had never seemed so inviting. But I had to stay focused. I needed to prepare briefing notes for what I hoped would be the next and final dialogue between Zeze and Luis. The clock was ticking.

Two hours later Humberto had sorted the money and divided it into the bin bags. I was drinking my sixth double espresso of the day at the company offices when Zeze called again. Luis answered. I put the headphones on and listened in as he read from my list of instructions.

Luis said, 'I would like to speak with Diego.'

'No!' Zeze snapped. Dogs were barking and yapping in the background. I could hear two female voices shouting over each other. 'Give me a question instead. You must trust me.'

'Look, Zeze. I'm going to deliver a mountain of money to you. I need to speak to my brother.'

'Doesn't matter to me.'

Luis gritted his teeth and closed his eyes. Sweat percolated down his forehead, drops of it drip-dripping into his eyes. 'Zeze, please. I need to speak to Diego. I want to do this but before we do business I need to know he's okay.'

Zeze was giving us the silent treatment. I urged Luis to keep pressing. In kidnap-for-ransom cases the response consultant, the industry term for hostage negotiators, rarely communicates directly with the kidnapper. More often that task is left to a family member or a trusted co-worker. In this case, Zeze had demanded that Luis be the one taking his calls. Luis had done well under the extreme pressure, but he sometimes struggled to impose his will on the dialogue. More than ever, I needed him to stay strong now.

'We're ready to go ahead,' Luis said, eyes flitting back and forth from me to the notes in front of him. 'We've got the money, we've put it in the bin bags like you asked. This is a sign of good faith from us. Now let me hear my brother's voice.'

We heard the dogs yap-yapping and the angry women bitch-bitching, but not so much as a shallow breath came out of Zeze. Finally, he said, 'Wait for a call. Then you can speak with him. There better not be any police.'

Zeze killed the line.

At 4.35 p.m. I was back at the Feola family home running through the exchange plan with Humberto and Lara and a friend of the family by the name of Jorge. On a family K&R case one of the first things I do is establish a committee made up of the lowest odd number of the hostage's family members possible. This committee convenes to discuss the options on the table and votes to decide on how to manage the case, how much to offer at various points, etc. I want a small committee to minimise the number of egos I have to massage, nerves to soothe and asses to kick. I want an odd number so there can be no deadlocks. In this case, the other two members of the committee were Humberto and Jorge.

THE PACKAGE

My iPhone buzzed. It was Luis. I tapped ACCEPT. He sounded ecstatic about something. He'd received a call from an unknown number and when he answered he immediately recognised the voice as Diego's. The call, Luis said, lasted twenty seconds. Diego managed to say that he was okay and according to Luis he seemed to be in good spirits. This was a good sign. We were within touching distance of the finish line.

But something didn't feel right.

Lara stubbed out another cigarette in the ashtray like she was tapping out Morse code and said to me, 'Can I speak with you for a moment?'

'Sure.'

She did a thing with her eyes that said, *In private.*

I checked my watch. It was 5.15 p.m. Zeze said he would call again at six-thirty with instructions for the ransom drop. I could feel each second ticking inside my head as I followed Lara towards the kitchen and out through the rear doors into a garden that in a smaller country could easily double as a national park.

Rio de Janeiro is at its coldest in August. The city gets battered by coastal breezes blowing inshore, winding the temperature down to the low twenties. To make matters worse, Antarctica sends wave after wave of grey cloud and freezing rain over the city, often triggering fatal mudslides in the surrounding mountainous areas. I stepped outside and felt the cold, wet air prick my skin.

'What's going on?' I asked.

Lara put another Marlboro to her lips. 'There's something I need to tell you.' Her breathing was shallow and erratic. Whatever she was hiding, I could see it was eating her up inside.

'Go on,' I said.

'No one else is to know about this.'

Go on.'

'It's about Henrique.'

9

'What about him?' I asked, a tingling sensation working its way along my right thumb and forefinger.

'My second marriage was a disaster. His name was Carlito. He was a bodyguard for a very important politician. This politician was corrupt and so were the men who worked for him.' She exhaled heavily. 'Including Carlito.'

'And you think your ex-husband is involved in this somehow?'

'I don't know. Perhaps. He used to be a policeman too.'

'Henrique?'

Lara nodded. 'The bodyguards and the police used to go drinking together. People say, the police kidnap more than the kidnappers.'

I stayed quiet for a while as I soaked up this new information. I had no reason to doubt Lara's suspicions about her ex-husband. Corruption is the norm, not the exception in many Latin American countries and the police are often responsible for, or complicit in, many, perhaps most kidnappings. This is the over-riding reason why many families in Mexico or Colombia, for example, will not call the police when they learn that a relative has been abducted.

'We need to tell the rest of the committee,' I said.

She didn't like that, but said nothing as she followed me into the living room where, at my behest, Lara revealed to both Humberto and Jorge the secret history of her second husband. Humberto took it well. As far as he was concerned, the past was past. What he – and all of us – were concerned about, was how this was going to affect the ransom drop.

Zeze's request for Henrique to be the driver had puzzled me. How did Zeze even know who Henrique was? The demand was highly unusual, but it tallied with what Lara had just revealed about her ex.

I said, 'It's dollars to donuts that this is an inside job. Henrique would be the perfect inside man. Diego is his boss. He knows

Diego's schedule, all his movements, the weaknesses in his security.'

'And,' Humberto added, 'he was off work the day Diego was kidnapped.'

'How convenient.' I turned to Lara. She had found something utterly fascinating in her fingernails and was scrutinising them closely. 'You still talk to your ex-husband?'

Lara laughed weakly and said, 'It was a bad marriage and a worse divorce. We haven't spoken in four years.'

'But he still lives in Rio?'

'As far as I'm aware.'

'Then it's clear. There's no way we can let Henrique make that drop. If we do, chances are he'll pretend he got jacked, lost the ransom and we'll have to pay out twice. It's a classic kidnap swindle. No, Henrique is out of the question. Someone else has to do it.'

Problem was, Zeze had specifically requested Henrique. We needed a way of pulling the wool over his eyes. An idea flashed across my brain. I said, 'What does this Henrique guy look like?'

Lara dug her phone out of her purse and scrolled through the pictures gallery. 'He's tall, about your height. Light-skinned. Same blue eyes as you. And the big shoulders. In fact,' her voice drifted as her thumb paused on a camera shot, 'have a look for yourself.'

'What are you talking about?'

Lara handed me her BlackBerry Torch. I stared at a portrait shot of Henrique smiling into the camera. She was right. Henrique was practically my twin brother.

'Aw, hell,' I said.

I called Luis immediately.

'Where's Henrique?' I said. I felt everyone's eyes boring holes into me.

'I'm still about ten minutes from his house.'

'Listen carefully. Park at the side of the road and call him. Say you're stuck in traffic. Tell him that someone else will be along shortly to pick him up. Don't stay on the phone and don't invite any questions. I don't want the guy getting suspicious. Got it?'

'What's going on, Ben?'

'Henrique is dirty. We have to keep him away from here and occupied at all costs.'

'But Zeze thinks he's making the ransom drop.'

'I know.'

I terminated the call and paced back into the living room, Lara trailing in my wake. Humberto was nervously tapping his foot up and down like he had a tic. Of the three, Jorge seemed the calmest and most at ease. I made a note to speak privately to Humberto about his anxiety. He was on the heart drug Zonor, a mild medication that he took once a day. Kidnaps are one of the most stressful experiences a person can go through – perhaps more true for the relatives than it is for the hostage.

First though, I had to figure out a way to control the exchange. The answer was staring me in the face. Problem was, I didn't want to acknowledge it. You see, there are two golden rules that a negotiator should never, ever break. One, you don't use guns. Two, you don't do the exchange yourself.

I was about to break one of the two rules I swore I'd never break.

'Do me a favour,' I said to Humberto.

'What's that?'

'Get me Henrique's work uniform.'

At 6.31 p.m., Luis's BlackBerry sparked into life. He hit the green key while I stood close next to him to listen in. We were in Diego's study, which afforded us some peace and quiet away from the nervous energy unsettling the rest of the family.

Zeze said, 'Tell me what I want to hear.'

'The money is ready. Henrique is going to make the drop.'

'Let me speak to him.'

'He's on his way.'

Zeze seemed to accept this excuse without complaint. 'What car will he be driving?'

'A blue Honda Accord,' Luis said.

'And the cell phone?'

'We have it.'

'Give me the number.'

Luis cradled the BlackBerry on his shoulder as he frantically wrestled with the packaging on the burner. A burner is a pre-paid mobile phone and SIM card used to make one or two calls before being thrown away and thus impossible to track. For that reason they're popular with drug dealers.

I scribbled Luis a note.

Slow down and keep breathing, it read.

Switching on the phone, Luis located the number and recited it down the phone to Zeze. The kidnapper asked him to repeat it. 'Good,' Zeze said. 'Tell Henrique to head north on the motorway. I will be in touch.'

The call ended.

There was no time to lose.

Dressed in a black suit and pristine white shirt and black tie, I threw the two bin bags loaded with the ransom money on the front passenger seat of the Accord and set off north out of the city, leaving Jorge with instructions to pick up Henrique and make sure he didn't use his mobile phone. Luis was to be on standby beside his BlackBerry at all times. I would contact him immediately if anything seemed wrong, using my iPhone, which I would also be carrying. Lara was to keep a watchful eye on her father-in-law Humberto and do everything in her power to manage his stress levels.

As I neared the motorway the burner belted out a cheap tune. I answered on the second ring. Zeze spoke first. His voice was wavering. The tension was getting to him. Me too.

'Are you heading north?'

'*Sim*. Yes,' I said.

'Make a U-turn and head south.'

I eased my foot down on to the brake pedal and U-turned in the middle of the street. Zeze had planned this well because there was plenty of room to turn around. A catcall of car horns shrieked inside my ears. Irate drivers were the least of my problems. I was about to make the exchange with the kidnapper I'd been manipulating for the past week. And to make matters worse, I was impersonating someone who was part of the plot.

'Are you driving south now?' he asked.

I grunted, '*Sim*.'

'Head south until you join the Avenue of the Americas,' Zeze replied. 'Take the road west. Once you are past Sepetiba Bay you will see a sign indicating the route to Itaguai. Take the road all the way to Itaguai. When you enter the city head towards the Engenho neighbourhood. There is a footbridge. Park underneath it.'

I drove a steady fifty towards Itaguai, following Zeze's instructions to the letter. My hands gripped the wheel tight, like I was dangling over a precipice. I felt sweat leaking out of the palms of my hands and making the plastic wheel sticky. Sweat trickled down my spine. I've been doing hostage negotiations for the better part of twenty years, but nothing in the manual had prepared me for what I was about to do.

I hit Itaguai thirty-six minutes later and arrowed west towards Engenho. It was a grimy neighbourhood with all the usual hallmarks of civic neglect. Crumbling brick façades, gloomy warehouses and barren streets. The only nice building in sight was the local church. After several minutes navigating my way through the streets I spotted the footbridge. No sooner had I brought the Accord to a halt than Zeze was calling. He was obviously watching me. That's what I would do. He had spotters at key points along my route, ensuring that I followed his every command and that I was alone.

'Okay,' I said, glancing down the street in my rear-view mirror.

'Get out of the car. Take the bags and cross over the footbridge. When you reach the other side you will see a man dressed in a red, black and white Botafogo football club hoodie. Do not look at or speak to him. Drop the bags at his feet and immediately return to your car. Do not look back. Understood?'

Again I grunted, '*Sim.*'

I grabbed a bin bag with each hand and hurried up the footbridge. My heart was beating so hard I could feel it moving my sweaty shirt. Blood was rushing inside my ears. I was walking into the unknown. The guy in the Botafogo hoodie was visible on the far side of the footbridge. He was facing east, his profile side-on to me. He was dressed in black jeans and the red, black and white hoodie with the hood up. He pretended not to notice me.

What the hell are you doing, Ben?

At ten metres' distance the guy angled his body towards me and put his hands behind his back. He's got a gun, a voice inside me said. He's taking out his gun. He's going to grab the bags and pop one right between your eyes.

Five metres away and my legs were numb. Like someone had injected them with Novocaine.

Then I was two metres away, then one. I dumped the bin bags by his shoes. I noticed he was wearing scuffed Nike trainers. The white material had dirtied to a kind of arsenic grey. The man gave the bags a gentle tap with his left foot, as if testing their weight. I did a one-eighty and slowly paced back along the footbridge towards the Accord. My heart wasn't in my mouth. It was on the floor. With every footstep I waited for the gunshot.

It never came.

I slumped in the Accord and fumbled to put the key in the ignition. The hole suddenly seemed like the eye of a needle and the key the size of a log. I was exhausted. Every muscle in my body seemed to be coiled up with tension, but I felt weak. Collecting my thoughts, and after taking a deep breath, I fired up the Accord and took the return route towards Rio de Janeiro. Two minutes after I exited Itaguai, Zeze hit me on the burner.

'Throw the phone into the field.'

Those were the last words I heard Zeze speak.

At a random point on the toll road east I rolled down my window, removed the SIM card from the burner and chucked the phone over a wire fence into farmland. Then I fished out my iPhone and called Luis on the Feola household landline, just in case Zeze tried to reach Luis on the BlackBerry.

'It's done,' I said.

'My father wants to know, what happens now?'

'We wait,' I said.

Forty minutes later I arrived at the mansion. Lara, Luis and Humberto were in the living room. No one made eye contact. No one said a word. Everyone stood and stared at the BlackBerry lying on the glass coffee table, as if willing it to flash up with the call. I called Jorge from my iPhone. He was still escorting Henrique around town on a wild goose chase.

Two hours later and still no word from Diego.

'He's not calling,' Humberto panicked. He fell short of breath and lifted a hand to his chest. 'He's not coming home. They've killed him.'

'No,' I said. 'Kidnapping is a transaction. They got what they wanted.'

'Then why's he taking so long to call?'

'Maybe he's been taken to a hospital,' I said. That gave Lara an idea. She rang a special helpline that cross-checks every hospital and Red Cross clinic in the city for admissions. Using a fake name, she put in a request for Diego Feola. The search came up empty-handed.

Three hours since the drop. Humberto was picking at the calluses on his hands. 'Maybe they want more money.'

'I doubt it. That doesn't tie in with the final demand and the instructions to deliver the cash.'

One of my special skills is to make kidnappers feel like they have squeezed every red cent out of the victim's family. If they believed there was no more money on the table, there would be little point in making another ransom demand as Humberto was suggesting.

And then, at 10.49 p.m., the phone rang.

Luis scrambled for it.

'I'm on Copacabana, brother, all the way on the right end,' the voice said. 'I'm free.'

Twenty minutes later, Diego was reunited with his family. He had been blindfolded and handcuffed and taken from his cell into the back of a van that had dumped him on a side street in downtown Rio. He looked dishevelled, had a beard and sported a couple of bruises on his jaw and upper arms, but nothing serious.

As Luis, Humberto and Lara lined up to embrace Diego, I quietly slipped away and returned to the Hilton. I doubt the family even knew I'd gone. That's how it is for negotiators. We're there to reunite families torn apart by criminal gangs. And we'll do whatever it takes to bring the hostage back home safe.

Even if it means having to impersonate a chauffeur.

Abduction – **Captivity** – Proof of Life –
Negotiation – Ransom Drop – Release

Part Two

THE BUSINESS

'If you only have a hammer in your toolbox,
every problem is a nail.'

Lt Larry Bridge, Ph.D.
Commander (Ret.) NYPD Hostage Team

2

RUBBER CHICKEN

Police officers and soldiers carry guns to a hostage scene.

I carry a rubber chicken.

Several years ago I was invited by Scotland Yard to evaluate the national hostage negotiators' course held at the Peel Centre in Hendon. The course is closely modelled on the NYPD original. The guys at Scotland Yard decided that I was qualified to observe and provide feedback on the Peel course because of the high regard that they had for the NYPD course, which I had completed and helped design.

On each of the four training programmes held each year, at least one student will be a currently serving SAS officer or soldier. This helps to facilitate liaison between the law-enforcement and military teams during a hostage crisis. The SAS need to be aware of how the negotiators operate so they can integrate their activities with those of the police, and vice versa. To carry out an effective and peaceful operation, you need your hostage negotiators and armed response units – the hats and bats guys – singing from the same hymn sheet.

On my evaluation I was introduced to an SAS student on the course. He had shoulders shaped like arrow bows and hard as bags of nails. His name was Danny. He was a Geordie, a fitness fanatic – and one of the best negotiators I'd ever seen. Even though he used to joke that the negotiator's only job was to manoeuvre the perp in front of the window so a sniper could take him out, this guy absolutely got it. He understood the techniques and the mentality required of an expert negotiator. If I'm ever unfortunate enough to be taken hostage, Danny is the guy I'd want at the other end of the phone talking to the kidnappers.

I couldn't help but notice that during breaks and lunch periods, Danny produced a delicate porcelain teacup from his rucksack. Everyone else would be lining up at the coffee machine and filling up white styrofoam cups, while Danny would pour his into this dinky, feminine little teacup with pink and blue flowers painted around the sides.

'Why do you use that cup?' I asked him during a break.

'Because it pisses people off,' Danny replied.

'You carry that on operations too?'

'Don't leave home without it, mate.'

'You've gotta be kidding me!'

Whatever hellhole part of the world Danny inserted into, the teacup went with him. He'd be in the most uncivilised, backward part of the world, drenched in rain, covered in mud and filth, shitting into a plastic bag while manning an observation post for weeks at a time, and he'd be drinking his brew from the daintiest, most beautiful porcelain teacup you'd ever seen. The thing looked miniature and ridiculously fragile in his enormous granite hands. I was fascinated by this teacup and what it meant: why would someone take such a thing into hellhole combat zones?

The answer is that it allowed Danny to project a sense of complete mastery of his world to everyone else around him. You've got to be *somebody* to be able to cart this teacup safely round the globe and use it on a battlefield. It brings order to a situation that is, by definition, chaotic.

Danny then told me a story about a buddy in the same troop as him. Name of Tyrone. This guy had a habit of stashing a comic rubber chicken in the webbing that overlaid his combat gear. I was mystified as to why the guy would carry a rubber chicken into combat. For the same reason, I asked, that Danny packed his teacup when he shipped out to whatever catastrophe needed fixing? Not quite, Danny replied.

'Whenever things get a little dramatic, Ty looks at his webbing and thinks, It can't be that bad, I have a rubber chicken.'

This is a stroke of genius.

On the corner of the street I live on in London there's a magic store. That same day I popped inside and bought myself a rubber chicken. Ever since, that rubber chicken has been with me on every single hostage negotiation and kidnapping case I've worked on. I don't carry it out of luck or superstition – I don't believe in luck. It's more a reminder for those stressful moments when you've got the blinkers on, you're in tunnel-vision mode and focusing on how badly things are going with the case, the hostage is going to die and it's going to be your fault and your life and everyone else's will be ruined . . . in those dire moments, I look at my chicken and think to myself, You know what? Things can't be that bad. I've got a rubber chicken. It's a small thing, but it helps me get back to reality and appreciate the absurdity of the situation.

The atmosphere inside a negotiator's cell can get incredibly tense. Sometimes it feels like everything is tight: the air you're breathing, the chair you're sitting on, the faces of the people around you. Athletes who feel this way usually fail to perform when it comes to the big stage. Tension affects negotiators in a similar way. We can freeze up in our thinking. But like a great joke or a good night's sleep, the chicken helps to keep me loose. When the kidnappers are giving you hell and the client is giving you hell, when you're going back each night to an empty, lonely hotel room and you can't sleep because you're worried about the case, when you wake up the next day having barely slept a wink and the world seems darker because you're sleep-deprived – that naked, comedy chicken loosens me up every time.

It's also got an added benefit of coming in handy at checkpoints. It's never failed to get me through. As a negotiator I've had to cross over from Israel to Gaza or Ramallah in the Occupied Territories a million times. Getting into the Territories isn't easy. Making the return trip to Israel is even more fraught. But IDF soldiers at the checkpoints always laugh when they find the chicken in my pack. It lightens the mood.

I've yet to meet a border guard who doesn't laugh at the sight of the rubber chicken. There are bombs that can bust open bunkers and assault rifles capable of firing a thousand rounds per minute. But no weapon on earth opens as many doors, and helps smooth the way as much as a rubber chicken.

It's my totem. Indians have warrior feathers.

I have my chicken.

I became a hostage negotiator because I'm six-foot-five.

When I was an undergraduate and finally decided that I wanted to be a psychologist, a friend of mine said to me, 'Why don't you go to the psychology unit at the local hospital? They'll give you a job. It'll be a good opportunity to see if you like this psychology business.'

So I went, and to my surprise, they gave me the job on the spot.

It was only afterwards that I understood why they had given me the job so readily. The staff needed somebody to restrain the patients when they started throwing chairs and tables around the unit. Having someone as tall as a basketball player helped. The PA system would flare up with an alert, 'Doctor Strong to the ACCEPT Unit, Doctor Strong to the ACCEPT Unit.' Doctor Strong was the codename for me. I'd hear the alert, break into a run and jump on the patient.

Pretty fast I discovered that I liked the work. I didn't like the violence particularly, but the adrenalin of the situation gave me a real kick. It was like being a fireman: when the alarm rings, you run.

But it was more than that. There were times when it seemed like I had a pipeline straight into the patients' heads. After a while, I realised that I could get them to do what I wanted them to do just by talking to them. I didn't have to physically restrain them.

I guess I had a special talent for de-escalating crises. I was even better at making things go my way. I'd say you can't call yourself a hostage negotiator unless you have both these skills.

Hostage negotiation has been a part of my life in one way or another for more than twenty years. But my interest really began when I was a kid. While other boys dreamed of being a cop or a soldier or an astronaut, I wanted to be the guy talking people out of killing everybody on a commercial airliner.

In 1976 my family moved to Venezuela. My father was working for the International Monetary Fund at the time and had been transferred there for a long-term assignment, so he took us with him. Moving from New York to Caracas was something of a culture shock. At the time, Venezuela was enjoying a massive boom as a result of its oil deposits and the government had initiated a vast modernisation plan. The city was a mismatch of old Spanish colonial buildings alongside modern skyscrapers, huddled together in a yawning valley that stood three thousand feet above sea level, surrounded by the slopes of the Avila National Park on one side and a bunch of rundown settlements on the other.

Caracas might have had postcard sunsets, but scratch beneath the surface and you'd find lots of darkness. And it didn't take a whole lot of scratching. At about the same time we moved there, Ilich Ramirez Sanchez, now better known as Carlos the Jackal, was coming to international attention. I was only a school kid, but I followed all the reports of Carlos's terrorist activities. He became a figure of huge interest to me. The fact that he was a Venezuelan citizen by birth who'd studied in Caracas only made me even more curious about him. Like me, Carlos had a link to Cuba – he'd trained in Havana, and I had relatives from the island. But our similarities ended there. Carlos had gone on to join the Popular Front for the Liberation of Palestine (PFLP), best known for pioneering notorious airline hijackings by terrorists, and taken part in several terrorist attacks against Western and Israeli figures. Only months before, after several bungled bombing operations, he had achieved the notoriety he craved by carrying out a raid on the Organization of the Petroleum Exporting Countries (OPEC) headquarters in Vienna, in which three people were killed and seventy taken hostage.

I read with fascination about the negotiations between the Austrian government and Carlos. How he had said that he would execute a hostage every fifteen minutes unless they agreed to read a communiqué about the Palestinian cause on local radio and TV stations at two-hour intervals. While I was still at school, Carlos remained on the lam.

It was at about this point that a hostage crisis unfolded even closer to home.

There was a kid in the American school I went to by the name of Niehaus. His father, William Frank Niehaus, was the president of the glassmaker Owens-Illinois, which was at the time – and in 2011 still is – one of the largest companies operating in South America. I was sitting on the school bus one morning and happened to spot this Niehaus kid on the seat to my left. It was a blisteringly hot morning, the kind of heat that makes you feel like you've got hot towels pressed against your skin. The bus was packed full of the usual crowd: boys horsing around, girls gossiping and screaming, everyone making a racket. Except Niehaus. He was sitting alone in what appeared to me an almost visible bubble of sad quiet. It isolated and separated him from us, as if he were stranded on an island of silence amid an ocean of screaming children. His shoulders were slumped and his head hung down. He rarely looked up. But when he did you could see that his face looked tired and worn, incongruous in a sixteen-year-old kid. Now, the other kids will often taunt a kid acting like that. But on this morning everyone left him alone. No one bothered him.

I turned to a friend of mine named Gary.

'What's this kid's problem?' I asked, nodding at Niehaus.

Gary shot me a wide-eyed look.

'Haven't you heard?' he said. 'His dad got kidnapped.'

I did a double take. 'Kidnapped? You're joking, right?'

Gary shook his head. 'It's on TV.'

Six Marxist guerrillas had stormed the home of William Niehaus and bound and gagged his wife, daughter and maid in the drawing room. His wife managed to escape a short while later, but Niehaus himself was not so fortunate. The kidnappers injected him with a sedative and carted him off to their remote jungle base. As with many kidnappings that took place at the time, the motive wasn't financial, but designed to get the group international exposure and oust the incumbent Venezuelan government. They also made populist demands, stating that Owens-Illinois should raise the salaries of all their workers, distribute food packages to the poor and publish the kidnappers' lengthy denunciation of Owens-Illinois and the Venezuelan government, in the national and foreign press.

The kidnappers knew they had little or no chance of persuading the government to agree to its demands. But they were trying to curry favour with Venezuela's poor, casting themselves as the heroes of the downtrodden. Venezuela's very own Robin Hood and his merry men. Problem was, nobody on the street was buying it.

The episode with the Niehaus kid, and the actions of Carlos the Jackal, planted a seed in my mind. Maybe some kids thought Carlos was cool because he was this mysterious international terrorist in shades and people called him the Jackal in hushed tones. But I had a different opinion on the whole thing. To me, it just seemed that what Carlos was doing was fundamentally stupid.

His actions were never going to achieve his aims. These were not the actions of someone who really cared about other people, but rather those of someone who wanted the spotlight on himself. What I would later call my 'clinical antennae' had jumped to attention. Even though I didn't know the psychological terms then, Carlos was justifying his behaviour in terms that Joseph Conrad described as 'personal impulses disguised into creeds'.

Later, as a professional negotiator, I came to call people like Carlos 'a pathology in search of a cause'.

In other words, Carlos used Marxism as a vehicle to satisfy his own personal agenda. He was a narcissistic personality who believed that he was somehow special and superior to ordinary people like you and me. Because he was superior, he felt entitled to special treatment and privileges. Rules are for other people, so he wasn't bound by them. It was very important that he received recognition, praise and admiration, and equally so that others had no right to criticise him. He acted according to the fixed and rigid belief that 'if others don't respect my status, they should be punished because no one's needs and desires should interfere with my own'.

I thought to myself, This isn't right. There's something wrong with this guy, and he shouldn't be allowed to get away with this stuff. And while the media focused on the persona of Carlos, I had witnessed myself the traumatic effect their actions had on innocent lives. Niehaus junior had done nothing wrong; the same goes for his father. Yet they had found themselves inextricably caught up in the malignant, twisted pathology of terrorists and kidnappers.

The consequences of the Niehaus kidnapping would have a direct influence on my future career. William Frank Niehaus was held hostage for more than three years. He was chained to a tree and lost sixty pounds during his captivity. He was freed after a shootout between the Venezuelan military and the guerrillas. But as a result of the capture of such a high-profile Western figure, a lot of major companies began to build kidnap-for-ransom (K&R) insurance into the contracts of their executives. K&R would subsequently become standard for anyone deemed to be under threat of kidnap. In a strange way, my personal experiences of kidnapping and the industry itself grew up together.

In the early 1980s my family's Venezuelan adventure came to an end and we returned north to the US. My parents sent me to a private boarding school in a sleepy New England town, one of the many preppy-type institutions that had been established along the English public-school model, with class forms and everything. When each student graduated they were given a book. The choice of book was supposed to say something about who you were. On my graduation I was given a book entitled *A Dictionary of Euphemisms and Other Doubletalk* by a guy called Hugh Rawson. I've always been verbally adept. When I was in sixth grade I had a twelfth-grade reading level. I was a bright kid, but more importantly I had the ability to make a compelling case and argue like a lawyer could. So by giving me this book, my teachers were basically saying, 'You should be thinking about a career in language.'

I took the book, read it in a couple of days, placed it on my bookshelf and forgot all about it. At college, I started off studying political science, but when it became clear it wasn't going to answer my questions about why people did things, I switched to psychology.

In the late nineties I met my future wife, Emily. She was from London and in terms of family background she couldn't be more different than me. I was brought up in New York in a Latino household. She was the wealthy European type with rich relatives sprinkled all over the continent. I was six-five. She had short hair and a spiky attitude and I guess she was a little different from the type of women I'd dated up to that point. She had a certain exotic quality that found expression in her alluring eyes, her charming, sophisticated English accent and the way she argued her point fiercely on any number of issues. In my naive American eyes, she was a world apart from your average American woman. After one date I was hooked. In the end I decided to move to London to live with Emily, reasoning that I could also balance life in a new city and country with the completion of my graduate school studies back in the US.

I had been studying psychology in one way or another for the best part of a decade. By now the years of research and seeing patients had convinced me of one thing: I did not want to spend the rest of my life as a conventional psychologist. However, I was damned if I was going to abandon my doctorate. I decided that I would complete my doctorate, get my ticket punched, and then do my own thing. The alternative – listening to the marital woes of middle-aged housewives – seemed too awful to contemplate. There has to be something else out there, I said to myself.

I was having dinner with Emily and her friends one night at a restaurant in Mayfair when my life changed for ever.

At the time I was working in what's called a 'locked' or 'secure' unit at a famous psychiatric hospital. These are wards where literally the entrance doors are locked, controlling who enters and who leaves. There are pros and cons to the locked psych unit that are too numerous to get into here – but the bottom line is that there are people who need to be locked up. Trust me. Whichever way you look at it, locked units are among the most violent and difficult places a psychologist can operate.

The unit I worked at was one of the first of its kind in the UK. With typical British understatement it was called the Challenging Behaviour Unit. Inside were rapists, arsonists and murderers. I guess it's safe to say those are some pretty challenging behaviours.

I thrived on the work and loved trying to understand the patients' violent behaviours. I was intrigued by violence. Its forms, its applications. But the pay was terrible and I was of a mind to jack it in. If I have to spend all day dealing with unpleasant, crazy people, I thought, then I should get a job in business. At least I'd be better paid.

At dinner the truffled chicken breast and cabernet merlot helped take my mind off things. I happened to be sitting next to a guy named Simon. He mentioned to me that he worked for an insurance company in the City. As soon as the words tumbled out of his mouth I began to switch off, thinking that this guy was another banker and therefore boring as hell. Except Simon had an interesting life story.

'So old boy, I hear you're looking to get out of the psychology gig,' Simon said.

'Yeah,' I replied, sipping the merlot. 'I'm not gonna be a shrink. No way.'

'Any idea what kind of work you want to do?'

I shrugged and gestured to the waiter for a refill. 'Maybe in business, something like that.'

Simon's eyes narrowed. 'You speak Spanish, right?'

'Sure. My mother was Cuban and my father's American. I grew up in a bilingual household.'

'Well, you really ought to talk to these guys I know.'

Simon told me about a security firm called Forefront Security International (FSI). I had never heard of them before, but it turns out that they were a very big deal.

The K&R insurance industry was created when a guy from an insurance background, who I'll call Brian, was drinking in a bar in Colombia in the mid-seventies with a friend I'll call Paul, who came from a military background. At the time Paul was working as a professional kidnap negotiator. Over drinks in the bar in Bogota, they suddenly hit upon a genius idea: why don't we sell insurance against kidnap? Brian would sell the insurance and Paul would manage the cases.

However, this business model was a two-legged stool. To make it a three-legged stool, they needed an underwriter to take the financial risk. The law states that there has to be a separate broker and underwriter, because of their conflicting interests: fundamentally the underwriter doesn't want to pay out, while the broker, however, works for the client who bought the policy. The other leg is the security company, who provide the advice, personnel and expertise on how to manage the cases.

Central to the K&R insurance industry is the Box.

The Box, as the name suggests, is a small walled-in area that each insurer occupies in the underwriting room on the Lloyd's trading floor, one of the oldest and most famous trading rooms in the world. It has become the K&R insurance capital of the world and is where the K&R underwriters sit and do business.

Though it's a relatively new glass and concrete building in London's Square Mile, traditional-church or public-school architecture permeates every aspect of this very special room. It is dominated by the Lutine Bell, which used to be rung whenever a Lloyd's insured ship sank. Now, it is only rung on special occasions.

Each syndicate has a box from which they transact business with Lloyd's brokers. Brokers represent people like you and me who want to buy insurance. A syndicate is a group of 'names' or underwriters who come together to financially stand behind any insurance claims that may arise and keep the premiums when they don't.

The syndicates received a steady stream of brokers, sitting on stools, presenting their clients' salient facts to the underwriters, who sat peering into computer screens. The broker would say, 'Client is a forty-five-year-old married accountant, with two children, lives in Mexico City, never been kidnapped before, has personal security. Lives in a good neighbourhood. He wants to renew his policy.'

The decisions were made quickly.

'He's been with us six years. No red flags. So yes, let's go ahead.' Then the underwriter would either consult a table or just stick his finger in his mouth, hold it up in the air for a moment and confidently quote a figure, apparently out of thin air. Three thousand dollars a year, or whatever the price may be.

When it comes to K&R, there is a hard and fast rule that every negotiator must bear in mind: the Box never wants to pay. Absolutely never. There is a natural and irreconcilable tension between the needs of the underwriter and the needs of the client. In its perfect world, the Box would pay out zero claims a year. Like anyone else, their fundamental goal is to keep the money they make. Say they sell a hundred policies a year, which equates to $300,000. The policies are only valid for a year. Let's say 5 per cent of the policyholders are kidnapped and the ransom in each of those five cases is $30,000. That means the underwriter has paid out $150,000 from the original $300,000 pot. The remaining $150,000 is theirs to keep as profit.

This is how the K&R industry makes money.

On most K&R policies, the underwriter is exposed to unlimited liability. Theoretically, at least. If a ransom is negotiated for say $5 billion, the insurer might kick and scream but they'd have to pay it. According to the terms of the policy, the insurer is obligated to pay whatever costs they've contracted to pay. Most policies will include the services of a response consultant, the ransom, the costs associated with collecting a ransom, psychiatric rehabilitation (a term I disagree with because it stigmatises people), and paying for a holiday for the family. The consultant is employed to get the hostage out safely, although a beneficial side-effect of the consultant's presence is that generally speaking the ransoms paid are significantly lower than the initial demand.

Over rhubarb and passion fruit tartlet and honey-sweet dessert wine, Simon explained that the jewel in the crown at FSI was the Reaction Division, which dealt with kidnapping and extortion. The men and women who worked inside that division were known as consultants. They were the ones who dealt with these cases, and there were usually no more than a dozen of them at any one time.

'They're the best in the business,' Simon said.

'How do you know these guys?' I asked.

'I work for the broker, old boy,' said Simon, quaffing more dessert wine. 'But it's FSI you really need to be talking to.'

'Why's that?'

'They're looking for someone who's fluent in Spanish.'

'And what are they doing that needs Spanish?'

'Practically their entire business is in Latin America and none of their guys speaks Spanish. Plus,' said Simon, now swirling his dessert wine, 'you know how it is with these Latinos. Bloody emotional. A psychologist could help calm things down. Give them a call.'

Simon scribbled a number on my napkin.

And there I was figuring that the dinner party was going to bore me half to death.

I called the number the next morning and got put through to a guy called Karl. Although Simon had explained everything to me, I still didn't quite understand the whole concept, and I worried that Karl would detect my ignorance. Instead, he graciously offered to meet me. I readily agreed; I had no idea what I wanted to do with my life, but I figured it could do no harm to find out a bit more about the job.

At the end of our meeting, Karl said to me, 'All right, here's what we'll do. We can put you down as a response consultant. How does that sound?'

It sounded great.

The fact I spoke Spanish counted hugely in my favour. None of the other consultants were fluent. They were all middle-aged white guys, some from Rhodesia and Hong Kong, and it just so happened that a lot of the K&R work centred on volatile Central and South American countries like Colombia, Peru and Mexico. These were countries whose histories are soaked in bloodshed.

In my spare time, I read up on this strange and secretive industry, and the countries where kidnapping was most endemic. It seemed that socio-political, economic and civic instability went hand-in-hand with a culture of kidnapping.

Colombia, for example, has an egregiously violent past. The period of La Violencia in the 1950s saw thousands of people slaughtered by rival factions who employed particularly sadistic methods of execution such as the Colombian necktie. This is where the victim had their throat slashed with a knife. The killer then pulled the victim's tongue out of their throat and left it hanging on their neck. Since then insurgency groups like the Revolutionary Armed Forces of Colombia (FARC) and the National Liberation Army (ELN) had moved into the kidnapping industry. Not for any great political motive – although they usually claimed otherwise – but rather, to fund their political and criminal activities. In this respect these groups were similar to any organisation in the corporate world: they did not really exist to achieve their stated goals, but rather to perpetuate themselves. A classic example of this is the March of Dimes, an American charity founded by President Roosevelt to find a cure for polio. So they did. Nobody got polio any more. Then it became a case of, great, we cured polio. But what do we do now? Odd as it may sound, FARC and the ELN were in a similar kind of boat. By the mid-nineties FARC's leadership had probably figured out they were never going to overthrow the government and establish a Marxist state in Colombia. But they had a lot of recruits and they weren't about to kill themselves off.

Despite Karl's offer, I ended up not getting a job at FSI. They seemed to take an eternity to come back to me, and I became impatient. I started ringing up from my office each day to see what was going on. I assumed they were being incompetent, but in hindsight they were testing me. They wanted to see how I would handle the Wait.

The Wait is what every negotiator must endure on a case. It's one of the kidnapper's most potent weapons. Sometimes it might take weeks for the kidnapper to get back in touch. Sometimes months, or even years. The Wait is usually torture and creates a lot of pressure on the consultant. But he has to be able to stay

calm at all times. Or at least appear to be in order to communicate a sense of calm and manage the family while they're going
crazy. By ringing up multiple times and revealing my impatience,
I'd failed the test.

Although they didn't take me on, it did start my relationship
with FSI. And it had definitely piqued my interest in K&R.

I was hooked.

3

COLD CALL

With the offer from FSI falling through, I had little choice but to go back to the US. My research period in the UK was drawing to a close and in order to tick off the final requirements of my doctorate I needed to spend my post-doctorate year at a hospital in New York.

The hospital was a world-class, Grade-A shithole. There's no other word for it. Look up the word 'shithole' in the dictionary and you'd see a photograph of this place. The Hope Charity Medical Center was established in Brooklyn by the local Jewish population to provide medical and psychiatric services throughout the local community, from Crown Heights to Bedford-Stuyvesant, to people from every denomination, whether Jewish or Catholic, Protestant or Muslim. In its early years, the hospital gleaned a solid reputation. That was back when this part of Brooklyn was considered a nice neighbourhood.

By the nineties, that reputation had been shot to pieces. This same part of Brooklyn was now a ghetto slum. On my route to the hospital I'd pass the Brooklyn Botanic Garden. By day the garden was lovely, with its lush greenery and cherry esplanades and copper statues. But at night? Watch out.

The Center's location meant that the majority of patients at Hope Charity were underprivileged people of African-American or Caribbean heritage, a significant number of whom were substance abusers. Mostly crack. The hospital lacked funding and the surrounding area was a haven of crime and inner-city neglect. The staff at the hospital, who were predominantly white, would flee to the subway together at night to avoid travelling alone. Brooklyn back then was that kind of neighbourhood. One police friend of mine from the local precinct told me the story of a guy who got shot right outside the A&E entrance. As medical staff scrambled to lift him on to a stretcher, he screamed, 'No, no, Downstate! Take me to Downstate!' The victim would rather have travelled to another hospital two miles away than get treated at this one.

My office was in the psychology department. Rudimentary wasn't the word. It looked like a 1930s classroom, all bare floorboards and sash windows. On my first day of work I pulled open the desk drawer and in the gutter, where pencils are kept, I spotted a bunch of nail clippings.

The whole hospital was falling apart. One day I arrived at work and discovered four or five great drooping patches of swelling on the latex ceiling paintwork, like giant blisters. Something had obviously leaked from the floor above into the latex. I told myself, I'm gonna go check it out. I found out that the rooms directly above mine belonged to the kidney dialysis department. I had bubbles of foul smelling dialysis water suspended over my desk. A couple of hours later a janitor swung by and said he'd fix the problem. I told him, go ahead. The janitor took his broom and prodded the handle at the bubbles until they popped open. A hideous brown liquid splashed down on to the floor of my office. For weeks the place smelled like an open sewer.

I remember turning to the psychologist working in the next office, a guy by the name of Mike who would later become a good friend of mine.

'Hey,' I said to him, 'do you know we actually leave work dirtier than when we get here?'

'Yeah,' Mike said, cringing at the dirty floor. 'This job should come with a compulsory Hazmat suit.'

Touch any surface and you'd be caked in a layer of filth. Right across from my office was a toilet. It seemed like the toilet was overflowing with piss and shit practically every other day. I'd sit at my desk trying to clear a stack of paperwork and this vicious smell would crawl into the room. It got especially bad in the summer, when the stifling heat made the air heavy with the stench, as if we were inhaling raw sewage. On the really bad days Mike and I spent a good deal of our time fighting our gag reflexes.

The hospital was split into two buildings connected by a footbridge. Crossing that bridge was not something you did on a full stomach. Debris hung from the roof of it, where a net made out of cables had been strung over the bridge to shield staff from the crap (literally) being thrown out of the windows by the crackheads who received their treatment inside. In my mind, Hope Charity looks a lot like the Bates motel, only dirtier and less welcoming.

As for my patients, they were the cream of society.

One guy was a schizophrenic who called himself Stoneface Jackson.

Stoneface was also cross-eyed. His left eye gazed ahead and the right stared off at a forty-five-degree angle. I could never be sure which way he was looking while I treated him. In addition he suffered from a thyroid problem, so he had the unfortunate double-whammy of looking like a cross- and bug-eyed frog.

'Where'd you get the name Stoneface from?' I asked at our first session. 'Is it a name your friends gave you?'

Stoneface scratched his cheek. 'Nah, nah, dog. It's like the other Jackson dude. The Stonewall Jackson nigger, from the war,' he said, referring to Stonewall Jackson, the Confederate general from the American Civil War. I had to admit, the link was lost on me. I guess Stoneface had interesting friends.

At our follow-up, Stoneface looked perturbed about something. I asked him what was up.

'This thing been bugging me.' He scratched his elbows and shifted in the plastic seat. 'There's been a movie about Batman, right? And one – no, five! – on that Superman nigger. Hell, even the Phantom got his own movie.'

'Right. So what's your point?'

'Well why ain't Spiderman got a movie coming out? That ain't right. I mean, yeah, Peter Parker's a pussy but when he gets into Spiderman, he kicks more ass than Superman and Batman combined.'

The very next day, Stoneface Jackson burst in to see me. He was clutching a newspaper folded in half and hopping up and down on the spot, a big excited smile breaking out across his face. 'Youdidityoudidit,' Stoneface said to me. 'Ican'tbelieveit . . . That you would do something like that. For me. Thank you.'

Stoneface seemed close to tears. He thanked me profusely, over and over, gripping my hand and staring at me with his eye at a right angle.

'What did I do?' I asked, genuinely confused.

Stoneface pulled a face on me. He gestured to an article in the newspaper. It was from the entertainment section, and reported that Tobey Maguire was to star in a new Spiderman movie.

'You got Hollywood to make the Spiderman movie. You told them to make me happy. You're the best, Dr Lopez.'

Dealing with my patients at the Hope Charity Center was an intense experience that forced me to adjust the way I worked with people. Many people I saw came from poverty-stricken backgrounds and consequently had poor educations. Many were addicted to alcohol, crack cocaine or heroin. I had been used to a system whereby patients made an appointment and stuck to it. Or else they called up a day or two in advance and apologised for not making it and asked for another date to put in their diary. The patients at the hospital, however, did not behave in this manner. Half the time they failed to show for appointments. Maybe they were having a hard time. Maybe they couldn't be bothered to get out of bed that morning. Maybe they plain forgot.

So I recalibrated the way I worked, double- and triple-booking in order to increase the chances that one of my patients would actually show up for their appointment. On the rare occasions when two or three patients did arrive all at the same time, I simply told the others to wait in reception for an hour. These people had been crapped on by the government and their neighbourhoods their entire lives. Asking them to hang around – they almost expected that. Certainly no one ever complained. Other times we'd triple-book and still none of them would turn up. It appeared to be accepted practice at Hope Charity.

We idled away a fair number of hours waiting for patients who never showed. During those lulls Mike and I would browse the internet. The World Wide Web was still in its infant stage at that point. No Google, no YouTube, and shitty modems that took for ever and a day to download a single page. One day we stumbled upon a website designed by a grad student at MIT that described in great detail, complete with illustrations, how to make your own lock-picking tools out of street-cleaner bristles. The bristles on the brush are made out of ultra-thin spring steel, but they're also very stiff and hence ideal for picking locks. With our patients failing to keep their appointments, we spent the next month and a half making bespoke lock-picking tools. Mike brought in a vice-clamp, I supplied some small files. In our spare time we went around the building cracking locks. By the end of our stay, there wasn't a lock at Hope Charity that hadn't been picked by either Mike or myself using nothing more than some steel bristles and a bit of insider knowledge. I still have the tools. You ever lock yourself out of your home, I'm your guy.

Although the hospital was shitty, the psychology department had a lot of really smart people in it. Guys like Mike were seeing outstanding results with their patients. They were going places. The department was like a gem in the middle of a dump. And because we were surrounded by a hostile environment, everyone in the psychology unit developed a strong *esprit de corps*.

Although I was doing a lot of good work with guys like Stoneface, I really couldn't see myself eking out a twenty- or thirty-year stretch at a hospital. This wasn't why I had signed up to study psychology.

I was sitting in my apartment on the thirty-third floor of a new block on the West Side one morning, watching the sun rise over the Manhattan skyline, rays splashing down over the river. I'd just moved in to this place and had zero furniture. Emily was still living in London at this point, but we had made plans for her to come over and join me while I finished up my Ph.D. The place was lonely. I'm talking not even a mattress. Just one plastic chair in a 1100 square-foot apartment. I looked at the phone and thought to myself, I need to get into this negotiating gig. That's what I really wanted to do. My imagination had been captured by my earlier encounter with FSI, and I simply had to follow up my interest. So I made a cold call.

I dialled local directory assistance and said, 'Give me the number for the New York City Police Department.'

The operator was quiet for a beat. 'What number exactly, sir? The front desk?'

'That works.'

When I got through to the front desk at the NYPD I said, 'I want the direct line for the hostage negotiation team.'

I knew the NYPD had one of the leading hostage negotiation teams in the world. The operator gave the number to me. No one answered, so I left a message.

'My name is Ben Lopez,' I told the machine, 'and I'm a clinical psychologist. I'm interested in doing some work with you. If you'd like to give me a call back, my number is . . . '

Two days later, the phone rang while I was resting between shifts at Hope Charity and reviewing some case notes. I answered, not expecting anything but a sales call. No one had my number.

A confident, friendly voice said, 'I'm looking for a Dr Ben Lopez?'

'That's me,' I replied.

'This is Lieutenant Larry Bridge. I'm the commander of the NYPD hostage negotiation team. I got your message. Listen, I can't promise you anything. But why don't you come on in and we'll talk.'

I was kind of surprised the NYPD returned my call. I'd rung them out of the blue, with not much of an expectation that it would go anywhere. I was casting myself around and hoping something would stick. When you think about it, most people who cold-call the police department are crazy. So I was surprised and delighted they did return my call. I sensed my whole life was about to change.

COLD CALL

I turned up at the department headquarters for my meeting with Larry two days later. The NYPD HQ is situated at One Police Plaza in downtown Manhattan on Park Row, not far from the East River. In the nineteenth century the area was known as the Five Points and was a notorious rat's nest of vice, squalor and violence that rivalled the East End of London as being the most violent, disease-ridden, destitute urban block in the Western world. The twenty-first century had been moderately kinder.

The NYPD headquarters was set in a brown-brick building with a glass front. I entered the atrium. It was dark and gloomy inside, despite the glass. Almost as if light had given up on the place. And despite being quite large, the building gave off the impression of being a cave. I signed myself in at the main desk. Street cops were hanging around, coming and going. A few minutes later Larry came down to get me.

He escorted me up to the Chief of the Detective Bureau on the thirteenth floor. The department looked kind of drab. Breeze-block walls painted that dull beige the colour of filing cabinets. We wormed our way through a maze of desks and wires and cabinets until we reached Larry's office. Years later, when I was shown around Scotland Yard for the first time, I would encounter an almost identical layout. They say that whatever the NYPD does, Scotland Yard follows. I didn't realise that philosophy extended to depressing, institutional office furnishings.

My first impression of Larry was that he looked like a favourite uncle. He was a middle-aged man with grey hair and the slightest paunch, charming with it. And like all negotiators, he loved to talk. You can't be a negotiator if you're a Silent Bob type. Larry also introduced me to Tanya Watkins. She was a detective, first grade. In the NYPD, becoming a detective first grade is like winning the George Cross. It's a big deal. Tanya was one of the department's brightest stars. She was plucked out of the NYPD training academy to do undercover work before she had even finished her training. She was that good.

Larry Bridge was, and still is, a legend. He was the longest-serving commander of the negotiating team at the NYPD. Working in a city as messed up as New York, with more than its fair share of kooks, Larry had worked on thousands of cases. From the moment I met him, Larry inspired me. He had a philosophy towards police work that resonated with me. He liked to say, 'If you only have a hammer in your toolbox, every problem is a nail.' Another of his sayings was 'We are *peace officers* first and foremost.' In Larry's eyes, every single hostage case could be resolved non-violently. This might not seem like such a big deal now, but he came from a background and an era in which hostage crises ended in one of two ways: either the perp comprehensively surrendered or else the cops stormed the barricade like they were in a John Wayne movie, guns blazing. Neither method was particularly effective but in the world of law enforcement, Larry Bridge was preaching a radical message. And I loved it.

The art and science of hostage negotiation began with the NYPD. Two incidents led to the creation of the NYPD team. The first was the Attica prison riots in 1971, when around a thousand prisoners rioted and seized control of the facilities, taking thirty-three staff hostage. After four days of negotiations, state police moved in to take back control of the prison. The uprising left thirty-nine people dead, including ten correctional officers and civilian employees.

The second was the 1972 Munich Olympic Village massacre, when members of the Black September terrorist group took Israeli Olympic athletes hostage at the Olympic Village complex. During a rescue attempt eleven of the athletes were killed, along with one West German police officer.

NYPD Lieutenant Frank Bolz and Detective Harvey Schlossberg are widely credited with developing police negotiations. The newly formed Hostage Negotiation Team – HNT – unit was thus created in early 1973. As the first unit dedicated to handling crisis management in this way, it was a groundbreaking moment in the history of hostage negotiation.

Larry was full of fascinating statistics and bits of knowledge he'd acquired over his many years of experience. He told me that he was in the process of trying to break down the frequency and origin of crisis interventions. What was the most common cause behind a hostage crisis? Bank robberies gone bad? Or cases where the kidnapper had a mental disorder? Did some disorders feature more often than others? He'd discovered that those with anti-social personalities were more likely to be involved in a bank robbery kidnap scenario. Individuals with avoidant personality disorder were overrepresented in the area of unplanned kidnaps. People who've been frustrated their whole life and let their resentment boil up inside them over a period of days, months and years, until eventually they crack. Maybe they're behind on their rent. The landlord says, 'You have to leave,' they reply, 'Fuck you, I have a gun,' and all of a sudden you have a hostage situation.

Anti-social personalities, on the other hand, do exactly what they say on the tin. They are self-centred narcissists. The world is all about them. Nobody else matters. Other people are only useful when they can be used to further their own gains. But they have few emotional relationships with other people. They have no remorse or sense of guilt over the terrible things they do. Jails are full of people with anti-social personality disorder, for obvious reasons. These are the guys who find it easy to rob, rape and kill fellow human beings.

When you're negotiating with a bank robber, he will often have an anti-social personality and therefore he will care less about the welfare of his hostages. They won't mean as much to him as people. Saying, 'Please don't hurt Frank or Julie,' won't work because the bank robber totally lacks compassion. Anti-social people can appear suave and sophisticated, but when you scratch the surface there's not much going on behind. They are often liars, swindlers and cheats. They'd steal money from old ladies and it wouldn't bother them.

Larry emphasised the motto of the NYPD negotiation team: 'Talk to me.'

'It's not "listen to me",' he stressed. 'Everyone thinks a nego-tiator has to be a good talker. And we all are. But it's more important to be a good listener. We're here to listen to the guy on the end of the line. They talk. We listen.'

Advice that I have found invaluable ever since.

At the end of our meeting I shook hands with Larry and Tanya and we went our separate ways. I still had no idea if this was going anywhere or not. I think they were trying to get a feel for me. A friend of mine who taught at Columbia said that she knew some of the psychologists who worked at the NYPD, and that she had reservations about them. I parked the meeting at the back of my mind and went back to work at Hope Charity.

A couple of months later Larry called me out of the blue.

'Say, Ben, you want to appear in a documentary?'

Larry had been approached by a commercial TV company that wanted to do a show based around the exploits of the nego-tiating team. Though the NYPD had a few psychologists working for them Larry chose me to take part in the documen-tary. My role would be to train the next negotiating class. Before the cameras began rolling, Larry explained, I would have to put together a specialised training programme for the class. Larry was only offering the work for the documentary. I was more interested in working with the negotiators than being on TV, but I got the sense that if things worked out, it would open up more doors for me in the future.

'I'm in,' I replied.

COLD CALL

The thing about Larry was that he was an iron fist inside a velvet glove. There's an old maxim that goes something like this: 'You know you're dealing with a diplomat when he tells you to go to hell but you look forward to the trip.' That was Larry's style. Most of the time he got what he wanted. The NYPD made his department jump through a ton of hoops in order to clear the documentary crew, since every other branch of the NYPD was pissed off that they weren't being filmed for a nationally screened TV show. But Larry danced the dance and he got approval and I knew that I simply had to be part of this.

I had to get a fortnight off work at the Hope Charity Center, so I knocked on my boss's door and said, 'Look, this is what I want to do, I really need the time off.' He knew he was going to let me go, and I knew he knew that. But he was the boss, so he had to put on the stern face and the rest of it. Made it seem as though he was doing me a favour and cutting me some extra slack.

Needless to say, he granted me the leave.

I spent the next couple of months preparing the class. The pressure was on: I would be teaching the class myself, with a little help from Larry and Tanya. There was a lot of stuff surrounding the psychological aspect of negotiation that I needed to learn, and fast. I had to learn about containment, police tactics and the standard operating procedures (SOPs) governing any siege or kidnap situation. When a guy is holed up in a stronghold, you have to move quickly to establish an inner perimeter (IP) and an outer perimeter (OP). Access to the IP is restricted; it's designed to contain the movement of the perp. The OP acts as a back-up, in case the perp manages to breach the IP. The negotiators will generally operate within the IP, although advances in telecommunications mean that these days we can work from virtually anywhere in the world. (I've worked cases in Somalia from the comfort of a business conference room in central London.)

I learned all this stuff on the fly while preparing to teach a room full of cops how to talk to sociopaths. By the time the film crew showed up, I was more than ready. For two weeks the crew followed a bunch of us around. They shot footage of me teaching the class. One of my students, Ryan Arnold, is the current head of the negotiating team.

I had no formal training in hostage negotiation. Much of my success comes from the fact that I'm too stupid to realise I can't do something. I wasn't worried about my lack of experience because what I did have – and could offer to these officers – was a background in understanding the mind of a criminal. In most law-enforcement scenarios, the officer doesn't need to understand the perp. A guy shoots a bunch of people, he's gonna get shot or arrested. A guy deals drugs, he's breaking the law. But hostage crises require some basic understanding of what's going on inside the perp's head. That's where I came in.

The more elite the cop or soldier, the more they are interested in psychology. It's something they want to get to grips with because it helps give them a tactical advantage and these are guys dedicated to being the best of the best. That said, there is a popular aversion to shrinks. As psychologists we're seen as the bearded Freud types who let people lie back on the sofa and tell us about their dreams. The first thing I did was to bury that perception.

'I'm not here to talk to you about the time you didn't go to Disneyland when you were seven and how that fucked up your chances of going to Harvard,' I said. 'I'm not interested in any of that. But the bottom line is that you're cops, and human beings are the raw material you have to deal with.'

In other words, if you're a carpenter it behoves you to know about how nails and wood and glue work together. Otherwise you're gonna suck at carpentry. The raw material that police negotiators have to deal with is people. This is an opener I've employed in training programmes ever since. It strikes a chord with my audience – who isn't interested in knowing more about people?

Most people intuitively know when they're dealing with someone who's crazy. Maybe the guy's hearing voices, maybe he's saying bizarre stuff. The fact remains, when the cops are confronted with somebody like this, they need to modify their approach because they're not dealing with someone who's thinking the same way as them.

This approach also applies to hostage negotiation. Let's say you've got a hostage-taker who's paranoid. In that case, your negotiation strategy should absolutely not be to try to become that guy's friend. Why? Because he's paranoid! People who are paranoid believe that people are out to get them. They're not afraid that something *good* is going to happen to them. They're not afraid that they're gonna win the lottery or get laid. They fear that something *terrible* will happen.

People who are paranoid are also narcissistic. Everything is centred around them. One guy I know likened paranoia to a guy going to watch a football game. As he takes his seat in the stadium, the team comes out and engages in the pre-match huddle in the centre of the pitch. Everyone else in the stadium knows the players are talking about strategies, about how to win the game. But the paranoid guy suspects that the players are talking about *him*. Even though he's just an anonymous guy in the crowd and the players could not care less about him.

So there's no point trying to get close to the paranoid hostage-taker or barricaded individual. He's not going to believe you're his friend. He's too busy wondering *why* you want to be his friend in the first place. Instead the best way to handle him is to take a very direct and blunt approach. You say what you do and you do what you say. You stay insistent, you stay boundaried and you always keep a distance between yourself and the perp.

I gave the cops insight not into logic but *psycho*-logic. This is essentially the multiple thought patterns that mentally disturbed individuals suffer from. It's not a logic that you or I could necessarily relate to, but in its own way, in the mind of the subject, it makes sense. Helping switch this light bulb on in the cops' heads allows them to make a reasoned judgement about seemingly bizarre behaviour, and leaves them better equipped to respond to it.

A month or so after the filming was over, Ryan Arnold called me up. I first met him during the negotiation course, when he struck me as someone who had the potential to be an outstanding negotiator. 'Ben,' he said. 'Can I get a piece of advice from you?'

Larry was up for retirement at this time and Ryan had been in the Emergency Service Unit for longer than a little while. ESU is the NYPD's answer to the S019 unit of the Metropolitan Police. The ESU guys have their own specialised transport – blue vans that carry everything from assault rifles and shotguns to rope and breaching equipment. Ryan was a senior commander in the ESU and had been involved in several hostage scenes.

'I've been offered Larry's job,' Ryan said. 'Been thinking about it a lot. I don't know whether to take it. What do you think?'

'You enjoy the ESU stuff?' I asked.

'Christ, I love it. It's good work. I'm master of my own domain, you know.'

'Well, the only thing I can think of is this,' I said. 'When I was twenty-one I quit college and went to work on cruise ships. I spent a glorious year doing nothing but partying. It was great. In fact, it was so great I couldn't do it for more than a year. So I went back to college.'

'Where are you going with this, Ben?'

'Hear me out. About the same time that I re-enrolled, my house burned down. Space heater blew up, it was a nightmare. I was really low, I had no clothes and no possessions. Life sucked.'

Ryan said, 'Okay.'

'I started thinking, I'm gonna go back on the ships. Then I bumped into a friend of mine. And he gave me the best piece of advice I ever heard. He told me, "Don't ever go backwards. Go forwards. If you're gonna go, do something else. Don't do the ship thing again." So it's like this, Ryan. You've already done ESU. I don't think it will happen, but if for some reason you crash and burn at the hostage team, you can always go and do something else. But try going forwards first.'

Ryan was silent for a period. Then he said, 'Thanks Ben. That means a lot to me.'

He took the job and never looked back.

Finally, I got my licence to practise psychology in the US. That was it. Ticket punched. All my ducks were in a row now. The first thing I did after becoming qualified was that I quit being a psychologist and put my negotiation skills to work for various big businesses, mainly helping these companies change the way they work. I also got to travel to offices all over the world.

The money was good but it wasn't inspiring me. Problem was, my dream of being a negotiator remained out of reach. At the turn of the millennium there were only a small number of hostage-takings or barricaded individuals in New York or London. Too few to warrant me having a full-time career in hostage negotiation.

Then 9/11 happened.

One of the unintended consequences of the terrorist attacks of September 11 was that every UK special forces operator and his brother at or near retirement age suddenly quit the army to go set up their own security companies on what's known in the trade as the Circuit: the world of security and close protection work that has become one of the most lucrative industries of the past few years.

This surge of private enterprise lit a lightbulb in my head. If the K&R industry had originally been a three-legged stool – security, underwriter, broker – I was going to be the fourth leg. To evolve the system from a purely physical security structure to one that had a psychological component.

To put it in six words, it was about a *safe mind in a safe body*. My business idea was that there should be parity between physical security and psychological security. My reasoning was that the majority of the value in companies is in the heads of the people who work in them. That's why companies spend lots of money and effort on protecting their bodies, including their heads. So why wouldn't you protect what's inside them as well?

To me this was a massive gap in the system that desperately needed to be filled. Kidnap is a uniquely human crime. More psychological than just about any other crime, kidnap takes advantage of the fact that human beings are social animals. We live in flocks and take comfort from being around each other. Animals don't kidnap each other. They kill and rape and steal, but the concept of holding one another hostage is alien. Kidnappings inflict severe trauma on not only the person being held captive but the families too. I took the idea to FSI and said, 'You should be doing something like this. It's an important part of the K&R circle and it's currently being neglected. At least it'll differentiate you. At most it could represent a significant revenue stream.'

They loved the idea. Not only that – they loved it so much they wanted me to go and work with them, providing my services on their behalf as subcontractor. I'd come up with the content, they'd sell and market it as part of their K&R offering. It made sense for FSI to jump in enthusiastically; there are a lot of competing companies in the K&R industry, a lot of sharks, and by having a psychological component of their package, FSI were able to say they were first in providing a *complete body and mind* security package to the market. After all, security guys are there to provide security. They don't have the training or mind-set to both negotiate with psychopaths and comfort grieving mothers.

I was privileged to sit in on the reaction meetings to discuss live hostage cases and provide feedback and talks to the security guys. They liked me, I guess because I'm not an academic by nature or in my approach. I don't speak down to people, and I don't try to mask my insecurities or lack of knowledge by using big, complicated words.

One of the talks I gave to the security guys was about stress. I got around to mentioning the effects of adrenalin – which the body produces in massive quantities when faced with a stressful situation.

'Adrenalin is a vasoconstrictor,' I said. 'In other words, it shrinks the size of your blood vessels, thereby increasing your blood pressure and making you a better athlete.' These big, burly British guys nodded approvingly. 'It also helps with wounds because you bleed less. Basically it has a lot of effects that allow you to survive a crisis situation.'

I paused and looked around the room. These guys had heard this stuff before. It was nothing new to them.

I went on, 'But because adrenalin is a vasoconstrictor, it's incompatible with the presence of an erection. You see, you need your blood vessels to open up to get a hard-on.'

The moment the words left my mouth everybody shifted uneasily in their chairs. Each and every one of those guys, I'm sure, knew exactly what I was talking about. I'd struck a raw nerve. But I presented it in a way they could relate to. I didn't dress it up with bullshit.

At the same time as I was teaching ex-SAS guys about erectile dysfunction, I went on a course to learn about K&R negotiations. The media and Hollywood tend not to discriminate between them, but K&R and law-enforcement negotiations are two entirely different things. Law enforcement is fundamentally about saving lives and apprehending the perp. K&R is also about saving lives but the negotiator is unconcerned about apprehension. When I'm talking to Somali pirates or Afghan insurgents, I don't care what happens to the kidnapper. I just want to get my hostage back alive and well. It's a business transaction. And no matter what they tell you at school, crime does pay. Or at least the right type of crime. Most of the time, in most places in the world, kidnappers in K&R situations will get paid and they won't go to jail. When I go into a job, I fully expect to pay something. I'm not there to apprehend anybody, I'm just there to hand over a plastic bag full of cash in exchange for a human life.

That's one of the reasons K&R cases are rarely publicised. There are a few exceptions, such as the year-long kidnapping of Paul and Rachel Chandler by Somali pirates in the autumn of 2009. In that instance, UK news outlets essentially became communication vehicles, with the pirates issuing a ransom demand of $7 million in a phone call to the BBC and subsequently sending a video to Channel 4 News in which Paul Chandler expressed his fear that the pirates would kill them within a week unless negotiations began. But that is very much the exception to the rule.

There are a couple more reasons why K&R cases are kept out of the public eye. One, it complicates things. When the press gets involved, it often has a disastrous effect on proceedings. At its base level, kidnap and hostage negotiation is a game about communication. If the negotiator controls the communication and controls the message, he has the power to exert influence in a situation that by definition he has little control over. Media involvement dilutes the negotiator's ability to manage the message. Worse, extensive media coverage and hype usually inflates the self-worth of the kidnapper in their own mind. Kidnappers come in all shapes and sizes, but they tend to be of a common type. They're uneducated, unsophisticated people. For the kidnapper, seeing the hostage getting airtime on the national news must mean they're filthy rich. Because only rich people are on TV, right?

Kidnap for ransom is not a problem for people living in London or New York or Berlin. It's a phenomenon peculiar to semi-failed states. In countries like the US or the UK, the police forces are generally pretty good, they get paid enough and aren't corrupt. Which means the kidnappers stand a high chance of getting caught. But K&R doesn't happen in *completely* failed states either, where the situation on the ground is too chaotic even for the kidnappers and anyone worth kidnapping has high security or lives in a compound.

A semi-failed state is somewhere like Colombia. Here the government has control over the cities but not the countryside. As long as you travel by aeroplane between Medellin and Bogota, you're as safe as you would be walking down Bond Street or Fifth Avenue. Step outside that security bubble, however, and you might find yourself being kidnapped at gunpoint by a bunch of Marxist rebels armed with AK-47s.

Your choice.

While learning the basics of K&R I networked with several ex-special forces operators. And it was through these connections that my career really began taking off. After 9/11 and the rise of private security firms, a few of the ex-SF guys got in touch with me. They offered me the opportunity that I'd always dreamed of: to become a response consultant and work as a subcontractor on hostage negotiations.

Consultants are called consultants because that's what they primarily do. We don't make decisions, we provide advice. In most cases he or she will be guiding a designated communicator that they might help choose and almost certainly will help train. There are numerous reasons for doing this. The response consultant might not speak the local dialect or they may want to use a family friend to handle the talks in order to play up the idea to the kidnappers that the hostage's company is not helping out, financially or otherwise.

As a subcontractor, it would simply be a case of waiting for the phone to ring, agreeing terms and my fee, and hopping on the next flight out of Heathrow. I'd moved back to London by this point and any excuse to leave its grey skies and bleak weather behind sounded good to me.

I accepted, didn't need to give it a moment's thought. This was what I wanted to do and I was psyched to be part of the inner circle finally. I barely had time to sort out my paperwork when I was dispatched to handle my first case.

I would be travelling to Mexico.

4

THE LONGEST WALK

It was April 2003, and thirty-four-year-old Miguel Osorio had just returned to his office from a business meeting at a client's offices in downtown Mexico City when his mobile phone squawked inside of his breast pocket. It was an unknown number. Probably another company trying to sell me something, Osorio thought. He answered.

'Congratulations!' the voice on the other end of the line said. Male, twenties or early thirties. 'You've just won a mountain bike!'

'I didn't enter any competition,' Miguel said.

'No, no, you did, you did. You entered automatically when you used your credit card in the supermarket last month. Don't you remember?' The guy sounded nervous.

'But that's impossible. I never use my credit cards in the supermarket.'

Click.

As he listened to the dial tone, Miguel felt his stomach knot up involuntarily with tension. The call had been surreal. He was sure the caller hadn't been from a company and there was no real prize. So why had the person rung? He shrugged it off as probably another new scam in a city teeming with criminal opportunists and creative thieves. At seven o'clock he left his office and headed for the gym nearby and forgot all about the crank caller. After a serious workout he climbed into his silver Honda Accord saloon and set off for home.

Miguel was two blocks from his house when he noticed a jet-black Mitsubishi Shogun in his rear-view mirror gunning its engine and overtaking him. The road was narrow and winding and Miguel thought the Shogun driver was driving recklessly. He slammed the brakes as the Shogun screamed past him. Right in front of his stalled Accord, the Shogun braked in the middle of the road, blocking Miguel's path. Before Miguel could reverse away, a Toyota Hilux pickup truck came racing down the street to his rear. It stopped a metre to his six o'clock, blocking the exit. Miguel was trapped.

Two men debussed from the Hilux. They were packing Sig Sauer 9mm handguns and wore beige combat pants and dark T-shirts.

'*Manos arriba!* Hands in the air!' one of them shouted at Miguel. Ants crawled up his spine. He recognised the voice from the phone call earlier. Prize guy. He had dark skin, curly black hair and a five o'clock shadow, against which his light-blue eyes seemed ghostly.

The second guy was five-six, a little chubby. Miguel thought he looked nervous.

'I said hands in the air!'

Miguel presented his open palms.

'Out of the car!'

He climbed out of the driver's seat. The man with the blue eyes grabbed him by the scruff of his collar and forced him into the rear passenger seat of the Accord. Miguel was made to lie face-down across the seats. Blue Eyes took the wheel and raced two blocks south to a side street, where they transferred Miguel to the Shogun and relieved him of his wallet and mobile phone.

'You're Miguel Osorio?' Blue Eyes asked him as they sped away from the Accord.

'Yes, yes, that's me,' he said, his voice cracking. Miguel was trying hard to keep it together. He'd read the stories about kidnappings in Mexico City. He knew his status as a successful businessman from a rich family made him a target. Lots of people get kidnapped, but no one ever expects it to be them.

'What's the telephone number for your house?'

Miguel gave it to them without protest. As he spoke, Blue Eyes tapped the digits into Miguel's old mobile. Then he hit the DIAL key. Miguel stilled his breath. He could hear the ring tone coming out of the tinny speaker on the phone. On the fourth ring, Sienna, his mother, picked up.

Blue Eyes said, 'Is this the home of Miguel Osorio Torres?'

Torres was Miguel's dad.

Sienna said, 'Who's speaking?'

'A friend of your son. I have Miguel and need to speak with Don Torres. Put him on the line.' The Shogun jolted as it burned down a potholed road. The line was silent for several seconds. Then Torres came on the line.

'Yes?' he said.

'I have your son. I want five million dollars, American. Talk to you again soon.' Blue Eyes spoke almost too quickly, like a bad actor rushing their lines on stage. He pressed the phone against Miguel's ear and nodded. Talk.

'Papa, I'm well. Please don't worry. Be calm—'

Blue Eyes killed the call. And it hit Miguel, right there and then, that he'd been kidnapped. The reality and gravity of his situation suddenly struck him. It was real and unreal all at the same time. And terrifying.

Twenty minutes later the Shogun came to a halt inside a garage in a rundown part of town. The garage was built into a house comprised of two adjoining parts surrounded by a three-metre-high wall. It looked newly built.

Blue Eyes put a towel over Miguel's head and marched him through a door and up two flights of stairs. He was dumped in a bare, dark room. Wooden boards had been nailed across the windows, blocking out the sun. The skylight on the roof was locked and had a blue plastic tarpaulin taped across it that had holes in it. A thin, stained mattress had been dumped in a corner.

Miguel didn't have time to orientate himself. Blue Eyes ordered him to face the wall and strip naked. The gang seemed worried that he had a subcutaneous GPS tracking chip injected in his arm and looked particularly attentively at them. They don't really exist, but that didn't stop the kidnappers from being paranoid. They continued to look for GPS devices in Miguel's clothes and threatened to kill him if he lied to them. An underling brought Miguel some dirty sweatpants and a T-shirt. He was allowed to turn around. Now the gang were all wearing balaclavas.

Blue Eyes took a call on his mobile.

'Keep watch on the hostage,' he said, leaving the room. As soon as he left, several other members of the gang beat Miguel up. Blue Eyes promptly returned and shouted at them to stop.

'No one touches the hostage without my express permission,' he said with barely disguised rage. This was a ploy to demonstrate that Blue Eyes had all the power and control. Miguel was at his mercy.

The rest of the gang departed, leaving Blue Eyes and Miguel alone in the room. For the next forty-eight hours Blue Eyes would hardly leave the room. Nor would Miguel be allowed to sleep. Sleep deprivation is one of the most effective torture weapons available to kidnappers and it's no surprise that SF outfits like the British SAS and the US Delta Force are instructed on how to deal with it if they are tortured. It's a fact that hostages are commonly denied this most basic human function. It weakens their inner resolve. If you want to break somebody, depriving them of sleep is one of the fastest and best ways to go about it.

'I know everything about you,' Blue Eyes said. 'I know your family. Your brothers are called Hector and Luis. Your sister is Margarita. They all work for your father's company. Your papa is very rich.'

'I don't know,' Miguel lied. 'We fell out a few years ago. I don't really talk to my papa any more, or my brothers.'

'Tell me about your papa's company.'

'Like I said, I don't know. You're asking the wrong person. Me and my family, we're not close.'

'You still work for your papa.'

'I'm leaving in a month.'

'Bullshit.'

'It's the truth, I swear.'

A few hours later Blue Eyes briefly left the room. He returned with a TV. Placed it on a chair, propped the chair against the far wall and put the volume all the way up to full. It had been tuned in to a kids' TV station. Blue Eyes sat opposite the TV, arms folded, and watched *The Simpsons* dubbed in Spanish. An hour later he fired the same questions at Miguel. How much money did the company make? What jobs did the rest of the family have? How many children did his brother Hector have? Asking someone the same questions again and again is a standard interrogation practice. Cops use it all the time. It's designed to pick up holes in a story. Anyone can lie once. But people tend to forget the details of a lie once they're told. That's why repeating them isn't easy. Thankfully for him, Miguel wasn't lying except for the fiction about the family being distant. He didn't slip up.

Miguel came from a wealthy family who had numerous business concerns in the US. He ticked all the boxes when it came to a privileged upbringing: he had been raised in a walled compound surrounded by lush trees and servants. He had the model good looks and the MBA. He got parachuted into the family business after college, where he proceeded to make millions of dollars, just like his father had done. He had more women than he knew what to do with and could have anything he wanted.

Around noon the next day – Miguel wasn't sure of the precise time – Blue Eyes announced he was going to get some takeout. 'What you want?' he asked Miguel. 'KFC? Pizza? McDonald's?'

Miguel rubbed his eyes. The stress of being abducted, combined with the lack of sleep, was taking its toll.

'Anything. As long as there's no chilli.'

Blue Eyes nodded at the TV. 'You want a DVD or an Xbox up here? You're gonna be here a long time. It could get very boring for you.'

'I don't want either.'

When someone finds themselves in a situation over which they have no control, the only effective means of protest is denial. It's the most primitive form of protest human beings have. Small children practise denial every time they spit out a mouthful of food. Miguel was doing the same thing.

Blue Eyes unlocked the door. There was a guard posted outside the room at all times. No way Miguel could escape.

The door slammed.

An hour later Blue Eyes returned with the food. He'd bought Miguel an eight-inch pizza – topped with extra chilli. Probably a punishment for Miguel's lack of cooperation. Blue Eyes sat his own pizza down on the floor. A fourteen-inch chilli-free meat feast with extra cheese. Miguel didn't touch his pizza.

'Not hungry, huh?' Blue Eyes said. 'You need to think long term.' He tore off a slice and chewed loudly on it. 'Try and think of this as a vacation. Shower, eat, don't hurt yourself. So when this is over, your family will be happy to see you. They will see that I took good care of you. I'm not a bad man. I want the money. That's it. As long as you and them both cooperate with me, you have nothing to worry about.'

On the second day, Blue Eyes announced that he was leaving.

'Don't think about doing anything stupid or my escorts will fucking kill you.'

'Escorts' was a strange expression to use for bodyguards. Miguel had only ever heard one or two people using the word in that way: police officers. Blue Eyes also used 'affirmative' instead of 'yes'. It got Miguel thinking the kidnapper was probably a corrupt cop. He hoped to God that his family hadn't notified the authorities about his abduction. That would only make matters worse.

For the next forty-seven days he settled into a grim routine. When he woke up each morning he would kick on the door, alerting the guards. Then they'd enter, blindfold him and make him put his hands behind his back.

The blindfold or hood is one of the most powerful tools in the captors' arsenal. Not only does it protect their identities, but it has a huge psychological effect on the hostage. It makes you compliant. If you can't see, you can't tell where you're going. You bump into things. You have to walk at a shuffling pace and you end up relying on your captors to guide you. The hostage is dependent on their kidnapper both physically and now psychologically too. Third, it prevents eye contact. If you look someone in the eye, they instantly become more human to you. A crude but effective bond is established between the two individuals.

The blindfold precludes that possibility. This is one reason why soldiers who face firing squads are blindfolded. That way the squad doesn't have to look into the eyes of the man they're executing.

With the blindfold on, Miguel's guards would then escort him to the bathroom down the hall. Breakfast would be a piece of hard bread and a glass of tepid milk. At around two o'clock the guards would enter – same routine, face the wall, blindfold – and give him some food. Ham and eggs mixed into pasta, with a couple of tortillas, apple juice and a bottle of mineral water. He always had two people guarding him, twenty-four-seven. The guards changed every six hours. They were not allowed to speak to Miguel. A week into his incarceration, one of the guards asked Miguel his name. The guy was promptly removed from the team.

Miguel would not see Blue Eyes again until the end of his time in captivity.

Four times a day the leader would telephone the guards on a pre-paid mobile to give them an update on negotiations. They spoke in low voices in the corridor, but the door was not thick and by pressing his ear against it Miguel could make out snippets of the conversation. Progress was slow and Blue Eyes became frustrated. He berated the guards if he thought they were slacking and they often got into shouting matches on the phone, with the guards claiming that the ransom demand had been set too high and they should settle for a more realistic figure.

'He's fucking paranoid,' one of the guards said to the other after Blue Eyes had hung up the phone. 'Either he gets real or this ain't gonna end pretty for nobody.'

'If you were wearing his shoes, you'd be the same,' the other guard replied.

Life went on like this for a month, until forty days later Blue Eyes showed up again and told Miguel he was going to speak with his father on the phone.

'Your papa doesn't believe we treat you well.' Blue Eyes laughed. He was wearing a balaclava. 'Turn around and face the wall.'

'Why are you blindfolding me to make a phone call?'

'The call is not being made from here,' Blue Eyes said.

Miguel was confused. He didn't understand why they had to make a mobile phone call from another location. He figured maybe they were worried about someone triangulating the signal and getting a fix on their location.

'Now listen carefully,' Blue Eyes said turning off the TV. 'When your papa answers, you cry. You cry fucking hard, okay? Tell your papa to pay the full ransom. Beg him. Tell him that if he screws us around, you die.'

They drove aimlessly around a nearby district, weaving through traffic. But Blue Eyes couldn't get through to Torres.

'He's not picking up. Fucking unbelievable.' Blue Eyes turned in his seat and faced Miguel. 'Looks like your papa doesn't give a shit about you. No cops, no professionals involved. You're in trouble, my friend.'

Despite his tough exterior, Miguel began seriously to worry he would be killed. They drove back to the prison and locked him in the room.

Three days passed with no news. On the Monday, at eight o'clock that evening, he was pacing the room to keep fit when he heard the rumble of car engines out front. He heard multiple voices in the corridor. His guards stayed put. People were coming and going. Then – silence. At three in the morning, the guards cracked the door open and put a towel over his head.

'Do anything stupid and I'll kill you,' one of them said. They took him out front to a minivan parked just inside the gates, its engine gently humming. The guards shoved Miguel into the back of the van. Blue Eyes was frantically chewing gum by the door. He looked on edge. The brash demeanour had gone.

'Forget this ever happened. Forget our voices. Forget where this place is. Forget everything. If you ever remember anything and tell anyone, we'll find your family and kill them.'

Blue Eyes didn't wait for a response. He slammed the rear door shut, locking Miguel inside a well of darkness. A minute later the minivan wobbled and jerked as it lurched out of the gates. Miguel had no idea where he was going, but he feared something bad was about to happen. He heard the ecstatic rush of traffic as they hit the freeway. Twenty minutes later they got off the freeway and stopped. One of the guards unlocked the rear doors and ordered Miguel to climb out.

They had parked at the side of an empty stretch of road in the middle of Nowheresville, Mexico. Heat shimmered off the tarmac in waves. The sun beat down from a stark, naked sky and the light almost blinded Miguel. He'd been in dark places for a long time. The guard gestured to the road.

'Walk down the road and don't fucking look back.'

The nearest building, a convenience store, was a ten-minute-walk away. It was the longest walk of Miguel's life. With every foot he put forward he thought, This is it. I'm going to be shot. But the bullet never came and Miguel walked and walked and finally he reached the convenience store, and freedom. Sweating profusely, he collapsed on the steps and cried to the store manager for help. The manager found Miguel outside pleading to borrow his mobile so he could ring his father. He looked like shit. The manager called Torres and said, 'Your son is here.'

It was over.

Except that it wasn't.

The psychological damage from a kidnap can be severe and disabling. As a general rule, people are going to come out of a kidnap about as psychologically healthy as they went in. If someone is still feeling traumatised twenty-eight days after a crisis event such as a kidnap, it's likely they are suffering from post-traumatic stress disorder (PTSD). Kidnapping messes people and families up in a way that few other crimes do. Partially it's because of control. As normal, healthy people mature in life, they tend to get ever-increasing control over their lives. When you're a child, there's always somebody to tell you what to do, where and when to do it. As you grow up into young and mature adulthood, your control over your own life increases to the point where sometimes you're managing the lives of other people like employees and your own children. Whether this is actually true or not is besides the point. It's the illusion of control that is important to people. But when someone is abducted, that control evaporates. They're told when to go to the bathroom, when to eat, when to sleep. They depend entirely on someone else for survival. They become infantile again. So what often happens after they're released and they have physical control of their lives once more, is that they find themselves breaking down in tears in the lift at work. They feel like they've lost mental control.

My work in the corporate and business field had shown me that this stuff was not rocket science and that I could do it for myself. To that end I set up my own company, registered in the UK as Lopez Consulting Group, LCG. Most of the work was business consulting. But now I had the added drama and excitement of getting calls from FSI, asking me to work cases for them as a sub-contractor. The calls came out of the blue and I might be asked to fly out the next day or the next month. To begin with I worked from the kitchen table at my London home. It was a world away from the steel and glass skyscrapers that housed some of the businesses I had advised in the past. I was a newly married guy with little money in the bank and a constant stream of bills to deal with, as well as the added pressure of running my own company. But the thrill of a call from FSI made that all worthwhile.

I took a call from FSI on a frosty morning. The cultured English voice on the other end said, 'Ben, can you respond to a case in Mexico?'

'Sure,' I replied.

He proceeded to bring me up to speed on the Osorio case.

I flew to Mexico and met and assessed Miguel at his family home shortly after he'd been released. They lived in an exclusive suburb located outside the city with a large outdoor swimming pool and a tennis court. The hallmarks of the rich, the world over. I shook hands with Don Osorio, the dad, and was introduced to Hector and Luis and Margarita. Unlike some wealthy families, they seemed relatively grounded. I put this down to the parents creating a sound, safe environment in the home.

'Where did you fly in from?' Miguel asked.

'London. Via Madrid,' I said.

Suppressing a smile, Miguel told me that he'd earned his MBA at an English university in the north of the country. He talked me through the kidnap and his time in the prison. It appeared to me that the whole thing had been pre-planned for some while before. Blue Eyes was either a rotten cop or a gang member and his group was newly formed. Hence his desire to stamp his authority on the guards and the reason for emphasising to Miguel that they were treating him 'well' – his treatment would act as a presentation card for future victims. In other words, Blue Eyes wanted to carve out a reputation as a guy who doesn't kill his hostages. If he was planning to forge a career out of kidnapping, this made good business sense. Because no one's going to negotiate with someone who has a track record of blowing his victims' brains out.

Blue Eyes was intensely paranoid. Miguel told me that in the moments leading up to his release, Blue Eyes had ordered that the hostage's arms be wrapped in aluminium foil, seemingly in order to jam any subcutaneous GPS tracking chip on his person.

I ran through my standard checklist of debriefing questions with Miguel. One of them was, 'Have you ever thought about killing yourself?'

'Yes,' he replied. 'But it was years ago.'

'What happened?'

'When I first got to the university in England,' he said. 'They showed me to my room. It was in this dark, damp cinder-block building. The walls were weeping with water and there was a cast-iron bed in one corner and a thin, pissed-on mattress on top. My first day in England.' He had a smile creeping across his face. 'Man, it was miserable. I wanted to kill myself.'

I laughed. As an American living in London and surrounded by southerners, I'd heard countless stories about how grim life was north of Watford Junction. It brought to my mind that scene in *Monty Python's The Meaning of Life*, when a shot of Yorkshire is subtitled, 'The Third World.'

'At least the MBA helped me in one way,' Miguel said.

'How's that?'

'It prepped me for kidnap.' When he saw the look of confusion on my face, he went on: 'For managing depression and loneliness.'

I laughed again, but there was an element of truth to what Miguel was saying. Unlike special forces operators or CIA agents, Miguel had received no formal training in how to deal with the effects of abduction or what they call 'conduct after capture'. Yet he hadn't cracked under pressure, he had done nothing to undermine the negotiations and the lie about the rift between himself and the rest of his family was inspired.

Behind all this, the love of his family helped Miguel stay strong.

'Those thugs tried to tell me otherwise, but I knew Papa and my family were working for my release,' Miguel said as we took coffee in the living room. 'I thought about everyone in the family, all the good times we had together. It was nice to think about those things.'

This is what's known in the trade as mental stimulation. A hostage spends a lot of time isolated from the world. Human beings are social creatures; cutting off interaction with other people can often lead to extreme depression. By thinking about the good times with his family, Miguel had managed to stay upbeat about his chances of survival.

'They had my body but never my soul,' he said.

'It sounds like you behaved impeccably,' I said.

'It was not easy,' said Miguel wringing his hands. 'When they took me out of the room, I really thought I was going to die.'

'You're back home. The way you feel now is part of the healing process.' I looked across to Don Osorio and asked him how the rest of the family was holding up. The old man shrugged with his bottom lip.

'Margarita, she's scared to go out.'

Agoraphobia. 'Perhaps she should talk with me.'

I spoke at length with Margarita and concluded she was suffering from a mild form of agoraphobia. It wasn't acute to the point where it affected her ability to live a normal life. I gathered the family around and explained to them about tell-tale signs of PTSD and that future events – such as the anniversary of the abduction – might trigger stressful episodes in the future. But this was by no means unusual and such periods were likely to pass quickly. I felt this was a healthy nuclear family and if anything, the kidnap had actually strengthened the bond between them.

The Osorio case was one of several I worked on in a short timeframe down in Mexico. I was slowly establishing myself in the K&R industry. On the same trip I worked on a case that proved the maxim that sometimes the hardest part of the kidnap comes after the victim is released.

Jesus Soldado was a typical fourteen-year-old kid on his way home from school on a stifling summer day. His family lived in an upper-middle-class district of plush condos and penthouses. Soldado was just another teenager dealing with the same frustrations and urges as his peer group. Until a black Mercedes pulled up at the side of the road and two guys smacked him on the back of the head with a pistol butt before bundling him into the back seat.

As is usually the case, the kidnappers demanded a ton of money for his release. And as is also often the case, the kidnappers had made a grave and fairly basic miscalculation about exactly how much money the family had. Kidnappers tend to come from impoverished backgrounds. They are not generally a cross-section of people who hold down regular jobs and have credit cards and overdraft facilities. They see a family living in a big house with a gate at the front and three cars in the driveway, and they think to themselves, This family must have millions in the bank.

When in fact, as any middle-class person knows, the parents are probably mortgaged up to the hilt and up to their eyeballs in debt. They probably don't have a lot of cash sitting around in their bank account.

In those semi-failed states like Mexico and Colombia, the targets of kidnappers are increasingly middle-class people. They have the trappings of wealth but most don't have the elite's security guards and armoured cars with bulletproof windows. For whatever reason, the Soldado family came to the attention of the kidnappers and they hatched a plan to snatch Jesus.

This case was what's known as an express kidnap. In the world of K&R, there are several variations on kidnaps. Express kidnaps involve rapid abductions of individuals with the intent to secure as quick a ransom as possible. At the crudest level, an express kidnap can mean a victim being dragged to a nearby bank or ATM and forced to withdraw their own ransom payment. They are often abducted late in the evening so they can be taken to the ATM twice: before and after midnight, when they can withdraw up to their daily limit again. The gang shakes them down and relieves the poor guy or woman of their watch and wallet and other valuables, and sometimes breaks into their house and steals more stuff. Express kidnappings are an urban phenomenon, where the sheer number of ATMs makes it easy for a gang.

High-net-worth individual kidnappings, on the other hand, require a lot more advanced planning. The perps need time to gather intelligence on the target's personal habits, routines and security procedures. Only experienced kidnap gangs carry out these type of operations because of the risk involved and the difficulty of abducting a highly visible target. On the plus side, the payoffs can be significantly higher than a regular businessman.

Then you get tiger kidnappings, where hostages are taken not for the purpose of extracting a ransom but to force the relatives of the victim to take part in a criminal activity, such as robbing a bank or jewellery store or planting a bomb. The IRA carried out tiger kidnappings during the Troubles in order to force the hostage's relative or spouse to plant car bombs. The tiger name comes from the fact that the gangs stalk their prey and study their movements intensely before striking. As in all other forms of kidnapping, the gang's ultimate target is not the hostage but someone related to them.

Virtual kidnappings rely upon the absence of information to extort money from people within a very short period of time. The 'kidnappers' will wait until the target is unavailable, then reach out to the target's family or employers and claim they have him hostage and will kill him unless a ransom is paid within the next few hours. The ransom is usually modest because the gang needs a quick payment before the target is online again, and the funds available at such short notice tend to be fairly small.

In one incident in Buenos Aires, a businessman paid out a

ransom after being tricked into believing his brother had been abducted. The businessman received a call from a man who said his brother had been in an accident. He was told to hold the line and give his mobile phone number so they could provide him with more information before hanging up. A short while later the same man called back and said, after describing the brother, that he would be killed unless the brother paid a ransom of $10,000. The businessman said he didn't have that kind of money and settled on 5000 pesos. He delivered the cash to a nearby park – and later discovered that his brother had merely been out of his house on business. The businessman had been scammed. Five thousand pesos – equivalent to $1250 US – might not seem like a big ransom, but it's only taken the kidnapper a couple of hours to make that money.

In the Soldado case, Jesus's family had paid up the ransom and secured his release by the time my services were engaged. But the fallout from a hostage crisis doesn't end with the ransom payment – and this is what I mean by the psychological component of K&R. I had been specifically called in to deal with the psychological aspect. Jesus had only been a hostage for four days, but he'd been left extremely distressed by the ordeal. In fact the whole family was upset and finding it difficult to cope.

His experience had been somewhat rougher than many other hostages. The kidnappers had denied Jesus food and given him little water for the duration of his captivity. They also refused to dress the head wound caused at the abduction. Nor would they allow Jesus to go to the bathroom.

Jesus had a sister. Her name was Theresa. She was about to turn sixteen, which in Mexican culture means you host a coming out party, called *La Quinceañera*. This is one of the highlights of a family's social calendar and involves organising a big celebration with hundreds of guests invited. But the mother was not looking forward to it.

'What happens if we invite someone and they know the kidnappers?' she asked me. 'What if they're casing our house, to rob from us?'

This paranoia is something that often occurs when a family is reunited. My job was to help the parents and Jesus rebuild a sense of trust and get back to a mental state where they didn't have to wake up each morning stricken with fear and dread. I created a series of taglines for each of them to memorise and recite whenever they were feeling low. The taglines emphasised key points about the reunion. One of them read, 'It's not about coming home, it's about coming back to where you were before.'

Coming to grips with trauma is a key part of my job and how you go about it with the client depends on who they are – and where they come from. I once spent some time working in the Gaza Strip with news agency employees who were referred to me for treatment for post-traumatic stress disorder. One of my clients was a decorous, polite Israeli Arab called Ghezzal. He'd been struck by multiple rubber bullets fired by IDF soldiers while he operated a video camera feed for a news team covering a night-time demonstration. At the same incident Ghezzal's best friend had been killed. The event caused him great distress.

I decided to try a technique on Ghezzal known as Eye Movement Desensitisation and Reprocessing, or EMDR. No one knows exactly why this technique works so well, but we do know that it does. It's been very well researched and validated. If you were to watch someone receiving EMDR treatment, it would look a little like hypnosis. The psychologist asks the patient to remember part of the trauma. As they're remembering it, the psychologist moves a finger left and right in front of the patient's eyes and asks them to follow it with their eyes without moving their head.

Though we don't know the exact mechanisms, some people

think that traumas work on what's known as a feedback cycle. In other words, the trauma is stuck in the patient's head. While it's normal to suffer trauma after a certain event, after three or four months an individual shouldn't still be struggling to sleep or jumping with shock every time they hear a noise. People with PTSD get trapped in a vicious pattern where the fear doesn't dissipate as it normally would. Like the feedback in a sound amplifier. Somehow the eye movement process breaks the logjam in the patient's mind. You can get dramatic results with EMDR in literally one or two sessions.

But one of the prerequisites for effective EMDR is for the client to have a warm, safe, happy place they can go to, in their mind, so that the trauma doesn't get too overwhelming. This happy place can be anything. Getting a massage, snuggling in your sleeping bag or laying by the pool in a holiday resort. The only criteria is that it has to be someplace safe and disconnected from the trauma.

I asked Ghezzal to think of a safe place in his head.

'Tell me about somewhere warm and comfortable from your childhood,' I said. 'Maybe you were in your grandmother's arms? Or in your treehouse?'

Ghezzal frowned. 'We didn't have a grandmother,' he said. 'I never had a treehouse.'

For the next three hours Ghezzal and I tried to find a safe place. He didn't have one. When you've grown up in a perpetual war zone, where a guy can be shaving in front of his bathroom mirror only for an Israeli tank turret to smash through the window, there's no such thing as a safe place.

So I created a safe place for Ghezzal. I took him to the gym near my office and we hung out in the jacuzzi. Having spent all of his life in the Gaza Strip in the desert, Ghezzal had never laid eyes on a jacuzzi before. He'd never been fully immersed in water. He thought the jacuzzi was the greatest thing ever.

Although I opted against using EMDR on Jesus's parents, my work with them began to bear fruit. Gradually, the family learned to trust other people again. I held their hand through this process. By the end of my time with them, both mother and father were beginning to break through the paranoia barrier. They had hopes for the future once more. They realised they didn't have to live their lives under a cloud. The healing would not happen overnight, but that's okay. Just like a physical wound, these things take time.

Jesus's case opened the floodgates. Word got around that I'd done wonders for this family and within the space of a week a dozen clients got in touch asking for my help. All of a sudden I was busy as hell, running from home to home to help families through the trauma of a kidnapping. And there were plenty of families in need of my expertise: several thousand people a year are kidnapped in Mexico, and a large number take place in Latin America.

When it rains, it pours.

On that same trip I worked on the case of a thirty-one-year-old woman called Giuliana. She lived with her husband Mariano in a small town in Paraguay. Population about twenty thousand. It was a laid-back place in the mountains.

Giuliana was taken at six o'clock on a Monday evening as she was parking her car at the doctor's surgery. She was a few minutes late for her appointment and in a hurry. The kidnappers dragged her away from the vehicle. There were no witnesses. An hour and a half later, she was told to call her husband. When Mariano answered the phone, he was confronted with the chilling words spoken by his wife in a trembling voice: 'I have been abducted. Please do not tell the police.'

Giuliana was gone for a week. The family decided not to report the matter to the cops. Agreement was reached for a ransom of $41,000. The drop went ahead as per usual: the money was stuffed into a plastic grocery bag and the kidnappers led the person charged with making the exchange on a merry chase through places where they could safely observe him and check he wasn't being followed. The money was then dropped by a bridge underpass.

Giuliana's release was not the end of the story. In fact, that's where the trouble really started. Mariano believed that his wife had been raped during her time in captivity, an accusation she vehemently denied. Her protestations only fuelled Mariano's anger. He started lashing out at everybody. Matters were not helped by the financial burden the couple had suffered: this was an uninsured case, where the victims ended up having to pay the ransom and negotiation fees out of their own pocket.

I believed Giuliana when she said she hadn't been raped. Although her abduction had caused some psychological trauma, there is generally an awful lot more PTSD casualties when someone is sexually violated. The casualty rate can be around 50 per cent.

One of the reasons for this is that man-made events cause more psychological casualties than do natural disasters like fires or tsunamis. Ultimately this is because if you suffer at the hands of an earthquake or a flood, you can do something about it. You can move to the desert or relocate to the top of a mountain and never see water again. We evolved in a world where natural disasters happened all the time. People got eaten by lions, they moved away from the lions. Bingo, problem solved. But you can't live alone.

So when the tragedy is caused by your fellow human beings, it creates a major problem: how the hell do you protect yourself from people, when you need to be around them? That's one of the problems that Western governments are having to deal with now with the likes of al-Qaeda and the Taliban, because these terrorists are among us. When this occurs, it harms a person's sense of security and belief in an orderly universe. Trust goes out of the window.

The first time I met the couple I noticed that Giuliana's hand was shaking and Mariano was a mess. His leg was trembling and twitching nervously. Their faces displayed their emotions. Mariano was smiling and telling me there was nothing wrong, but it was a fake smile. How could I tell? Because real smiles happen up in the eyes.

Both Giuliana and Mariano were in a state of extreme agitation and stress. I knew Giuliana had been having trouble sleeping. She was dosed up on sedatives and temazepam, which is generally prescribed for patients who have severe insomnia. Helping out this couple was as much about salvaging their relationship as it was coping with the reality of being a hostage victim.

'Talk to me about what happened,' I said to Giuliana.

She nodded slowly and brushed her silky brown hair behind her ears. Despite the physical symptoms of their stress, both Giuliana and Mariano retained their good looks and charm. Giuliana was five-seven with azure blue eyes and the kind of sexy, bronze-blonde skin that made women want to sign up to tanning salons. Mariano was five-ten and had the classic Latino dark good looks. Deep-set eyes, smooth jaw, dark hair. They made a handsome couple and had made a ton of money in finance.

'I remember the older man,' Giuliana said. Her voice was weary and tired. 'He was nice to me. They blindfolded me and made me live in a room under the stairs. The younger man was a local chief.' Her fingernails dug into the palm of her hand. 'He was not nice.'

I listened intently as Giuliana described the classic good-cop, bad-cop scenario. The older guy, I figured, had to be the leader. He would butter Giuliana up and placate her while his number two, the chief, would shout at her and make threats. She also had a distinct memory of her keeper – the guy charged with watching over her.

'He had very hairy arms,' Giuliana said. 'And they called him *la muchachito*.'

As hostages are typically blindfolded, denying them a look at the face of their abductors, a hostage's memory of the people around them during their incarceration is often of hands and shoes: that's all they ever get to see. The *la muchachito* thing intrigued me. In Spanish nouns are gender-specific. *El* is male, *La* is female. *La muchachito* kind of means 'little girl'. But if I call someone *el mucha chito* it means 'the little girl who is a boy'. Like a ladyboy.

Giuliana's keeper was gay.

La muchachito repeated a phrase several times to Giuliana. '*No me tutees.*'

In Spanish there are several levels of formality when you address somebody. To say *tu* is very informal, *tu usted* is how you would communicate with a stranger, and *vosotros* is how you would talk to the King. Depending on where you are and who you're talking to, misuse of these terms can be very offensive. It'd be like paying a visit to your doctor and calling him or her 'dude'. You just wouldn't do it. And this is what *La muchachito* was saying to Giuliana, in effect: don't call me dude. She was using the *tu* form to address him. The fact the keeper got so highly strung about a relatively minor thing told me he was an unstable, volatile person who was very dangerous. As are nearly all kidnappers.

Mariano was a very macho guy. His anxiety about Giuliana having been raped was more down to paranoia than any evidence. It was also the kind of deep-rooted fear that many men suffer from to some degree. From an evolutionary perspective, marriage and monogamy really only works for men. If there's no monogamy, then the man is unsure whose children he is raising.

Giuliana and Mariano had been separated for several months before the abduction took place. They were trying for a baby, and failing. Giuliana was freaking out that she might never have children and Mariano was too immature to deal with it, so she moved out.

I patiently explained to the couple that being taken hostage is one of the most emotionally powerful experiences a human being can go through – and that goes for both the hostage and their relatives. That sense of joy someone feels when a loved one is free? It's a temporary thing. What quickly sets in afterwards is a rollercoaster of emotional highs and lows, and it can take a long time to finally get over these bumps and return to normal everyday life. Part of my reason for giving them this psycho-education was so that they would better understand their emotions after the fact. It's like what the sign outside the Australian Army's Parachute School says: 'Knowledge dispels fear.'

As I spoke to them, I felt instinctively that Giuliana and Mariano's relationship wouldn't survive. Hostage-takings either cement or expose the cracks in a relationship. Rarely do they leave things exactly as they were before. Sadly for Giuliana and Mariano, the kidnapping was likely to rip their world apart. I spoke to Mariano separately and said, 'Look, Giuliana says she was not raped. There's no reason to doubt her. But let's imagine for a moment that she was. So what? She's back home now.'

Mariano couldn't get over the idea that someone might have violated his wife. From my observations, I had the distinct impression that he was mentally checking out of the relationship and, whether consciously or subconsciously, the possibility of Giuliana having been sexually assaulted while captive provided him with another reason to leave.

'There is one other thing,' Giuliana told me as I prepared to leave for my next assignment.

'What's that?' I said.

'My brother, Hugo. He says he wants to find who kidnapped me. He says he wants to make them pay.'

The look in her eyes said that this wasn't an idle threat. Clearly she thought Hugo was capable of killing the kidnappers. I asked her what Hugo did for a living.

'He runs a car-rental business. He rents out cars to tourists.'

'You think he might be able to find them?'

'Maybe,' she shrugged. 'It's a small town. People know people.'

I never did find out what happened to the kidnappers. But something tells me that Hugo might just have made good on his threat.

Latin America taught me a lot. It's a market leader in kidnap. I worked on all kinds of cases, got to witness at first hand the multiple crises that arise when someone is taken hostage by a gang. Talking to the kidnappers is only a small part of a negotiator's work. After all, he can only speak on the phone as and when the perp feels like it. If the perp doesn't want to return the negotiator's calls for a week or two, there's little the negotiator can do. Aside from the actual negotiation, he or she has to be able to bring order and organisation to a chaotic situation. I'd come in to the family or the firm and work hard to make everyone feel better. Sometimes my very presence was enough to chill people out. They saw me as the specialist – the guy who was going to make everything all right again.

But I realised that if I wanted to succeed as a negotiator, I'd have to be able to juggle a million things at once and not crack under the pressure. I was confident in my abilities, but what I was really looking for was a job where I could conduct my own negotiations and direct the operation from top to bottom. My skill sets had prepared me for this moment.

I caught a red-eye flight back to London direct. Spent half the flight staring out of the window and figuring out my next move. When I landed at Heathrow I made a point of stopping at the newsagents to grab a paper for the train journey back to central London. The headline on that morning edition described another terrorist attack in Pakistan. According to the editorial, Pakistan was a hotbed of insurgent activity spilling over from the war in Afghanistan. The presidency of Pervez Musharraf was coming under intense pressure and the whole country looked ripe for further strife and instability.

Jesus, I thought. Who the hell would want to travel there?

Abduction – Captivity – **Proof of Life** –
Negotiation – Ransom Drop – Release

Part Three

DROP ZONE

'Have you seen the Sheikh when he cuts the heads off?
We will do the same thing.'

Samar Yussuf

5

INITIAL ACTION

In the summer of 2003, around the time that Iraq and Afghanistan were going to hell in a handbasket I was sitting in my joke of an office when the landline rang. I'd rented premises in central London from where I could run Lopez Consulting Group. I soon regretted not sticking with the kitchen table. The business did need an office, owing to the amount of work I was having to deal with, so the move kind of made sense. Sadly about the only thing exclusive the building had was the postcode. The office itself lacked any heating. It was a freezing cold morning and I wasn't doing myself any favours by hitting the bottle every night.

I was not in the mood to take that call.

Being a hostage negotiator takes its toll on your body and mind. Most negotiators are paunchy, middle-aged guys with a house in the country and a legacy of strained personal relationships. The constant travelling and working in far-off locations is partly responsible for this, but it's also because of the type of person attracted to a career spent talking to sociopaths and hardened criminals. Negotiators are frequently people who require a high level of stimulation. Any relationship gets boring after a period of time. My relationship with Emily was beginning to suffer for precisely that reason. I was becoming obsessed by the work and had started to view her in a different light. The things I had appreciated about her at the beginning – her exoticness, her fierce intelligence – I now found grating and unappealing. Little by little, distance opened up between us. Those who crave normality and routine need not apply.

Neither is it a job for people who can't cope with being lonely. When you've eaten in the same restaurant in the same hotel for three weeks and know every single item on the menu by heart, you start to feel empty inside. You realise you're living a soulless existence. And you're in the paradoxical situation of being bored stupid but stressed to buggery.

I used to counter the boredom by drinking heavily. Dark, aged rum was my poison of choice. I spent some time living in Puerto Rico in my twenties teaching scuba-diving to tourists and the local liquor of choice was dark rum. I'd drink it straight because in the local convenience stores, the Coke cost more than the rum and I thought to myself, Why bother with the Coke? I took to having my rum neat with some ice and a slice of lime, and I carried this habit into my negotiating days.

Returning from a case is the world's worst comedown. When the pilot announces you're coming in for the final landing at Heathrow and the cloud cover breaks and you see the gridlocked, iron-grey mass of London laid out in front of you, that's when you start to feel the exhaustion your body has been building up for the past weeks or months of a case. I'd think to myself, I'm back in the land where nothing works.

INITIAL ACTION

From the moment I disgorged myself from the plane and hit the luggage carousel, everything at Heathrow appeared to have a vaguely shitty veneer. I'd head over to the train and find it was running late, if at all. And when it did arrive it seemed to take for ever to depart. Then I'd be coughed up at Paddington in rush hour and the taxi rank line would stretch around the station while dark clouds seethed sheets of pissy rain. The cold chilled me to my bones.

I'd arrive back at my flat on the third floor of an apartment block in east London. The apartment was great, a sweet little place with enormous rooms, stylish furniture and a roof terrace that overlooked downtown. But to come back to it after several weeks away was a dejecting experience. I'd look in the fridge and find nothing but a container of curdled milk. Rotten fruit in a basket on the counter. I'd be starving hungry and on a Sunday night at eleven o'clock, even in the middle of London, a guy's options are limited to either greasy kebabs or a late-night curry.

There was an off-licence located a ways down the street and they offered a home delivery service. So each night I'd call them and place an order for a bottle or two of Rhum Barbancourt. They were happy to deliver. Being American, I'd always tip the guy generously. I'd polish off a bottle in a couple of days.

On top of the boozing, I wasn't sleeping properly, and because my business was divided between New York and London and God knows where else, I was perpetually jet-lagged. In a single year I was doing maybe fifteen trips to the US and back, and double that to other hotspots like Mexico. I must have lost fifty IQ points on the jet lag alone. Add in the drinking and you could easily double that. Believe me, I couldn't afford it either.

That morning the arctic temperature did me no favours. And the hangover was chronic. Like someone had taken a pickaxe to the back of my head. I rubbed my hands to get some warmth back into them and picked up the receiver, trying to block out the rumbling London soundtrack of traffic and police sirens. My marriage to Emily was not working out the way we had both hoped, and we were now living separately, almost separate lives. Practically the only thing that was saving me was the job. When I sat down to negotiate or act as a response consultant, I felt completely at ease, in the zone.

I overheard my PA Inga Svensson answer the phone. Inga was an elegant Swedish blonde with a teasing smile and a body that wouldn't look out of place in a Victoria's Secret catalogue. For some reason she seemed to flash that smile at me a lot. If she hadn't been such a diligent PA, I would've asked her out for dinner.

For the first months of my business it had been just me and Inga, but after a while it became apparent that the workload was more than the two of us could handle. So I asked my brother, Tony, who at the time was scouting about for something new and different. He'd been teaching English in France and the timing was right for both of us. Tony was the younger of us and had a good business head on his shoulders. My parents used to say I leaped before I looked, whereas Tony looked before he leaped. Together we made a good team. I brought him on board to be the operations manager, handling the day-to-day side of the business.

'Ben, it's John, do you want me to put him through?'

'Yep, I'll take it.'

I was staring blankly at the pile of bills and notices that had stacked up on my desk during my absence. I had a lot of work but was beginning to realise one of the truisms of running your own business: people are always quick to demand your services but slow to pay up. I probably wasted more time chasing unpaid invoices than anything else.

'John, good to hear your voice. Get to the point.'

'Ben, can you respond?'

John was a former SAS warrant officer who'd started up his

own private security company, and I knew him well from the Circuit. 'I've got this case and I need a negotiator. Are you interested?'

I cradled the phone and flicked through the bills. Red letter, red letter, red letter. I needed the work. My first question, as usual, was 'Where?'

'Karachi,' said John, his heavy laugh coming down the phone like stones shaking inside a bag. 'Sorry, Ben. One of these days I'll get you a job in Hawaii.'

'One of these days, my friend.' I rubbed my temples. 'The short answer is yes. But how about you tell me what's going on?'

John explained that the company was a distribution outfit based in the sprawling metropolitan centre of Karachi on Pakistan's south coast. They had a contract delivering vital equipment to US forces in Afghanistan. The company had just finished a delivery job for which they were paid $530,000 in $100 bills. When the company received payment in Karachi, the money was split. Half was dispatched to Hyderabad some sixty miles to the north-east, with the other $265,000 remaining in Karachi, kept for safekeeping in the house of a company employee. A few days later, that same employee was taken hostage.

From the off, the timing between the delivery of the money and the abduction seemed too close to be a coincidence. It just didn't seem right. In this business, there are a lot of inside jobs, and on this case I had my suspicions immediately. But I didn't have time to investigate that side of it further.

'Are we sure that this isn't a self-kidnap?' I asked.

'This one's genuine,' John replied.

In the world of K&R, the first thing you have to do is rule out self-kidnap. It's one of the universal truths of life that people will go to extreme lengths to get a payday, and that includes hiring some goons to kidnap them in order to rip off their insurance company. As a negotiator you really don't want to find yourself caught up in this kind of mess, so you make it a priority to find out the lay of the land first.

'Okay, I'll do it,' I said.

We got the business terms out of the way, then John suggested I call the owner of the company direct and get up to speed on events on the ground. The owner was a guy called Aamir Rehman. I put the phone down, washed a couple of aspirin down with a glass of tepid tap water. Aqua de Ken, as I called it. I dialled the number in Karachi. After a series of clicks and whirrs, a voice as rough as gravel answered in rudimentary English.

'Yes?'

'This is Ben Lopez,' I said. 'I'm the kidnap consultant. May I please speak to Mr Rehman?'

'Please, call me Aamir,' the guy replied, sounding relieved. 'Thank you for helping.'

'Thank me later. We've got a lot of work to do. Tell me, how can we be sure this isn't a fraud? Or maybe the guy isn't abducted at all? Maybe he's just out with his girlfriend for the weekend.'

'No, no,' Aamir said. 'I can assure you, this is not a false alarm.'

'But how can you be sure?'

'I am sure,' Aamir snapped.

I decided to leave this line of enquiry alone for the moment. 'Before I fly over, I'm going to need to know the ins and outs of the case. Have the kidnappers been in touch yet?'

'They have not. But I have an email. I sent it to John earlier. It has all the details we know so far. Times, dates, locations. Maybe you find it interesting. I send to you now. Okay?'

'Sounds good.'

A few minutes later my inbox pinged with the forwarded message. It laid out the facts in more detail. At approximately 1800 hours the previous day, the employee, Jadid Khan, was driving his white BMW 3 series into a trailer park located outside

Karachi to meet with some of the company's drivers and give them their way bills. He stopped to chat with the owner of a shop located inside the trailer park. Khan often went to the park to deliver the way bills and he knew the shop owner well. After chatting for a while, Khan received a call from a security company. These guys had a contract with Aamir. The security guy asked Khan where he was. Khan told him, hung up and thought nothing of it.

Several minutes later, Khan heard the angry revving of engines. He stood up from his chair outside the shop and looked towards the gates at the trailer park entrance. They were open. Usually four guards manned the truck gates but today there were none, which seemed a little unusual. Plumes of dust swirled above the gates like a mini sandstorm. Four tattered, black Mercedes Benz coupes raced into the park.

Twelve men spilled out. They all wore dark trousers, tan shirts and keffiyehs covering the lower halves of their faces. They were all armed with AK-47 assault rifles with the exception of a fat guy at the front wearing an olive-green shirt covered in sweat patches. He wasn't wearing a head scarf. He had small, pig-like eyes and a beard so thick and straggly it could moonlight as a thicket. He gripped a Glock 17 pistol in his right hand, his chubby finger wrapped around the trigger like a grub on a branch. Despite the beard, there was a youthfulness about his face that made Khan think he must be in his early or mid-twenties.

The fat guy aimed the pistol at Khan. The employee found himself staring down the menacing black hole of the barrel.

'You,' the guy said in a rough voice. 'Are you Jadid Khan?'

Khan said he was.

'You're coming with us.'

The guys behind the fat man dragged Khan into the back of one of the Mercedes. Despite the drama of his situation, Khan was sharp enough to note that the kidnappers referred to the fat guy as 'sir'. He was definitely the ringleader and called all the shots. I would later learn that this was one of the guys we were negotiating with on the phone. He called himself Samar Yussuf.

The kidnappers also took away Khan's car. That detail made me sit up and pay attention. For me, that's a diagnostic sign. It virtually ruled out the possibility that they were al-Qaeda or some kind of affiliate terrorist group. If it was al-Qaeda, they probably wouldn't bother stealing the guy's car. Stealing the car told me these guys were a bunch of crooks who wanted to get the most bang for their buck. They'd set eyes on Khan's BMW and figured they could sell it on for a profit.

In a way this was good news because it made the kidnappers less likely to bring serious harm to Khan. Kill him and they wouldn't receive the ransom.

I finished reading the email and called Aamir back. 'All right,' I said. 'Here's the first thing we're gonna do. I'm going to send you an initial action checklist. Have a look at it and call me back.'

The IAC is essentially a memory aid. It helps to prepare the client for the kinds of problem that kidnapping presents. If you're doing business in a country where the press is an issue and the victim is a high value target (HVT), then you'll need to release a carefully worded holding statement to the media. It will look something like this:

There has been an abduction of one of our personnel in the [area / country].

No details are available at present, but our emergency response plans have been initiated. We are communicating with the Government and other local agencies for an early release of our personnel.

Further statements will be released as information is received.

No further questions.

Thank you.

The IAC also establishes the communications standpoint. In negotiation, the golden maxim is: he who controls the communications controls the case. You absolutely do not want multiple people communicating with the kidnappers because these Chinese whispers are how you get and receive mixed messages. This usually ends up in the case taking longer than it could have. The problem is much worse nowadays because everybody who gets kidnapped has a mobile and the kidnappers will just start calling people at random. So you also have to make up a list of people who might be called. This is essentially family – the people who have influence and an emotional bond to the hostage. Once this list is put together each relative has to be called and told, 'Here's what you do if they call you.'

The first person to talk to is always the wife or husband of the hostage. We try not to scare or alienate them, but we always tell them the truth because no matter how traumatised or upset they are, we would much rather have them inside the tent pissing out than outside the tent pissing in. We want them on our side.

Tony booked me on a Qatar Airlines flight from Heathrow to Karachi connecting at Doha International Airport in Qatar. It was agreed that I would travel by car to the premises with an armed personal security detail (PSD) provided by John's company. I didn't want to use my client's security, since I wasn't sure they weren't involved in the kidnap. Whereas I trusted John and his people. In negotiations, we always follow the first rule of any kind of rescue.

Don't become the second victim.

I have a 'go' bag always ready, filled with fresh clothes, toiletries, chargers, any meds I might be taking at that moment, and Pro Plus and Red Bull to keep me going. Also into the go bag goes a crisis management programme (CMP) checklist, phone-line recording equipment, a printout of the database of the contact details and pertinent information on every single employee in the company, a list of family contacts, plus local law-enforcement agency phone numbers and those of any relevant embassies, NGOs and individuals in the media known to the company management.

I always say to my students in negotiation classes, what's the first thing you do when you agree to work a case? Hands go up in the air. Most of them answer that you pack or send an email. I say, wrong. The first thing you do is take a pee. Because from that moment on, you don't even know when you're gonna have the chance to take a pee. Your schedule becomes sadistically frantic, and all your energy and time are focused on resolving the case. Not toilet breaks.

As my taxi shuttled me towards Heathrow, in the back of my mind I knew I was taking a risk by operating the case from inside Karachi. Sometimes consultants can work a case from London when the kidnapping is the other side of the world. But this case needed a hands-on approach. All I knew was, Karachi had been in the news a lot. The place was in turmoil. Terrorist attacks, suicide bombings and corruption were part of daily life. In 2002 terrorists had launched an attack on a bus carrying French naval engineers and suicide bombers had struck at the US Consulate. A poor intelligence network, widespread corruption within Pakistan's Inter-Services Intelligence agency (ISI), combined with hundreds of sectarian organisations and a thriving port and industry drawing people from all over the country, meant Karachi was a city where militant Islam thrived. It had become a key funding base for the terrorists' ongoing conflict in the tribal regions. Perhaps, I speculated, Khan's abductors were trying to raise funds to launch attacks in neighbouring Afghanistan.

The flight took ten hours with the stopover and refuelling, and I touched down at Karachi at a little past six o'clock in the morning. My hangover finally receded somewhere over Austria, I think.

Meeting up with my security detail, we raced towards the centre of Karachi. It seemed to me to be a nondescript, shithole industrial town like thousands of others around the world. Particularly as we made our way through Korangi Industrial Area (KIA). Gridlocked traffic, air pollution so bad it felt like I was choking on a pack of cigarettes and drab tan-coloured buildings. Nothing much was going on there.

I had a room booked at the Marriott Hotel, a four-star gig with a swimming pool a little under ten miles from Karachi Jinnah International Airport. I had a window view overlooking the MCB Tower, the gleaming 116-metre-tall skyscraper that dominated the Karachi skyline. When you're in somewhere like Pakistan you make damn sure you stay in a good hotel, purely for the security it offers. You do not want to be based in some exposed two-star joint where anyone could walk in off the street and grab you. Security aside, I wouldn't be enjoying the hotel's creature comforts. Once that phone rang and I was on the case, I knew I would never rest, rarely sleep, barely eat. You drink a lot of coffee and Red Bull. You have to be ready to respond twenty-four-seven.

And you're thinking. Always, always, always thinking. Thinking about every possible angle. Negotiations of this kind are the most demanding and exhausting mental process that I know of. It's also the most exhilarating. I chucked my go bag on the lumpy mattress, sploshed some cold water over my face and necked a Diet Coke. My body ached for a precious few moments of shut-eye but my sense of duty said that I had better hit the ground running. So I checked out of the hotel and jumped in my security detail's ride towards the company offices.

I took in the surroundings of the place where I'd be spending the next few weeks. Downtown was a stockpile of electronics stores, coffee shops with smeared windows and pudgy guys sitting outside in groups and sipping tea. They eyed me, the foreigner, suspiciously through the spicy haze of their fuggy cigarettes. Every road was potholed and filled with accumulated rubbish. The concept of a highway code seemed to be alien to the residents of Karachi. It was August, the height of the summer, and the temperature was in the low forties. The roads were practically melting.

The office block was utterly anonymous. I could have been in some suburban industrial estate in London or New York. And it was empty. I'd arrived way early in the morning. A porter let me in, an old guy with a face like crumpled sandpaper and teeth the colour of old bones. You get guys like this in every office in places like Pakistan and India. He's a porter and a security guard rolled into one. He didn't speak any English. Somehow we communicated through hand signals and established that the boss was expecting me. He gestured to a chair and I sat there and waited for Aamir.

Several minutes later Aamir showed up and the rest of the office crowd began trickling in for the day's work. There was a weird vibe among the employees. Khan held a reasonably important position at the company and word of his kidnapping had spread quickly through the watercooler grapevine.

I shook hands with Aamir. The guy had a firm shake and a determined look in his eyes, and my first impression was that he was a smart operator.

Aamir introduced me to Khan's wife, Shadah. She had delicate hands and a quiet, shy manner about her. Dark hair that reached down to the small of her back. Electric green eyes and softly drawn lips. In her own way she was quite attractive. I smiled at her to make her feel better and said, 'Please don't worry. I'm here to get your husband back alive and well, and I won't rest until that happens.'

She tried to smile back.

'How long have you been married?'

'Four months,' she said.

I smiled again. It's a simple thing but a smile can make a person feel that things are going to be okay. Even the very fact of me being on board was reassuring to Shadah. It's a sign that the professionals are here. We've been parachuted in to ensure her husband is returned home. There's a certain theatre to being a negotiator. As well as being skilled at understanding and manipulating the kidnapper, you also have to project a sense of control and authority to the people you're working for. That helps to tone down the tension and create a stable environment in which to get things done.

'Shadah,' I said, 'may I see your mobile phone?'

She took out a Sony Ericsson and handed it to me. I slipped off the case and removed the battery. Then I ejected the SIM card and showed it to her. 'We need to change this,' I explained. That way we could block any attempts by the kidnapper to harass or target the wife.

I repeated to Shadah that we would pay, and we would get her husband back. I turned to Aamir. 'Okay, let's get a situation room set up.'

'Situation room?' Aamir asked.

I explained what I needed. A situation room is similar to a negotiator cell: it has to be private, lockable, available indefinitely and around the clock, with access to telephone lines and the internet, computers, a printer and plenty of power sockets so I can record all the conversations with the kidnappers. And it has to be soundproofed as much as possible to avoid people listening in. Aamir leaned forward in his executive chair and nodded.

'We have just the place for you,' he said. He gave me a meeting room situated away from the employee offices and pods. I inspected the place. It was perfect. We wasted no time in getting everything set up. While that was being taken care of, I gave Aamir a task. Tasks are great. They provide a distraction from emotional turmoil and give people a sense of movement, of doing something, of being useful.

'I need you to find someone with the following criteria.' I'd written the criteria down on a piece of paper because when people are upset, they forget things. At the top of the piece of paper was a single word: COMMUNICATOR.

The communicator is the guy who would be doing much of the actual talking to the kidnappers over the phone. There are several characteristics of a good communicator. They have to be someone with local knowledge, fluent in the local dialect and languages. Someone who is completely and utterly trustworthy. The person has to be available twenty-four hours a day, seven days a week, and they also have to be totally loyal and at my beck and call for the length of the case, however long that may be. The communicator is the conduit to the kidnapper. All the communications to the kidnapper must go through this person.

Abdul was our communicator. He was a chain-smoking guy, had eyes as black as button holes. A mid-level manager in the company with an impeccable track record, he knew Khan well. Abdul had a soft, lyrical voice that I felt would go some way towards shaking off the tension the kidnappers would be feeling on the other end of the line.

Abdul was a funny guy. One day while waiting for the kidnappers to come back to us, we had a chat over coffee and somehow ended up on the subject of the sea. Abdul let slip that he'd spent all of his life in Karachi and never once left the city.

He reminded me of a guy I'd met in the Gaza Strip, an engineer by the name of Jamal. He came from a long line of communists and had spent time in Israeli jails, where he claimed he'd been tortured. Jamal had to cope with the incredible burden of supporting an extended family of more than fifty people. He was fundamentally intact but stressed to breaking point. People in the West get worked up about supporting a child or two; imagine having fifty people relying on you. Jamal worked day and night and never took a day's holiday, which only added to the level of stress he was feeling. He refused to take a break.

I said to Jamal's boss, 'Here's what you do. Send him to Thailand for fourteen days. Give him two days' work and make him sit on his ass for the other twelve. Tell him that you'll phone him the next day with some work, but never call. Force him to have a vacation.'

I saw Jamal a month later and the guy was totally refreshed. That break had done him the world of good.

I made it a personal goal of mine to take Abdul sightseeing once the case was over. It was the least reward I could offer him considering his ability to work under pressure.

Next I needed to compose a crisis management team. It was my job to source an employee – whether it's the lawyer or the financial director or accountant – who could discreetly and quickly pull together a lot of cash: the ransom. This person also had to have the mental strength to stay calm and composed under pressure and to think logically.

I also had to locate that special guy, the one who's been there for ever, knows everyone on a first-name basis and is friends with the janitor and the CEO. Every company's got one. Somebody who knows where all the bodies are buried, who knows how to get things done. I call this guy the foreman.

Our foreman figure was a guy by the name of Naveed. He was a skinny guy with dark hair, dark skin, dark clothes. He would have ultimate responsibility for overseeing the logistics of the operation. Anything we needed, from computers to cigarettes, Naveed was the guy we'd go to see.

Aamir had also brought in some third-party assistance. Jaffar ran his own business across town and was related to Aamir in a way that I never quite fully understood, Pakistani families being inherently more complicated than American or British ones. I figured he was some kind of cousin. A successful businessman in his own right, Jaffar stood at five-ten and wore a beige suit with an open-necked white shirt, pristine and neatly pressed. He smoked cigars and this heavy, sweet and spicy scent drifted off him like a cloud in his wake.

He had something I needed and that I wanted to make sure stayed a secret. He spoke Arabic, Punjabi and Pashto. As much as Aamir trusted Abdul, I wanted to have some insurance.

After some initial niceties, I pulled Jaffar aside from the rest of the group. 'Are you listening to me?'

Jaffar nodded.

'I want you to listen very carefully to each phone call live as they happen.'

'I understand, my friend,' Jaffar said.

By employing Jaffar as a secret second translator, I created a fail-safe in the situation room. He could listen in confidence to the dialogue between the kidnappers and Abdul and report back to me privately on what was being said. For all the Punjabi and Pashto I knew, when Abdul was on the phone he might be saying, 'We'll do a deal, $100,000 and I'll keep fifty of it.' It's not that Abdul struck me as that kind of guy, and Aamir had personally vouched for him, but I had to consider all aspects of the situation. And a guy on a meagre salary, faced with the prospect of maybe making some serious cash for himself, might be tempted to put his morals aside.

As a New York rabbi friend of mine once said, 'Believe in God, but plant cabbages anyway.'

This was my CMT. Aamir, the CEO, was not involved in a hands-on role because when it comes to large companies, CEOs are the ones who have to make decisions. My job, whether it's law-enforcement negotiation or K&R, is to provide options. The CEO needs to be presented with the list of options and to make the decision on the path they want to take. I make options; they make the call. That's how it works.

All the hostage negotiators I know share a healthy – and sometimes not so healthy – contempt for authority. We're not afraid to speak our minds, and we don't automatically assume the person at the top of the pyramid is correct. In fact, in many cases, it pretty much guarantees they're not. This contempt hasn't created any problems for me on cases. I'm the outsider to whatever client I'm working for, and because of my expertise and the seriousness of the matter, CEOs will normally defer to me on all matters related to the negotiations. There have been a few directors who left me thinking afterwards, Jeez, what a nightmare it must be working for that guy. But negotiators will just shrug and get on with the job. We're not there to kiss anyone's ass. It's not a popularity contest.

I gathered up all the SIM cards from anybody in Khan's address book who we thought might be contacted by the kidnappers and replaced them with new ones. I gave this task to Naveed. Meanwhile, at my request, Jaffar went out and bought a bunch of unlocked mobiles and chargers to put the old SIM cards in. Now, regardless of who the kidnappers tried to reach, they'd be coming through to us. At the same time, I also opened Hushmail accounts for everyone connected to the case. Hushmail is an encrypted email provider that uses advanced encryption to keep communications secure. It uses techniques that even the CIA finds next to impossible to crack.

The kidnappers called the number of a friend whose SIM card we had not yet obtained. The friend's name was Iqbal. He took the call sometime around seven o'clock in the evening.

'Are you Iqbal?' the kidnapper said.

'Who is this?' Iqbal replied.

'A friend of Jadid Khan's. Tell me, where are you right now?'

'Who I'm speaking to?'

'Khan is here with us. We are the kidnappers.'

Iqbal felt his guts tie up in a figure-of-eight knot. 'What do you want?'

'The hostage says you are the representative from the company he works for. You are the one we are going to do business with.'

'I'm not from the company,' Iqbal said. 'I'm a friend of Jadid's wife. You need to speak with Abdul.' He read out the phone number we had given him.

'We don't want relatives! We want the company!'

'Call Abdul,' Iqbal replied firmly.

There was hissing down the line, muttered cursing under the caller's breath. Then he said, 'Have you seen the Sheikh when he cuts the heads off?' making a reference to the beheadings in Iraq that had been in the news. 'We will do the same thing with him.'

The line went dead and Iqbal got in touch with us. I told him well done and instructed him to take out his old SIM card and throw it in the trash. The next time the kidnappers called, they would be reaching out to Abdul. And I would be ready beside him.

The game had begun.

6

GOOD MONEY AFTER BAD

'We want two million rupees,' the voice crackled down the line. The kidnapper was on edge, his shrill voice jumping up and down like shares on a stock-market graph. From the kidnapper's perspective, this is the moment they've been waiting for. This is when they're about to get rich and all the hard work in planning the abduction finally pays off. Dollar signs flash before their eyes. Except their nerves were making them mix up their currencies.

'Yeah, yeah, no problem. Two million rupees, Okay.'

Two million rupees was about $22,000. I heard a rush of static on Yussuf's end of the connection as he snorted his frustration. 'No, no, no. You misheard me. Dollars, I said. We want two million dollars.'

'Are you sure? I could have sworn you said *rupees*, my friend.'

'No! Two million *dollars*!'

From the outset it was clear that these guys were not exactly the sharpest professional kidnappers in the world. Manipulating them would take time, but I was sure I could do it. We were not even a day into the case and they were already screwing up.

At the same time as we spoke to Yussuf, I had Naveed and Jaffar putting feelers out to discover what kind of assets the company had. If things went according to plan, we'd need to pay up a ransom to secure Khan's release and to do that we'd need to make an exchange locally. Two days before Khan had been abducted there had been a bomb attack killing more than fifty people. The atmosphere on the streets was one of fear, hostility and unrest. My immediate concern, given the deteriorating security situation, was that sourcing a reliable figure to drop off the cash was going to be a tall order.

Each time Yussuf called I prepared a script for Abdul. The script gave a list of messages that Abdul was tasked with delivering, depending on Yussuf's demands and questions. They ranged from questions about the hostage's heath – 'How is Khan today, may I speak with him?' – to warnings that obtaining any level of cash was not going to be easy – 'It's hard for us to get a large amount of money from the bank. The authorities will become suspicious.'

The fact they were talking in Pashto meant I wasn't able to come up with real-time notes to pass to him, but after each dialogue had finished I would get Abdul to play the tapes back and translate it word for word. Then I would read it to myself several times and analyse it, and double-check with Jaffar that the conversation was as Abdul had described it. That allowed me to help plan out the next call, and so on. By doing this, we could shape the direction of the negotiations and set traps for the kidnappers.

You'd be surprised how much you can tell about the way a conversation is going from tone of voice, speed and rate of fluency. And after you've been doing this kind of work for a while you start to get a sixth sense about that kind of thing, so you really feel as if you know what's going on.

The situation room had changed since Aamir handed me the keys to it. It was dark now, with the blinds pulled down so nobody could look in the windows. The walls had been covered with brown butcher paper, the kind you wrap meat in. It's strong and doesn't bleed through when you write on it with a magic marker, so prying eyes can't read what's written on it when it's over a window.

I'd scribbled key points on the paper for Abdul, Naveed and Jaffar to remember at all times. Everything was written in Pashto as well as English. 'Silent Running – Mobiles to be switched off at all times'; 'Proof of life', 'Proof of Possession EVERY TIME!'

When the negotiator's on the phone, the team enters something called silent running. Nobody talks. People will scribble messages and pass them to one another, but nobody will break the silence, so the negotiator can absolutely focus on the voice on the other end of the line.

Proof of possession (POP) and life (POL) are distinctly different. Proof of life comes in many forms: pictures of a guy holding up a newspaper with the day's date and headlines printed along the front, for example. But this is not a good way to ascertain whether the hostage is alive or not because it can easily be manipulated. On one case I was involved in, the hostage, a middle-aged man with a pre-existing heart condition, died quickly and suddenly of a heart attack during the abduction. Obviously this complicated the kidnappers' plans for a payday, so they put the guy in a freezer and pulled him out every couple of weeks, propped him up with that day's edition of the local newspaper in his hands. They would capture the shot on a blurry, grainy mobile phone camera in order to disguise the fact that we were looking at a dead guy. The unfortunate family received a corpse in exchange for the substantial ransom they paid. The fact that the hostage died early on and probably didn't suffer much was little consolation to the family.

It's even worse with video. You can shoot a video today, change the date stamp, hold on to it for three months and send it to the hostage's family another month later, and they would have no idea that their loved one was already dead.

The best proof of life is talking to the hostage on the phone. If I can't convince the kidnappers to let us talk to the hostage, I'll ask a question that only the hostage would know the answer to: where did you and your wife go on your first date? What did you buy her for your third wedding anniversary?

The problem with a proof-of-life question is that although it offers proof of life, it doesn't necessarily provide proof of possession. Sometimes the guys you are negotiating with are in a separate location to the hostage, which invariably complicates and delays the set-up and means there's an extra link in the chain before you can secure their release. With a simple proof-of-life question, the guy you're negotiating with might hold the line, call up his buddies and get them to speak to the hostage.

That first call didn't last long. They wanted two million dollars, but in K&R negotiations, like lots of other negotiations, your initial offer is usually drastically lower. So I told Abdul to make a counter-offer of $60,000, with the CEO's blessing. That might seem extremely low compared with the demands, but I was playing the odds here a little bit. I was betting on something called the 'escalation of commitment'. This is a term from economics originally used to describe the human tendency to justify increased investment in a project, based on the cumulative prior investment of time, effort, money, risk, etc. The phenomenon is reflected in such proverbs as 'Throwing good money after bad' and 'In for a penny, in for a pound.'

Put differently, the more time or resources you invest in something, the more you're driven to seeing it succeed. For Samar Yussuf and his gang, as well as for me, it follows that the longer this negotiation goes on, the more determined they will be to see it go right.

This is where my training as a psychologist comes in.

I use empathy to increase my understanding of the kidnappers' world. People have asked me how I can possibly be empathic with a bunch of ruthless kidnappers. Why would I want to know what they're feeling and thinking?

My reply is if I don't, I might get my client killed.

If I don't understand what it's like to be a kidnapper, then how can I get them to do what I want them to do?

Imagine this. You're planning to abduct someone you believe is rich. Even if the target is unguarded, you still need at least half a dozen guys to pull it off. You need to be able to trust these guys with your life because if they screw up, you could go to prison or worse. These guys must be available twenty-four hours a day, seven days a week, indefinitely. Why at least six guys? Well, you need at least two guys to guard the hostage in each eight-hour shift. Three shifts per day, two guys, that works out to six right there. You also need people to talk on the phone because kidnappers rarely risk talking on the phone from the same place that they hold the hostage. All these logistical problems can cause the kidnappers great headaches and my goal is to exploit these headaches to achieve my own aims.

Then there's the powerful human reluctance to kill.

The first thing most of us would do if we were going to kill someone is perform a set of complex mental manipulations. We would be unaware they were happening, but happen they do. This manipulation transforms the image of our victim from that of an ordinary human being, just like us, into that of a creature whose differences from us are so exaggerated, distorted and degraded that it becomes one of 'them' and therefore much, much easier to slaughter.

This process is called dehumanisation and it is an essential first step in creating killers.

This is not a new idea. It's been going on since human beings became social animals and realised they liked living with each other.

I once heard these bonds of affection called 'a tool of hostility' because by forming groups, we must by definition exclude others. This is often the first step towards dehumanising someone. The deep, primitive, yet very useful psycho-logic of group formation goes something like this: if they aren't in my group, they aren't like me. If they aren't like me, they must be dangerous. If they're dangerous, then I can kill them.

We good. They bad.

Religions have a long and distinguished history of demonstrating this. History shows us that religions continue to be quite effective in stressing the differences between the in group, which is 'with God', and the out group, which isn't. Once you start calling people unbelievers, infidels, blasphemers, fornicators, and so on, you've begun the dehumanisation process and it becomes pretty easy to persecute and kill them.

In the whole wide world, there is, thankfully, only a very small percentage of people – perhaps 1 or 2 per cent – who are genuinely antisocial personalities or psychopaths. These are people whose personalities are distorted in a way that means they don't have remorse, they don't have a conscience and they don't feel guilty about the terrible things they do to other people. That's why their lives are often characterised by a persistent tendency to manipulate, exploit or violate the rights of others. They love to take risks and are usually unconcerned about injury to themselves and others. They can and do live and operate with a degree of fearlessness that would incapacitate most of us. When you think about it, planning and actually abducting somebody requires an absence of anxiety that most people simply do not have. Normal people feel uneasiness and dread about a wide variety of things, from having an out-of-date tax disc to being robbed in the street. Antisocial personalities on the other hand, rarely have any experiences that begin to cause this sense of impending danger.

Part of where this distortion comes from is hereditary. Some people just have a genetic predisposition towards fearlessness. That doesn't mean that it's guaranteed that you will become a criminal if you are an antisocial personality. It just means that you're likely to be attracted to jobs and ways of life that provide you with the high levels of stimulation you require. Soldiers, surgeons, law-enforcement officers, bomb disposal technicians are all jobs that require an extreme level of fearlessness.

What can make the difference between somebody who's an antisocial criminal and an antisocial, yet productive member of society is often down to how they were raised. It probably won't come as a surprise to hear that if you raise a child predominantly with love, kindness, predictability and safety, chances are that they will grow up to be a decent, productive member of society. But if you raise a child in an abusive, unloving, unpredictable, violent, drug- and alcohol-infested manner, you are likely to end up with an antisocial criminal.

Some of them will be lawyers or firefighters or racing car drivers. A large number of them will be crooks: your Ted Bundys and Peter Tobins, and any one of the various serial killers active in the north of England in the past half-century.

In business, and kidnap for ransom is most definitely a business, it doesn't make any sense to destroy or damage the thing you're trying to sell. Though hostage killings do occur, they occur rarely and tend to happen during rescue attempts, which is probably the single most dangerous time for hostages.

We had the mobile number listed that Yussuf was calling from, but there was little point in us trying to reach it; when Yussuf hung up he immediately switched his phone off. He was evasive on the phone and I found it hard to piece together a profile of the guy. He wasn't a smooth talker and didn't seem like a religious fanatic. On the other hand, he wasn't a criminal mastermind either. It seemed to me that he was a low-level thug who'd stumbled upon a once-in-a-lifetime, get-rich-quick scheme.

When the next call came, Yussuf issued a threat.

'We'll sell him to al-Qaeda! They will give us more money than you are offering!'

'Al-Qaeda?'

'Yes, yes. We know many people in al-Qaeda.'

Bullshit, I told myself. These guys don't know anyone in al-Qaeda.

The next day I decided we needed a new negotiating tactic. When it came to my briefing with Abdul, I wrote a new message on the butcher paper and double underlined it. I asked Abdul to read it back to me.

'There is no company, only family.' Abdul frowned at the words, rereading them silently several times.

I said, 'We don't want them to think the company is paying. They have to believe they are dealing directly with the family, and that we are friends of the family. If they think that, they will begin to realise we don't have a lot of money.'

The primary goal of a negotiator is to secure the safe release of the hostage. Everything I do must be measured against this. But there are secondary and tertiary effects of my work as a negotiator that are pretty beneficial. One of these is to try to 'harden' my client enough so that the next time the kidnappers run out of money, they'll kidnap someone else from another client. I want the kidnappers to think twice before coming back to kidnap any of my client's people. I have to try to do a good enough job, and make my client's company seem hardball enough, that the kidnappers won't ever bother them again. Unless you make the kidnappers work hard, they will continue to target you again and again.

A classic example of this is a case I worked in South America that involved three brothers. Though it sounds a little like a fairytale, I promise you it's a true story. These three brothers ran a mostly cash business and the oldest was abducted on his way to work one morning. The kidnappers called a few hours after the brother was supposed to arrive at work and demanded a ransom of $50,000. The other two brothers get together and say, 'Yeah, we've got that, we can pay you right now.' They did. The brother was returned and the whole case was over within forty-eight hours.

About six months later when the money ran out – as it inevitably does – the middle brother was abducted, also from his car on the way to work. This time the ransom had doubled to $100,000. Again the brothers quickly paid up the full amount and got the middle brother back home within a couple of days. What they didn't realise is that, from the kidnappers' perspective, these brothers had become cash cows. They must have loved these guys: $150,000 for less than five days work.

The youngest brother was no dummy and figured that he wasn't going to let this happen to him. He thought, Screw this, these assholes are not gonna kidnap me, and he bought himself a handgun. Seven months later, when the cash dried up a second time, the kidnappers tried to abduct him from his car one morning on the way to work. He pulled out the gun – and was killed in an exchange of gunfire.

The other brothers were so devastated they sold the business for a song, picked up sticks and moved out of the country. To this day, no one knows where they are. The moral of the story is this:

if the opposition is making you pay in *money*, you make them pay in *time*. Had the brothers resisted paying for several weeks when the first one was kidnapped, the tragedy that followed could have been avoided. The kidnappers would have thought to themselves, Jesus, these guys make us work too hard, and they would've been much more likely to go somewhere else next time they were broke.

From a psychological point of view, there is no worse feeling than walking away from a deal thinking you've left money on the table. Thinking, Damn, I should've asked for more. This is exactly what the kidnappers thought when the brothers eagerly paid the initial demand the first time around. This convinced the kidnappers that they could tap the same family repeatedly.

So when it came to Khan and Samar Yussuf, one of my first aims was to slow the case down. As a negotiator, time is on my side. Time is the enemy of the kidnappers. It increases their costs and risks: the cost of maintaining the safehouse, paying the gang, etc. Not to mention the constant risk of getting caught.

Statistically, the longer a hostage case goes on, the higher the chance of the hostage coming home alive. Time applies pressure to them. I'm using my empathy and understanding of the kidnappers' world to my advantage.

This also worked in terms of preventing Khan from having the crap beaten out of him. To begin with I expected Yussuf to treat the hostage badly and beat him up some, maybe a lot. But if I played my cards right and dragged this thing out for a couple of weeks, by the end of it they'd be kissing his ass.

When the next call came, Yussuf was in an angry mood. He shouted at Abdul and harangued him, but Abdul played his part perfectly and put across the message: 'My friend, there is no company. They have washed their hands of us. I am working for the family. Please understand, Mr Khan's family does not have the kind of money you are asking for.'

Yussuf said, '*Kona ka dzha!* Motherfucker! The package is a rich man.'

But Abdul stuck rigidly to the briefing. 'Please don't hurt him. Jadid Khan is my friend. We want to reach an agreement with you, but I want to make it clear, we won't pay for damaged goods.'

'One million, then,' Yussuf said.

'We'll come back to you,' Abdul said. 'I need to speak to the family first.'

'Do not keep us waiting.'

Abdul persistently delivered his lines in a calm, authoritative voice. The combination of his voice and the assertive and firm but non-confrontational manner, peppering the conversation with 'my friend' or referring to the hostage as 'Jadid' rather than 'the package', was all designed to familiarise ourselves with the kidnappers and foster a relationship between them and us.

Yes, you read that right. I am trying to foster a relationship with the kidnappers. Why would I want to do this? Why would I want to foster a relationship with this bunch of murderous, ignorant thugs?

Because in the back of my head I was already looking ahead to the exchange. Part of what I was doing now was laying the groundwork for a safe, smooth swap.

The second most dangerous part of any kidnap is the exchange. That's where the money is given to the kidnappers and they release the hostage. The reason it's the second most dangerous part is that this is when the kidnappers come into contact with the opposition – namely us. They're exposing themselves, coming out into the open. They're afraid of getting caught or killed. They're afraid that Sod's law will make them somehow lose the money and they're nervous about all of the many, many things that can go wrong. That's why I want my 'relationship' with the kidnappers *not* to be one of the things that they have to worry about. I want them to trust me as much as they can. I want them to feel comfortable and confident about us.

The next call was from another member of the kidnap gang. He gave his name as Abu and reiterated the gang's demand – or so he thought – of $2 million.

'But my friend, this is wrong,' Abdul replied. 'The number we arrived at with Yussuf was one million.'

There was a long pause at Abu's end. 'Let me go check,' he said warily.

We could hear Abu speaking to someone else in the room. The exchange was frenetic. It sounded like Abu was castigating the person he was speaking to. He came back on the line and said, 'I don't know what you're talking about.'

'Yesterday Yussuf said five hundred thousand,' Abdul repeated. 'That is where we are. You are mistaken, Abu.'

'I need to check,' Abu said.

I had a settlement figure in my head of $250,000. That's where I believed we could negotiate down to. Discussions over the ransom amount were held between myself, Aamir, Naveed, and Jaffar. We'd sit around a table and run through the options over coffee. Throughout, Aamir never revealed how much money he was prepared to pay. Sometimes the clients prefer it that way. Maybe they don't fully trust the negotiator, which is reasonable enough given the circumstances. Or perhaps they think that if they tell me, 'I can afford $300,000', then that's the figure I will end up paying because below that I might not haggle so hard.

The next conversation was at two in the afternoon.

'We cannot have this confusion,' Abdul said. I'd advised him to be strong and feign outrage when Yussuf called. 'When we spoke yesterday the number was a million. This is not how we do business!'

Yussuf immediately hung up. Abdul looked at me, panic etched across his features. I told him not to worry.

'But we offended him,' Abdul said. 'Perhaps they will hurt Jadid.'

'Yussuf will call back in an hour. You'll see.'

'How can you be so sure?'

'Just wait,' I said.

Sure enough, exactly sixty minutes later the phone rang and Yussuf was back on the line. He'd had time to let off some steam and realise that if he was going to do business, it would be on our terms. He couldn't play us for fools.

Abdul now made the improved offer of $75,000. Yussuf had come down by a million dollars. We had increased our original offer by $15,000. I was hoping the message was getting through to him that the family had little money and he was going to have to settle for an awful lot less than his original demand. I was also counting on the comedown after the abduction. For a couple of days after the abduction, the kidnappers will often be in a highly agitated and excitable state, pumping with adrenalin. But once the high wears off, they depress. My deliberately slowing down the case and low initial offer was a way of helping get Yussuf to reset his expectations.

'It is not good enough,' Yussuf yelled. When I listened to his voice on playback and got Abdul to translate for me, I figured he was angry but would eventually come around.

'You haven't even given us proof of life yet,' Abdul said.

'*Spi zoe!* Son of a bitch! Do not worry about him. He is fine.'

'I want to believe you, Yussuf. But why should we talk to you if you won't show us that you've got what we want?'

'*Moor kwas!* Motherfucker! Shut up. I will let you speak with him when I decide. Not a moment sooner!'

In the negotiating game, this is known as encouraging fairness by focusing on objective criteria. You create a situation where, in order to do business, the kidnappers have to be fair with you. Simply asking questions was a much better strategy for achieving results than getting bogged down in endless arguments that only served to piss Yussuf off.

Some of the negotiators at the Waco siege in Texas infamously got involved in religious debates with David Koresh, leader of the Branch Davidians, a religious sect, over interpretations of Bible Scripture. Now I'm not saying those negotiators were responsible for the tragedy that unfolded there. But I am saying that for the purposes of this kind of negotiation, getting involved in an argument with a religious fanatic is a lot like arguing with a drunk. You're not going to convince him and he's not going to convince you and you end up going around in circles.

The Davidians believed the Bible predicted that the end of the world would come in a confrontation between true believers such as themselves and the US federal government. They also believed that Koresh was the chosen one who would usher it in.

That's why during the negotiations, much of David Koresh's attention was focused on proving to the FBI negotiators that he was the chosen one.

Of course the FBI could not accept that Koresh was the chosen one. Their approach as federal law-enforcement professionals simply ended up pitting God against the US government and it doesn't take a genius to see how that's going to end.

At the end of the day, the federal government caused a biblical prophecy to come true.

You cannot operate that kind of argumentative, conflict-driven strategy and hope to effect a positive outcome.

'No, no, no,' Yussuf said. 'It doesn't work like that. Money first. Then the hostage.'

Abdul stuck to his guns. 'I don't understand, Samar Yussuf. You want the money, and I have given you my word that we will pay you money. Now we want Jadid in return, but you say you won't let us speak to him. We have to know that Jadid is alive and well.'

Yussuf was silent. 'Wait one minute.'

Abdul clasped his hand over the speaker to hide his rapid breathing. Time seemed to stand still. Eventually Jadid Khan's voice came down the line, tinny and faint. I figured they were keeping him in a separate location and Yussuf was trying to establish a line by holding two mobile phones together. Abdul complained that he couldn't hear Khan.

'We will call again in thirty minutes,' Yussuf said, highly irritated.

Half an hour passed and Yussuf called us from a new number, confirming my suspicion that Khan was being held a few streets from wherever Yussuf was conducting the negotiations. Abdul spoke briefly to Khan.

'Jadid, my friend. How are you?'

'I am okay,' Khan said.

'Are they feeding you?'

A slight pause. As if Jadid Khan was looking to the kidnappers for approval to answer. 'Yes, Abdul. They give me food and water.'

'We are going to get you out of there very shortly,' Abdul said, reading from my pass notes. 'Please do not lose hope. Do as the kidnappers say and you will be back home with Shadah soon.'

'I will try, Abdul. Please tell—'

The phone was snatched away. Yussuf now returned to the subject of money. 'We will settle for five hundred thousand.'

Abdul said, 'We can offer ninety-seven thousand.'

Call ended.

I felt we could play hardball with Yussuf since he wasn't displaying any of the hallmarks of psychopaths or experienced professionals. For the most part Yussuf tried to come across as businesslike and level-headed, but the high-pitched tone of his voice told me he was fighting to keep a lid on his anxiety. Other days Yussuf came back and acted crazy as hell, when the stresses of negotiation evidently became too much for him.

I allowed myself a cynical thought: Why was Yussuf dropping his ransom figure so easily? I had expected more resistance to our low offer and perhaps more stubbornness on his part to stick closer to his original demand of $2 million. The case was quickly gathering pace, though, and I had no time to think about this properly.

Not yet anyway.

Like any twenty-five-year-old in the world, Samar Yussuf had a chip on his shoulder and was preoccupied with social status. Therefore he was going to be much more concerned about being 'disrespected'. He wouldn't have the equanimity of, say, a more mature, older man.

He was also worried about something else.

'You're trying to buy time to let the Americans find us. I've seen it on TV, my friend. They have spy planes and bombs. They're going to come and attack us, aren't they?'

'Of course not,' Abdul replied quickly. 'We haven't even been in touch with the Americans. No one knows about this matter but you and me and the family.'

'This is not a game! You fuck with us, *ghawl lun*, you shitter, and we'll chop his fucking head off.'

This was one of the points I'd especially briefed Abdul on. Violence must never go unchallenged. 'If you did that,' he said, 'how do you expect to make any money?'

'Don't try to play games with me,' Yussuf snapped.

'Are you Muslim?'

'Yes, of course.'

'So am I. And our Prophet says that you should never kill your fellow Muslim for a matter such as wealth or honour.'

'The package is working for the Americans.'

Abdul went silent.

'Are you there, brother?'

I had instructed Abdul to use silence at key points in his

conversations with Yussuf. Silence is a highly effective weapon, whether you're talking to someone on the phone or in person. It fosters anxiety in the other person. It forces them to end the silence, either by saying something or doing something.

'Talk to me, Abdul!'

What the person who breaks the silence says – or does – can be very revealing about their character and you can also use it to your advantage.

'I am not having this conversation with you,' Abdul said, reaching for his pack of smokes. 'Either we talk about the release of my friend Jadid or we do not talk at all.'

Yussuf muttered something inaudible.

'We talk again tomorrow. I will call you.'

Abdul said, 'Okay, bye'.

But we didn't hang up the phone.

One of the principles of silent running is that you never hang up. You always wait for the kidnappers to hang up. They might forget to do so and you'd find yourself listening in to private conversations that might give you a tactical advantage at the negotiating table.

That time they didn't talk about anything revealing. They were in a car and they were arguing over where to eat lunch. But the mere fact that they weren't attentive to details reinforced my opinion of Yussuf and his gang of toughs as a bunch of amateurs.

I was emboldened by the vividly expressed fear on Yussuf's part of the US military. This was a fear based on the slick marketing of American firepower and its limitless capabilities and, Abdul pointed out to me, fostered a widespread belief as to American perfection and invincibility.

We were killing time one day when the news on the TV switched to footage of a gun-mounted camera on an Apache helicopter. The camera was looking down at an Iraqi bridge, the crosshairs right on top of the bridge itself. Several vehicles were crossing the bridge: vehicles identified as belonging to the Republican Guard, and in the middle was an ambulance. The Apache waited until the ambulance had safely passed through the crosshairs and driven off the bridge before unleashing its Hellfire missiles on to the military vehicles. They were obliterated in a white-hot fuzz while the ambulance drove away unscathed.

'Perhaps you can explain something to me,' Abdul said. 'How come your army can do this and yet so many innocent people are killed on the ground?'

There was no easy answer to that question, and I didn't try and patronise Abdul by giving one. Instead I shrugged and conceded he had a fair point. On the one hand, the Coalition forces, mainly British and American, want the world to believe they're capable of magic. And from the air, to a certain extent, it is. But on the ground – where bullets don't automatically lock on to targets and people get maimed in crossfire – the reality is far from magic. It's thuggish.

Yussuf was scared, too, of the Pakistani police because he thought they might steal Khan and run the case themselves or perhaps steal the ransom money from him. I considered this fear to be reasonable, considering the questionable reputation the Pakistani security forces had at the time.

But in the way of the negotiator, I turned these fears to my advantage. Their fears were my secret weapon. The longer the case went on, the more paranoid Yussuf became that a crack team of Delta Force operators was going to kick down his door and machine-gun the shit out of everyone in sight. He couldn't have been more mistaken but this now explained why he'd been so quick to drop his original demand by a million dollars. Yussuf wanted to get paid, and he wanted to get paid *yesterday*.

7

SUBTERFUGE

On the afternoon of day eight we arrived at a settlement.

The previous day we had managed to get them down to $375,000. But we felt we should push a little harder. We went back and said $252,000 was our final offer.

'For that price, perhaps I cut his head off.'

Abdul read out a line I'd prepared for him. 'If you do that, you're not going to get double the money, my friend. We're not going to pay you more for two pieces.'

An exhausted Yussuf called us a short while later.

'We accept your offer,' he said. The excitement had drained out of his voice. He sounded lethargic and depressed.

'That is great news, my friend,' Abdul replied. 'Now, about the exchange—'

'I'm very tired, Abdul.'

'Okay, let's talk tomorrow, same time.'

The reality of K&R is usually sobering from the kidnapper's point of view. Usually they get paid, which makes it sound lucrative. Crime pays? Amazing. But look at the bottom line. $252,000 for two weeks' work, with at least six other members of the abduction team to pay? Any way you cut it up, Yussuf wasn't going to be able to afford that apartment in Monaco. His profits might stretch to a new car.

I was feeling pretty wiped myself. Eight days solid of negotiating, with two beforehand spent getting the case set up, twenty-hour days and enough caffeine in my body to juice a space shuttle. I went back to my hotel room and put a call in to John, my employer on this particular case.

'We settled,' I said, sitting on the edge of the bed and feeling the ache in my bones from a lack of sleep.

'Bloody great work, mate. What's the damage?'

I could hear John drumming his fingers on his desk, waiting for the magic number. The drumming echoed inside my head and formed a pressure point at my temple.

'Two hundred and fifty-two.'

The drumming stopped.

'Fuck me,' said John. 'From two million to two-five-two? That's ridiculous. What did you do, Ben, threaten to marry them?'

I laughed and shrugged it off. To me, negotiating a ransom of 12.5 per cent of the original demand was normal, even perhaps a little over the odds. Normally I can get a kidnapper down to 10 per cent. Time is on my side, and I'm good at working people and getting what I want from them.

Now my mind turned to the logistics of the exchange.

This is the point at which kidnapper and negotiator must meet, when everyone's adrenalin is up and the tension works its way thickly up your back and into your neck muscles. The slightest mistake can have catastrophic consequences. For the kidnappers as well as the victims. There have been cases where kidnappers have been killed during handovers. In the Dominican Republic, a local mob confronted a suspected kidnapper after he and a group of men came to a small town to collect a ransom they had been demanding for the release of a Santo Domingo merchant. The mob beat him to death and set his body on fire. Safe to say, that exchange didn't go according to plan.

First of all I needed to find someone I could trust to deliver the ransom to the kidnappers. This was not exactly an easy task. I don't know about you, but I just don't know that many people who I can trust to run around Karachi with $252,000. The person I was looking for had to know the lie of the land in the city and be utterly reliable.

I approached Aamir and sounded him out about using the company's own security provider. He stroked his chin while he listened, and when I was done he frowned at a spot on the wall.

'I'm afraid we can't use our own people.'

'Because they're not trained for this type of thing?'

Aamir pursed his lips. 'There is that. And also because of the timing.'

'With the money being transported?'

'You read my mind,' Aamir said, nodding. 'It's too much of a coincidence, don't you agree?'

I did. On top of that, I couldn't help thinking that the settlement figure we arrived at – $252,000 – was uneasily close to the $265,000 in cash that the company had stashed in Jadid Khan's own house just days before Khan was abducted. Yussuf probably felt that he couldn't ask for exactly the same amount because it would look too obvious. I figured that Yussuf and his friends were local toughs with some ambition and who had been tipped off by somebody in exchange for a cut of the ransom. That somebody had to have been an insider. Someone privy to the details of the half-million-dollar split. We had no evidence linking anyone inside the company or the security company to the kidnappers. Just a hunch that the picture didn't seem quite right.

Although we were reluctant to put our trust in the security company, I didn't want to sour them. If they figured we weren't using them because we suspected they were in on the kidnap, and that was in fact the case, then that might bring harm to Jadid or otherwise queer the pitch. So I followed an old trick taught by Don Corleone in *The Godfather*. He said, 'Keep your friends close but your enemies closer.' I befriended the security personnel and even requested they send photographs across to the office, 'so we can see all the great work you heroes are doing out there'.

As I said, we had no hard evidence linking anyone inside the security outfit to Yussuf and his toughs. But I didn't want to take any chances.

At this point I was just killing time until I found someone to deliver the money. I was beginning to exhaust my collection of standard delaying tactics, with Abdul telling Yussuf, 'We're getting a loan on the house but this is taking some time' and 'We're selling the cars but the dealer is stalling on giving us the cash, please be patient.'

To buy myself some time, I slowed the case down by creating an act of subterfuge: I insisted on a simultaneous exchange. Now, a simultaneous exchange never happens in the real world, only in Hollywood. Why? Because the kidnappers have the hostage, and the hostage is worth much more than the money, and therefore why would they expose themselves to the danger of a possible assault? What normally happens is that the kidnappers scout out a place for a couple of days, checking access routes, escape exits, police presence and lines of fire. Once they're satisfied they have a good drop location, they'll call the communicator and say, 'Drop the money off at X location.' The reason for this is very simple: kidnappers don't want to reveal to the authorities where the exchange is going to take place unless they have been there beforehand. That way if they're already in situ at X when they name it as the drop site and they spot three guys an hour later in plain clothes who don't look like they belong there, they automatically know that their cover's been blown and will get the hell out of there.

So first the kidnappers own the street. They also set the agenda. Then they tell you exactly where the money will be deposited – perhaps dumped in a trash bin or left in the boot of a parked car, using what has become the universal ransom delivery luggage, a plastic shopping bag.

I wasn't pressing for a simultaneous exchange because I thought Yussuf would agree to it. I did it to maintain the fiction that Yussuf was negotiating with the family, not the company. I had to give off the impression that everything was a little bit amateur, a little bit naive.

The next day we received another call from Yussuf. He sounded anxious, like a kid who wants to open his Christmas presents early. 'What's happening with the money?'

'We're just getting it sorted, my friend,' Abdul said. This seemed to appease Yussuf somewhat.

'I am glad to hear it.'

'But first we need to discuss the swap.'

A long pause followed. 'There will be no simultaneous swap.'

'Yussuf, please—'

'No!' Yussuf was now shouting in an attempt to drown out our proposals. He gathered his breath. 'You will give us the money and then an hour later we will give you the hostage.'

'We can't agree to that,' Abdul replied. 'We have to receive Jadid at the same time as you get the money.'

'You're complicating the case. Either you deal with us or we sell to another group. It would be so easy for us, my friend.

There are many who would pay us more money than you are offering.'

'It is not . . . Hello? Hello? Samar Yussuf?'

The line was dead.

Yussuf clearly did not like the idea of a simultaneous exchange. I didn't care for his posturing or his hollow threats to sell to someone else. There were more than enough people being taken hostage and I very much doubted that Yussuf or his goons had the right contacts. But his displeasure was buying me valuable time to source someone to make the ransom delivery.

Ten days into the negotiations, I hit the jackpot. My friend Mike, an operator on the Circuit, put me in touch with a guy named Leonard. He ran his own elite private security company. They provided details to Western journalists and diplomats in Iraq and Afghanistan and anywhere else where foreigners were not welcome, and they had a reputation for being highly professional and incredibly tough. I rang this Leonard guy and gave him the proposition.

'I can't do it, Ben. I'm sorry but it's going to take too much time and my men are tied up with the billion other shitstorms happening over in Iraq.' Leonard didn't sound English. More like South African or maybe from Zimbabwe. He was the kind of guy you could imagine surviving in the bush with nothing but a sharp stick and a bad attitude.

It turns out that Leonard was originally from Lebanon and had lived in America. He was a hell of an operator and a brave man.

He's now a good friend of mine but it didn't start that way

'I'm gonna pay you five thousand dollars for half a day's work. Half a day.'

'Bullshit, Ben. It'll take longer than that. All my resources are tied up in Baghdad.'

'I've got this figured out, Leonard. It's a simple exchange. It's going to take half a day. Twelve hours or less. That's it. And hey – if it takes a minute longer, you can keep the money.'

Leonard chewed on it for a while. Then he said, 'No, I can't do it.'

I couldn't believe it. Here was a guy turning down good money for very little work in almost no time. What a knuckle-head!

I tried to appeal to his humanitarian side.

'Okay, Leonard, look. I'm trying to save somebody's life here. Don't you want to be part of that? It'll be good for your karma.'

'Save somebody's life? Fuck that guy! Fuck that piece of shit!'

Click.

He'd hung up on me.

So I did what I normally do. I approached the problem in the way that a physician approaches disease. He does not approve or condone it but seeks to understand its nature in order have any hope of defeating it.

I also did this because it was better than what I wanted to do, which was to choke the living shit out of this fucking Lebanese asshole.

I began to cast about for strategies and tactics to get Leonard to do what I wanted him to do. Then it occurred to me as I was taking a shower that evening. I literally said, 'Aha!' Like all of the most elegant solutions to problems, this one was simple and easy.

I woke up feeling pretty good after going to bed feeling optimistic because I knew exactly what I was going to do. I had the solution to my problem so I had gotten one of the rare four hours' decent sleep I got on this case.

I called Leonard bright and early that morning and used one of my best Jedi mind tricks on him. Since it was pretty clear he was not in a humanitarian mood, I appealed to the better angels of his nature through an act of selective honesty. I said, 'Leonard, look. I haven't been fully truthful with you. You were right. I told you the job would take twelve hours knowing full well that I need you for twenty-four. I was trying to get you on the cheap. And I thought you'd fall for it. I'm sorry.'

I understood that a man like Leonard spends his life not trusting others. In his business, trust doesn't come easily. So I knew he'd find my selective honesty refreshing, maybe even disarming.

'I knew you were full of shit, Lopez! I knew the moment I heard you were a negotiator,' said Leonard. 'But this ... you're actually being honest.' He went on: 'Look, if you're sure it's only gonna take a day, then I'll do it. You've got yourself a deal.' I felt relief deflate me just like a balloon leaking air. 'But you'd better make sure it takes one day. It goes on for longer—'

'It won't. Don't worry.'

While psychological Jedi mind tricks are often very effective in helping bring people round to your way of thinking, I find that doubling their fees often gets the job done in less time.

Months later, after the case was over, I met Leonard face to face for the first time in a bar in Istanbul. I told him he was crazy and that he had been more difficult to negotiate with than that bunch of ruthless kidnappers. He put his head back and laughed and laughed and laughed. He really enjoyed having a psychologist tell him he was crazy and to this day brings it up whenever we meet.

I ran my hand through my hair. My palms were oozing sweat from the heavy caffeine intake that was helping me stay disarmingly honest.

'So who's the guy?' I said.

'He's a local. His name is Aziz. He's a former Special Services Group operator.' The SSG is Pakistan's special forces outfit.

'Jesus,' I said.

'Don't worry, Ben. Now he fights with us. Aziz has personally killed or captured more than seventy-five insurgents with his bare hands. He's tough as old boots.'

The fact that Aziz had a military background presented me with a problem. Yussuf had earlier expressed his fears about the military coming in and kicking his ass. I would have to set this thing up so that Aziz did not come across as a soldier from any army, so that Yussuf's fear about the Pakistani security forces didn't get in the way of a smooth and safe exchange.

I prepared Abdul for the next phone call from Yussuf. This was the critical point in the negotiations. Now that we had secured a delivery guy, I had to facilitate an exchange scenario that would suit us. Not easy when they had all the aces. But I had my social manipulation skills and I had faith in my ability to convince Yussuf to do things our way.

Then Yussuf threw us a curveball.

'We want the money tonight,' he said.

'That is not possible,' Abdul replied. 'We will deliver but it has to be tomorrow.'

'All right then, tomorrow morning.'

'Yussuf, it must be the afternoon. Five o'clock is the earliest we can do.' It wasn't but I wanted us setting the agenda every step of the way, so that it would seem to Yussuf that we were the ones in control of the situation.

'Why not the morning?'

'Our delivery man works at night and he will be very tired. He cannot do the morning. Please, my friend. Let us agree for five o'clock tomorrow.'

Yussuf clicked his tongue. 'Very well,' he said. 'Five o'clock tomorrow.'

Relief washed over Abdul and the rest of the team's faces. Mine too, I expect.

'That is great news. The family is very happy.'

'Tell your man to call me. I will run through the details with him. First he delivers the money. One hour later we will call him and tell him to go to a place. When he gets there, he must call us.

Then we will tell him to go to a second place and we will call him again. Then he goes to the third place. And then another and maybe another. As many as we want. The last one will be where he will find the hostage. He must travel alone. No funny business.'

'I like your plan,' Abdul said, massaging Yussuf's ego. This was all part of the policy of giving Yussuf respect, building him up and being careful not to disrespect him. It was important for me to reduce his anxiety prior to the exchange. The less nerves on both sides, the higher the chances of a glitch-free swap.

'Let us speak later.'

The line went dead.

With negotiations now focusing on the fine print of the swap, I turned my attention to the problem of Aziz. My fear was that Yussuf might pick up on the fact that Aziz was a former special forces operator and draw the conclusion that we were Pakistani police or US military, potentially undoing all the good work we had done up to that point.

I decided to play a risky game on the kidnappers – and on my own team.

On the pretext of going outside to take a walk to clear my head, I put in a call to Leonard and explained what I wanted Aziz to do. Leonard asked Aziz to join the call and both of them immediately grasped the plan. Fifteen minutes later everything was in place for the little game I was going to play.

Everything on our end was ready. Aziz was in possession of the ransom money and had even sent us a picture of it. $252,000 in hundred-dollar bills looks a lot less impressive than you think it would. I looked at the picture wistfully. There have been lots of days when I wished I had this kind of money. I shook my head to get rid of the thought and got ready for what was to come.

That evening we had our final conversation with Yussuf.

'We need half an hour to count the money. We count it, make sure it is all there, and then you can have your man.'

'That is good, Yussuf. But I want a guarantee from you.'

Yussuf sniffed down the line. 'What kind of guarantee?'

'That you will never again take Khan hostage.'

'You have my word.'

Getting a 'vaccine' for the hostage is an always crucial but often overlooked part of negotiating strategy. The vaccine means that the group wouldn't touch Khan in the future. Sometimes kidnappers find it irresistible to return to the guy they've abducted. They know his routine and his address and when their cash runs out, it's tempting to go and rob the same bank. Extracting this promise from Yussuf was a small but vital victory for us. There were more to come.

'Okay, now we are agreed. This is what you need to do,' Abdul told him. 'You need to call the number of our delivery man. His name is Aziz. Tell him where to go and what to do with the money. He's a friend of the family. He knows about the situation and will follow your instructions precisely.'

'Okay.'

Yussuf was impatient to get over the finish line now. In his head, I imagined, images were playing themselves out of Apache helicopters and Black Hawks circling the safehouse. Ready to bomb it back into the stone age.

Abdul hung up.

We had arranged for Aziz to report to us at every critical event so there was nothing more for us to do except wait to hear that the kidnappers had made initial contact. Once that happened the next call would be to complete the exchange, then he'd call us to confirm that Jadid Khan had been secured alive and well.

The tight expressions on everyone's faces began to ease. I felt the stress levels palpably drop. The exchange plan was in motion. We were in the end game now and we did not expect to hear from the kidnappers again. All communications were supposed to go through Aziz.

At least, that was the perception.

In downtown Karachi, Yussuf immediately got on the line to Aziz.

Aziz then did exactly what I had told him to do.

'Thank you very much for contacting me,' Aziz said. 'It is a pleasure to do business with you.'

'The same,' Yussuf said back.

'I am going to deliver this money to you—'

'That is good—'

'But in return, I want 10 per cent of the ransom off the top for my trouble, okay?'

There was a silence so sharp it could cut through steel.

Yussuf said, 'Huh? *What?* This wasn't part of the plan.'

'It is now.'

'Fuck you. No. No fucking way!'

'No cut, no deal,' Aziz said.

'I can't give you any fucking money. The money is not for us.'

'Oh, really? Then who is it for?'

'It is to be . . . it's for the poor. Yes, we are distributing the money among the poor people of our neighbourhood. This is for them.' Yussuf was clearly trying to ad-lib some bullshit excuse. Stumbling on his words, and perhaps suspecting that Abdul didn't believe his lies, Yussuf hung up in disgust.

Back in the situation room, the mobile burner we'd been contacting Yussuf on vibrated angrily on the meeting table. Everyone jumped a little. They stared at the mobile like it was a time bomb. This wasn't in the script. Why the hell was Yussuf calling back? they wondered.

It vibrated again. Abdul and the rest of the team looked at me expectantly. I shrugged my shoulders as if I didn't know what was going on and said, 'Answer it. See what they want.'

'There is a problem,' Yussuf said. He was fuming hard.

'What is it? What's going on?' asked Abdul, genuinely mystified.

The rest of the team looked on like they were at a tennis match, shifting their gaze from me to Abdul and back again.

'Shut up! It is your friend Aziz. He is a bad man. A very, very bad man!'

Abdul tried to calm Yussuf down, to no avail. The kidnapper lost his cool, shouting and screaming down the phone about how terrible Aziz was and complaining about his demand – engineered by me – for a cut of the ransom.

'Please,' Abdul said. 'I'm sure we can sort this out.' He was looking at me with confusion etched over his face, wondering what the hell was going on.

'No, we cannot work with this man. He's terrible. He wants to steal our money!'

Yussuf worked himself up into a white-hot rage, which was somewhat ironic given the circumstances. He was angry about someone having the effrontery to steal his money, even though he was stealing it from us!

The rest of the crisis management team looked at me, puzzled, confused and worried. I feigned shock. I'd kept my plan secret from Abdul and the others so that their reactions to the unplanned call would be genuine. I didn't want to place them in a position where they would be lying in order to make it convincing to the kidnappers when they came back to us. Which I knew they would do. I was so confident about my grip over Yussuf that I felt comfortable enough to pull off this subterfuge.

From 5.02 p.m. to 5.05 p.m., there was a flurry of phone calls going back and forth between ourselves and Yussuf. He was upset about Aziz's commission and asked us to call Aziz and resolve the matter.

'Do it yourselves,' Abdul told Yussuf.

'My friend, I cannot,' Yussuf complained. 'He is a very bad man! Please talk to him.'

We had Yussuf practically begging on his hands and knees for our help. Truly, the tables had turned and the negotiating party – us – were in control of the situation now. My job was halfway to being accomplished.

Abdul clasped a hand over the speaker and said, 'What should I do?'

I shrugged. 'Tell him to call Aziz back and ask again.'

Abdul relayed the message to Yussuf, who wasn't pleased about the idea.

I had instructed Aziz to demand a cut. In this way, they would figure Aziz as a crook and chancer just like them, as opposed to some super-smart operator working for the Pakistani police or the military. This plan had the added bonus of making Yussuf eat out of our hands. I'd informed Aziz that when Yussuf called him back a second time, he was immediately to drop his demand and go with the plan.

Yussuf called us back once more.

'*Za kha yam*. Thank you, thank you,' he said effusively. 'I'm very grateful for your help.'

'No problem,' Abdul said, trying hard to suppress a smile. I was too. It's a proud moment in a negotiator's life when you do your work so well that kidnappers are begging and thanking you.

Of course, I'd also briefed Aziz that in the unlikely event the kidnappers accepted what he proposed, he was to go ahead and claim 5 per cent of the ransom. That way we would have recouped some of the money from the kidnappers via Aziz. Thus reducing the ransom even more.

On day eleven, we received some sad news. Shadah, Khan's wife, had suffered a miscarriage. That dampened the mood in the situation room. Whether the miscarriage was in part caused by the stress of the kidnapping, I have no idea. I'm not a doctor. But I'm sure it didn't help. I felt sad for Shadah and was even more determined to make sure the exchange went smoothly now.

8

SHEPARD'S PRAYER

Dawn broke like cholera. The sky was pale and the sand was purple and pink. The air was bitterly cold. There were few cars on the roads. Vehicles zipped by as we neared Karachi city centre. I felt like a naive kid from the sticks arriving at Grand Central Station in New York for the first time, only minus the martinis and pretty women. A mixture of fear and excitement seized my guts. My detail and I were travelling low-profile to avoid drawing unnecessary attention. We were in a beat-up white Nissan SUV that from the outside was nondescript and non-desirable to car thieves, but underneath was in cherry condition. Thank God the aircon worked because it was hot as hell.

We had keffiyehs wrapped around our faces and worry beads hanging from the dash. The closer we got to Karachi the more tense we all got. There was something in the air that just plain made it feel dangerous. Downtown Karachi was still volatile and in the distance we could hear sporadic crackles of gunfire. The city gave me a bad vibe. I was relieved when we finally reached the security of the compound Leonard's company used for its local operations. It had dozens of such offices dotted around the continent.

A former dentist's property, a two-metre concrete high wall protected several whitewashed buildings surrounded by exotic plants and palm trees. Entering via the steel gates at the front of the compound, you could almost forget you were in Pakistan. The look and feel of the place was more like a luxury holiday retreat in Greece or Spain.

I worried that the security company I suspected of colluding with the kidnappers might try and snatch Khan again, or someone else connected to Aamir's company, in order to extract the other half of the money secreted in the north as a 'second ransom'. We were using Leonard's security people and I knew they were clean. But I wondered: What if the other security company was outside and watching us?

On day twelve, Aziz collected the ransom money from Shadah's house and delivered it to Leonard's security compound across town to count and bag it. I saw the cash on a simple wooden table in a dimly lit room, sunlight prodding through the shutters: $240,000 in twenty-four bundles of new, crisp $100 bills, with twelve of the bundles arranged in a serial number pattern. $12,000 in new $100 bills was in a separate stack.

I ran through the exchange protocol with Aziz one more time. Three people were to make the exchange, two from our side and one from theirs. I didn't think for a minute that this would be true because I was sure that Aziz would be watched at every step of the way by Yussuf's men. The kidnappers would tell Aziz where to go and when to be there. But at the end of the day there were only going to be two important locations. The ransom would be in one location and Jadid Khan in the other.

Throughout the exchange, open communications would be maintained between Aziz and the kidnappers. Aziz would drop off the ransom money where he would be told and would then wait for the kidnappers to call with Khan's location.

For me, this is the worst part of any kidnap. It's the point at which you have the least control and the most vulnerability. The kidnappers have the money and the kidnappers have the hostage. All you've got is nerves and the expectant looks of your team. This is the part I hate the most.

Though I am not a religious man, this is also when I silently repeat the 'Shepard's Prayer'. Alan Shepard was the first American to fly in space and is partly remembered for praying, 'Please, dear God, don't let me fuck up', as he sat atop his rocket shortly before blasting off. He was also the first man to play golf on the moon.

A concern at the back of my mind was that Aziz might find himself held at gunpoint by the kidnappers and be forcibly relieved of the ransom. I needn't have worried. When I met him in the flesh, Aziz had the kind of handshake that could bend pipes, a face constructed from granite and a square jaw that made him look like a cross between Mike Tyson and the Terminator. The overall effect was pretty intimidating. I'd figured Leonard was maybe exaggerating when he claimed Aziz had killed seventy-five bad guys with his bare hands. Now, standing in front of him, that claim didn't seem so outlandish. If anything, I thought it might be a little on the conservative side. There was something about the guy that brought to mind Hannibal Lecter.

Aziz had instructions from me to press for a meeting point inside Karachi. The last thing we wanted was for him to be dragged out into a town that he was unfamiliar with.

'Do you know the Farooq-e-Azam Mosque?' said the voice.

'Very well,' Aziz replied. 'I have been there many times.'

'Good. There is a street nearby called Maktoub. You are to proceed there.'

'I understand.'

'Come alone. If anyone follows you, Khan is a dead man.'

'Brother, you have my word.'

'We shall see,' Yussuf said. 'What car are you driving?'

'A white Nissan.'

Yussuf terminated the call.

I looked up Maktoub Street on a map and cross-referenced it with Khan's home. Barely a ten-minute drive from his house to the drop-off point. Choosing somewhere close by was a smart play by Yussuf's toughs, working on the principle of hiding in plain sight. Putting myself in the shoes of the kidnappers, Maktoub Street made sense as a meeting point. Sparse, low-rise buildings, one road in and out, mosque in the distance: with three guys, Yussuf could do more than merely dominate this street. He could own it.

With everything set in place, Aziz ventured out. At 3.15 p.m., he arrived at the Farooq-e-Azam mosque and parked outside. Soon after he received a phone call from Yussuf.

'Listen carefully, my friend. You are under surveillance at this very minute. Thirty-five of my men are surrounding you in nearby cars. Thirty-five, do you hear! If any of my men notices something suspicious, they will kill you, and Khan will die too. Do you understand?'

Aziz sought to placate Yussuf by explaining that his only wish was for the operation to proceed peacefully and that he would follow Yussuf's every instruction to the letter. This was a shrewd move on Aziz's part. It's not only the negotiators who get tense during the exchange. The kidnappers are on a knife edge too. Aziz could feel the waves of anxiety coming off Yussuf.

A short while later, Aziz called in to me, reporting that he'd received contact from the kidnappers and that he awaited Yussuf's next move.

Aziz was directed to a series of winding streets around Karachi. Upon parking his beat-up Nissan at each waypoint, he would then find himself contacted by Yussuf, who reassured him that the hostage would be released within thirty minutes of receiving the ransom. This wild goose chase around town was an entirely predictable turn of events in K&R terms. Aziz had the sense he was being watched every step of the way, and I'm sure that's true. He was establishing a level of trust with the kidnappers by following their orders.

Yussuf and his gang had previously mapped out every location that Aziz would visit. They knew the route he was taking better than their own mothers. I was sure that wherever Aziz was told to go, Yussuf had in advance ordered a couple of his goons to station themselves nearby and watch for Aziz's Nissan. The teams could observe Aziz up close, verify he was acting alone and according to Yussuf's precise instructions and radio in to the safehouse.

This charade continued for three hours and half a dozen waypoints. At last Yussuf directed Aziz to a main street near the local electricity station.

'Travel one hundred metres down the street,' Yussuf told him. 'Roll down your passenger side window and drop the money on to the pavement. Don't stop. Keep driving and don't look back.'

Aziz trailed his Nissan down the street. It was now 6.53 p.m. and the traditional hustle and bustle of the street was conspicuous by its absence. It was still very hot. Unlit houses and hollowed-out storefronts lined the street like gravestones. Sporadic streetlights painted the road sickly orange. The air was vacant black.

Slowing the Nissan to a fast walk, Aziz slid towards what he estimated to be the hundred-metre mark. At eighty metres he eased off the pedal. Crawling at a walking pace, he rolled down the passenger-side window and grabbed the plastic money bag lying on the seat. Cooked air sandblasted his face. When he was about a hundred metres up the street, Aziz chucked it out and saw the bag drop to the cracked, dirty pavement.

Then Aziz sped the Nissan up to thirty and carried on down the street. In his rear-view mirror he caught sight of a black BMW tearing around the corner, tyres screeching. The BMW raced up to the money bag and jerked to a halt. A guy debussed in a hurry. He was skinny to the point of looking malnourished and decked out in faded jeans and a drab olive T-shirt. He glanced furtively up and down the street, scooped up the bag and dived back into the car. The BMW was already screeching off down the street before the skinny guy had time to slam his door shut.

Ten minutes later, a call from Aziz interrupted my pacing. 'They are saying the ransom is a thousand short,' he said.

'Of course it's not,' I sighed. 'We counted it a dozen times. Tell them to count it again.'

The miscount was another sign of nerves. We were so close to the finish line now, we were desperate for there to be no hitches. Beads of sweat worked their way down my back. Karachi heat working its way into my veins, thick as fingers. I felt as if someone had tied up my guts.

Aziz received another call from Yussuf.

'Okay. The money is all there. Now go back to the Farooq-e-Azam mosque.'

'What about Jadid?' Aziz reminded Yussuf that he had promised to release the hostage within thirty minutes of the ransom being delivered.

'You will have him soon,' Yussuf said tersely.

Another goose chase followed as Aziz was directed to a number of locations between the Farooq-e-Azam mosque and the neighbouring district. At 7.22 p.m., Aziz was informed that the pick-up would take place at any moment. I drummed my fingers on the table.

Waited, pacing for the phone to ring with the good news.

Waited and paced. Then waited, pacing some more.

At 7.45 p.m. Aziz got in touch to say he was being instructed to head to yet another waypoint. We had now crossed the thirty-minute barrier and I started to wonder if things were being messed up. I repeated the Shepard's Prayer, faster this time, so I could get more in. Edging towards eight in the evening and still there was no word from Aziz about Khan. It's been almost an hour, I thought. They should have released him by now. This is taking too damn long.

Please, dear God, don't let me fuck up.

I paced up and down the room so hard I was wearing a trench line into it. What the hell is going on? I asked myself over and over. Dark scenarios played themselves out in my head: maybe they had reneged on their side of the deal. Maybe they weren't the amateur toughs I had figured them to be. Maybe Khan was lying face-down in an alley somewhere, a bullet hole in his temple, black blood oozing into the gutter.

Stop freaking out, I told myself. There was no way I would have gone ahead with the exchange if I hadn't been supremely confident that Yussuf would uphold his side of the deal.

Walk a mile in the shoes of a psychopath. Imagine a world where responsibility is unknown to you, except as an inconvenient weight that other people, suckers, seem to carry unquestioningly and pointlessly. Stupid notions like guilt or shame don't apply to you so you've got nothing to hold you back from doing whatever you want to achieve your desires. Since you have no conscience, it's all the same to you whether you're a ruthless murderer or just a plain old kidnapper. Either way, it's all about you getting what you want when you want it.

The good news was that though he might be a narcissistic, status-obsessed thug, Yussuf hadn't displayed the behavioural signs of a psychopath.

And we had him agreeing to a bunch of stuff in the negotiations, which suggested he was going to keep his word. I had statistics on my side too. In the world of K&R, as we know, the longer a case goes on, the higher the chance of the outcome working in my favour. There was no rationale for Yussuf killing Khan at this point. He'd only be shooting himself in the foot, having worked so long towards a successful resolution from his perspective. And he was still shit-scared of the US military. He probably feared that if he murdered Khan, he would only be encouraging military action.

Finally, at 8.05 p.m., almost ninety minutes after the ransom drop, the burner vibrated, shaking me out of my thoughts and obsessive reciting of the Shepard's Prayer.

A call from the kidnappers.

Abdul blurted, 'Where the hell have you been?'

'Oh yeah, brother, we went to the mosque to thank Allah for getting the money,' said Yussuf.

A disgusted Abdul asked, 'Where's Jadid?'

'You will have him shortly.' The phone went dead.

Some minutes later, a text came through from Aziz. It said, simply: 'We have him.' As I read the words I felt the tightness in my guts slowly start to unwind. The situation room erupted in cheers and whoops of joy that could be heard by the workers in the offices outside. I allowed myself a small smile. We've almost made it.

Shortly thereafter Aziz called me.

'Ben. Ben, dear brother. You can stop shitting yourself now. I'm here with Jadid. They told me to go to Fakhruddin Valika Road. So I go there and find him standing on the corner. No problem.'

'How is he?'

'A little confused and distressed,' Aziz said. 'But otherwise, not bad.'

The first thing was to notify Shadah. She picked up the phone on the first ring, her voice rushed and breathless, almost too scared to ask me the question.

'Your husband is free,' I said. 'We will be bringing him over to you now. He should be back with you in a few minutes.'

She didn't say anything for longer than a little while. I heard a soft weeping come down the line. When someone fears the worst, it's hard to believe in a happy ending. Shadah had been through a lot – the trauma of her husband in captivity, the loss of her baby – and in that moment I think everything just welled up inside of her and came out in one spontaneous burst. Shadah was crying because the ordeal was over and the weight had lifted from her shoulders.

After a brief reunion with his wife, and a shower, Khan was escorted onwards to Leonard's compound, where I was waiting for him.

I was delighted that Khan was free. During my time as a negotiator I've been lucky enough to secure the release of dozens of men and women. Every release gives me a special joy. To know that the job has been done right, that the person is going home – gives me a lot of satisfaction.

Khan shook my hand. '*Za kha yam*. Thank you,' he said.

At midnight on the day of the release I was exhausted but still had things to take care of. First, I gave the order for all documents associated with the case to be destroyed. Because from a security perspective nobody has a need to have this stuff to hand and you don't want anybody rooting through your garbage and finding it. It also has a symbolic meaning in that this is really the end of the case.

I had also arranged for a physical examination of Khan by a doctor I'd previously sourced. Being a hostage is physically as well as emotionally distressing and Khan was a middle-aged guy with a history of heart trouble so it was important to get him checked out.

The next day I sat down with Khan and asked him to tell me what he could about his time in captivity. He took a deep breath and kneaded the knuckles of his left hand into the palm of his right. In negotiation terms the place the hostage is held is referred to as 'the prison'.

'Tell me about the prison,' I said.

'There were no windows,' Khan said. His voice was hoarse. 'I remember ... yellow walls. No furniture. It was somewhere in the city. I could hear traffic through the walls.'

'What about running water?'

Khan shook his head. 'They brought me one big Pepsi bottle a day filled with cold water. There was only one toilet. It was not a Western type. They let me go three times a day. When the guards came into the room they told me to put a towel around my face.' Jadid frowned at a spot on the floor. 'I had no one to talk to. No radio. No TV. The days seemed to last for ever.'

'Tell me about the guards.'

'They were mean. They treated me like shit.'

'Did they threaten to kill you?'

Khan nodded, wiped his nose. 'They said they were from al-Jihad. They told me they had selected me because I was working for the Americans. I told them I don't work for Americans but they didn't believe me.'

'Anything you remember about them?'

He shrugged. 'All I could see of them was their ankles, feet and shoes.'

'What about patterns, behaviour, anything like that?'

Khan thought about this for a moment, then said, 'They never changed at the same time. Every day, the shifts were different. Sometimes early, sometimes late.'

This was more proof that Yussuf and his buddies were amateurs. Professional criminals pride themselves on efficiency. They would never tolerate a guard showing up late to his shift.

One of the things I've noticed about being a negotiator is that, when the case is over – especially in the first few cases – you think, When the hostage comes home everyone's going to be really happy and they'll throw a party and lots of people will be thanking me.

The truth is, there's very little of that. The negotiator has a lot more in common with the plumber. When someone's toilet backs up, the plumber comes and fixes the problem but at the end, the family just want him to get out so they can get their lives back to normal. Or if a doctor saves a cancer patient's life. The patient might be hugely thankful but it's not like they're going to send him Christmas cards. People want to see the back of you not because of any personal animosity but purely because you're a reminder of the worst thing that's ever happened to them.

I don't blame them.

No one wants to be reminded of bad times.

There's an interesting postscript to this case. A few years later I bumped into Leonard in London. He was staying at the Dorchester Hotel. It had been a while since I'd seen him and we hadn't spoken about the case since the day after it ended. I remembered that he had enjoyed it when I told him that it was easier negotiating with crazed jihadists than it was with him. In the bar, I asked him what Aziz was up to these days.

'Funny you should ask,' Leonard said. 'He's quite the character, isn't he?'

'Tell me about it,' I replied. 'What's he doing, Leonard?'

'Let's just say he got what he wanted,' Leonard said.

I pressed him for more details. Eventually after much alcohol and Jedi mind tricks, Leonard revealed that right before I showed up at the compound, Aziz was telling the rest of the guys about his own plan. Apparently he said, 'All right, so I'm going to deliver the money, get the hostage back, right? And then I'm going to kill the fucking kidnappers and take the money myself.'

According to Leonard, this is precisely what they heard Aziz did.

To this day I have no idea if Aziz killed the kidnappers or not. All I know is, he seemed to be the fearless type who might do exactly that. All I know is, it wouldn't be the craziest thing that ever happened in a kidnap case. All I know is what two decades of exposure to K&R has taught me: that when it comes to money and people, the money usually comes out on top.

Abduction – Captivity – Proof of Life –
Negotiation – Ransom Drop – Release

Part Four

THE NEW WAVE

'Hurry up. My life is in danger. Please help me.'

Michael Andersen

9

LAST RESORT

With every passing week, operating in the hot zone of Iraq, Afghanistan and Pakistan was becoming increasingly hazardous for foreigners. Between 2003 and 2008 more than two hundred foreigners were kidnapped in Iraq alone. Some were high-profile cases that ended in brutal execution, like the kidnappings of Ken Bigley and Nick Berg. Others, like the Italian reporter Giuliana Sgrena, were released after large ransoms had been negotiated.

Now I was going to be thrust into the middle of this mess.

In the spring of 2006 I received a call out of the blue inviting me to go to Toronto. By now my relationship with Emily had deteriorated. We were barely on speaking terms. On the rare nights I wasn't working on a case, I tried to avoid seeing her and sought solace in the bottom of a bottle of Barbancourt. We had two young daughters, Claire and Melissa, to consider and their welfare was upmost in both our minds when we agreed to try and rescue the marriage. At that point we really were in the last-chance saloon.

But marital woes had to be put to one side with the phone call from Toronto demanding my immediate attention. It was from a high-flying businesswoman who wanted to speak to me about a sensitive matter. She said her name was Megan Andersen, and from the anxious, edgy tone of her voice on the phone, I figured she wanted to do more than glean a few business-psychology tips from me. She was married to a guy named Michael Andersen, she explained to me, a geologist. His field work took him to some of the most dangerous places in the world. And several months ago, he had been kidnapped in Afghanistan.

My brother booked me on a Virgin Atlantic flight from Heathrow to Pearson. It had been a brutally cold British winter and even in March it was still as cold as a Russian smile in the capital. I left the icy cave that passed for my office, reminding myself to give the council hell when I came back. Inga, being Swedish, was wearing a mini-skirt and wished me good luck for the trip. I thought to myself I really should take her out to dinner when I come back.

Toronto was much warmer. Swapping my winter coat for a jacket and my sweater for a long-sleeved purple shirt, I hailed a cab outside Pearson and gave the cab driver the Andersen street address. Even before I showed up, I knew they'd done well for themselves. They lived in a private residential block located in a neighbourhood rich in two things: history and house prices. The cab nosed through a warren of redbrick row houses and arrowed down a well-lit street. We stopped outside a slick, expensive-looking apartment block on the corner of a leafy, tree-lined street. I fished forty Canadian dollars out of my pocket and pressed the entry buzzer.

Megan Andersen came to the door. She was in her mid-thirties, a naturally good-looking woman. But the strain of Michael's kidnapping had evidently taken its toll. She had dark patches under her eyes, her cheeks were chalk-pale and the smile she flashed at me was sad and forced. She looked exhausted. My first impression was that Megan was doing a very good job of holding it together but inside she was breaking up.

She ushered me into a living room that had definitely not come from the IKEA catalogue. I sat on the sofa opposite Megan and asked what I could do for her. As she went into the background of the case, it felt like the start of the Pink Floyd song 'Time' was playing in my head. Alarm bells were ringing.

Michael had been abducted in the notoriously violent Kandahar province, along with his Afghan driver. The gravity of their situation was compounded by the fact that their captors claimed they were the al-Hakim clan. A bloodline association of gangsters and warlords, the al-Hakims ruled the Kandahar roost with a mixture of fear, guns and more fear.

'Proof of life?' I asked Megan, taking notes.

'On Mike?'

I nodded.

'They sent Mike's employers a videotape, let me see, eight weeks ago.'

'And the driver?'

'I don't know.' She paused. 'I don't think so.'

'Anything on your husband since then? Have you heard his voice on the phone, have the al-Hakims released photographs of him, anything like that?'

'No,' she said, shaking her head slowly. 'Nothing.'

The absence of information is one of the most powerful tools the kidnappers have. They use it to torture the hostage's family because in a very large and important sense the family is the real target of the kidnappers. The hostage knows he's alive and however uncomfortable his situation might be, he has some grasp of what's going on. He knows when he eats, when he drinks, when he goes to sleep, when he's getting a beating, how bad it is, etc. The relatives do not and this is often what tortures them the most. Part of the reason for this is that people are information processing machines and like nature, we abhor a vacuum. So in the absence of information, we tend to make up our own. And we rarely make up good information.

Any Westerner operating in the Middle East has to bear in mind two cases. The first was the tragic execution of Daniel Pearl, the *Wall Street Journal* reporter who was abducted in January 2002 in Karachi by a militant group and subsequently beheaded. The brutality of his murder – his body was cut into several pieces and dumped in a shallow grave – and the crude video that the group released on the internet, sent shockwaves through the world. Of course, Westerners had been kidnapped before in other conflicts and in other parts of the world – but never killed in such a cold-blooded manner.

The invasion of Iraq in March 2003 saw thousands of Western civilians taking up contractor jobs in Baghdad. Ostensibly they were there to rebuild the shattered country – have an adventure and make tons of money. But their arrival precipitated a new wave of kidnappings – ones that ended in bloodbaths. It began in May 2004, when a video was leaked showing the beheading of American-Jewish businessman Nick Berg. The CIA believed that an Islamic terrorist by the name of Abu Musab al-Zarqawi was personally responsible for the execution. Berg's kidnapping was unique in that his kidnappers at no point made a demand, political or financial. Instead, the videotape was accompanied by the warning that 'You will not receive anything from us but coffins after coffins.'

Founder of al-Qaeda in Iraq, al-Zarqawi had been honoured with the title 'Emir of Al-Qaeda in the Country of Two Rivers'. He fascinated me from a psychological point of view. I think he was a classic psychopathology in search of a cause. If he hadn't been cutting people's heads off in the name of Allah and al-Qaeda, he would have found some other justification for acting out his depraved fantasies.

The complete absence of a ransom demand in cases such as Berg's demonstrated that these guys had no real interest in negotiating. The beheading of Nick Berg spearheaded a wave of similar incidents. South Korean translator Kim Sun-Il was captured in May 2004 and beheaded. The following September, US citizens Eugene Armstrong and Jack Hensley, along with Briton Ken Bigley, were abducted in the al-Mansour district of Baghdad. They suffered the same fate as Berg and Kim. In total more than thirty foreign civilians were executed by Iraqi militia groups for the purposes of propaganda videos.

The kidnappers' primary – probably only – concern was to create terror. It's important to remember that terrorists don't measure their success by the number of people they kill, they measure it by the number of people they frighten. And they were very, very successful.

Another unique factor about this new breed of kidnappers was that they appeared to be incredibly narcissistic. It's all about them. The world is fucking them around personally; so much so that they feel compelled to take some kind of action. Whether it's 'The world is fucking with my people' or 'The world is fucking with my God', the real message is 'The world is fucking with me.' These guys display no empathy and no remorse. To them, other people are mere instruments to be used and abused as they see fit.

Afghanistan had latterly taken Iraq's place as the hostage capital of the Middle East. It was a bad time to be a foreigner in Afghanistan. It was a bad time to be kidnapped. Securing Michael Andersen's release would prove to be one of the most difficult cases of my career, but not because of the kidnappers.

As I was only brought in originally to offer psychological help to Megan, I had come late to the party. By the time Megan engaged my services, Michael had been held hostage for almost six months. In that time in my opinion, the case had been managed by the Keystone Konsultants. From the outset, Michael's employer dithered as to whether they should be negotiating with the kidnappers at all. Being a company composed mainly of idealistic and somewhat naive scientists and academics, they took the stance that 'we do not negotiate with terrorists'. It's also very far removed from the real world. If the company directors thought that refusing to negotiate with the kidnappers was going to scare the al-Hakim clan or deter it from targeting their employees in the future, they were making a monumental error of judgement that could cost Michael his life. Westerners working in Afghanistan were already targets. Suddenly going all Jack Bauer on Michael's case wouldn't change anything.

I explained this to Megan very clearly. In K&R, you simply have to negotiate. There's no viable alternative. When I answer a hostage call, from the get-go I know that I'm going to pay a ransom and prepare to do so.

The company did fortunately have a K&R insurance policy in place. But that's where the problems began. The first guys they hired to negotiate with the kidnappers immediately set up a situation room in Kabul. However, the negotiators also made some fundamental mistakes, such as failing to route all communications through the Kabul situation room. As I stated earlier, you need to get everyone's phone number and have them direct any calls to one central line. Afterwards, those same numbers need to be thrown away. Failure to accomplish that simple goal had left Megan living on a knife edge. She was the one being harassed by the kidnappers, and the worst part was they didn't have to lift a finger. They reached her on the landline and her mobile phone. When I met her, she had become afraid to leave the flat in case the kidnappers phoned while she was out. This was torturing her and left Megan at the kidnappers' mercy. This phone arrangement was doing the kidnappers' work for them.

As Megan retold me the story I could hardly believe my ears.

In fairness, it has to be said that Megan initially wanted things this way. She'd been badly advised from the beginning and the hesitant posturing at Michael's employers had her convinced that they were not taking care of things. So being a competent, strong woman, she began to take over. But all it needed was for someone else to answer her landline and say, 'Megan's in the hospital, this is the new number to use, goodbye.' *Click*. Do that a couple of times and the al-Hakims would soon get the message.

A month into the kidnapping, the company stepped back from negotiations at the family's request. When the K&R policy is invoked the reaction consultant is immediately tasked with contacting the client and offering their services. In this case the consultants were a specialist outfit called Barringer. These guys had a solid track record when it came to K&R. During the first month of negotiations they had taken a back seat and allowed the company to steer the case. Now they took a more hands-on role.

But problems quickly developed between Barringer's representative on the case, a guy named Brad, and Megan. Brad, Megan felt, did not inspire confidence. He came from a special forces background and spoke in a clipped, static and aggressive style that had no doubt been drummed into him at Fort Bragg. Useful for barking orders when training local militias, but not really appropriate for speaking to an intelligent, successful female client. Making him harder to understand was his thick Alabama accent. It was a non-starter from the get-go.

The al-Hakims made an initial ransom demand of $15 million, plus the unconditional release of several prisoners being held at Guantanamo Bay. The prisoner demands were, I suspect, a smokescreen, since the al-Hakims were sophisticated enough to know that the company had no way to release prisoners. Negotiations were also muddied by the fact that another contact at Barringer received a ransom demand of $20 million plus prisoners. A third guy got told the ransom was set at $30 million plus prisoners.

The Chinese whispers over the ransom illustrates exactly why you absolutely have to have only one team managing communications. When you have multiple points of contact, messes like this occur.

In response, Barringer's negotiator, a guy by the name of Bill, made an offer of $424,000. That's an okay number. It's at the low, low end of expectations on the part of the kidnappers. As a negotiator you always make sure the offer numbers aren't too round or perfect. An offer of $424,000 works better than an offer of, say, $400,000 because it ties in with a universal rule of human persuasion. A psychology study carried out in the 1960s involved getting a university student working for the researchers to dress up as a homeless guy. They dispatched him to Grand Central Station to beg for money. Over the course of the day he'd accrue a certain amount in loose change. The researchers would then alter certain features about the student's appearance and begging strategy and document the effect on his earning power. If the student asked, 'Can I have *some* money?' he got perhaps forty bucks a day total. But if he changed the paradigm by asking for a *specific* amount, for example forty-eight cents, he doubled his income. The secret was the specificity of his request. It made the guy seem more genuine. People would hear the mention of forty-eight cents and figure that he needed to make up his train fare.

The same principle is at play in kidnapping and ransom payouts. The figure of $424,000 sounds like the client has really had to stretch to make up that extra $24,000. I personally would've made it $424,500 – the extra $500 tacked on to the end gives the kidnappers the impression that you've been rooting around the back of the sofa and underneath the cushions for every last penny.

But unsurprisingly, the al-Hakims rejected Bill's offer out of hand. They were under no pressure to reach a speedy resolution.

Then negotiations halted.

Out of nowhere, Bill quit in a fit of pique. Neither Megan nor Michael's employers ever heard from him again. His departure created a vacuum and caused a major delay in progressing negotiations. All this while, an innocent guy was being held in captivity several thousand miles away fearing for his life.

This undermined Barringer in the eyes of Megan and the rest of the family. Bill disappearing off the face of the planet, Brad's coldness on the phone . . . it did not play well. Another Barringer consultant had been inconsistent in his feedback to Megan. Eventually everyone grew tired of Barringer and it was agreed that a change of approach was needed. The company then interviewed two different security firms with a view to taking over the case. They decided to give the gig to Worldwide Security (WS), which employed several former CIA agents.

It's my belief (based on faith, I guess) that the CIA does a lot of good work, and they have many good people working for them in extremely testing circumstances and environments. I believe it because I know and respect a few of the people who work for them. They have much expertise to offer in a crisis.

But not a kidnap crisis. The CIA is an intelligence organisation, and though these guys might have been the best intelligence agents in history, they were simply not trained or experienced in K&R or managing a kidnap. In that regard they were no less likely to avoid making the same assumptions as would any average member of the public with only a Hollywood concept of how kidnaps actually go. Like the public, these former agents seemed to think that every kidnapping ends with a massive armed assault, that no ransoms are ever paid and that the bad guys get blown away in a hail of bullets. Therefore their automatic response was to play hardball, to say, 'We won't pay', and start loading cartridges into their shotguns. They failed to understand that violence must always be the last resort in K&R, not the first. Unfortunately, the guys at WS bought into the same doctrine. It quickly became apparent to me that negotiating a ransom with the kidnappers was not high on their agenda.

In the initial few weeks after Michael's abduction, negotiations had kind of stuttered along, hindered in part by the company's indecision over whether to enter into negotiations at all. Sure, some initial progress had been made. But the several months leading up to my arrival had seen little movement. In my view this inactivity was due in no small part to WS's attitude. It had been hired out of desperation by people who'd believed the 'CIA' PR message.

WS had convinced Megan that it could use its contacts to locate Michael and then bust him loose in classic American *Call of Duty*-style. To me, such a philosophy was not only hopelessly unrealistic and out of touch with the real world, but dangerously irresponsible and professionally incompetent. WS was dreaming.

Worse still it was burning a hole in the insurer's pocket. They had a burn rate of about $100,000 a month by keeping a small army of ex-special forces operators on permanent standby in the crazy belief that WS would need to deploy them at a moment's notice to rescue Michael. These guys were obviously used to spending Uncle Sam's unlimited budget.

As Megan explained this to me I thought, How the hell are you guys gonna pull him out when you don't even know where he is? Sure, their CIA backgrounds meant their intelligence-gathering skills were second to none and they might have had a guy or two on the payroll over in Afghanistan, but none of this mattered because if they couldn't get their heads around the fact that this was a kidnap-for-ransom negotiation, not a kidnap-for-rescue case, then Michael was dead.

Their secretive, cloak and dagger covert approach had yet to yield any significant results. I also felt they were being overly vague with Megan. If I was any less generous, I'd have said they were lying to her. Especially since I had a suspicion that the SF team leader was giving them a kickback.

'What exactly are these guys doing?' I asked her.

Megan jerked her shoulders. 'I won't hear from them in a week. Then I'll call Adam.'

'Who's he?'

'He's the one managing the case. I call him, he tells me that they're working on something at that very moment but it's sensitive and we can't talk to you about it right now.'

'And then?'

'Then they won't call me for another week.' She let out a heavy sigh and frowned at her hands as she explained that the following week she'd put in another call to Adam at WS and he'd reply that the lead from the previous week had gone cold but they had another thing that had literally just cropped up although they couldn't talk to her about it because of operational security. And so on and so on.

I struggled to believe WS was giving Megan such short shrift. If that had been me on the end of the phone I would have said, 'Screw you, I'm the goddamn client and I'm the one paying you. You had better tell me every little damned thing or I'll find someone who will.'

WS wasn't the only one with its grubby fingers all over this case. Megan strongly suspected that the CSIS (Canadian Security Intelligence Service), the Canadian equivalent to the FBI, had tapped her phone. Although I'm not sure who would have made the request or why, so did I. The thing about intelligence agencies like the CSIS and the FBI is that they do have a lot of bells and whistles and machines that go *ping*.

Organisations like these are resource-heavy because they are funded by federal government. But the FBI, for example, really gets involved in surprisingly few hostage negotiations, because of who it is and the way jurisdiction works between local, state and federal law enforcement. In the case of the Waco siege, for example, the best negotiator present wasn't from the FBI; he was the local sheriff.

Larry Bridge once related to me his very elegant theory about why the FBI and ATF (the Bureau of Alcohol, Tobacco, Firearms and Explosives) made such a mess of it at Waco. He calls it the 'Bunion Factor' and it goes like this: federal employees don't get overtime pay. Whether those guys are in the field for eight hours or eighteen hours, they get paid the same amount. Local cops do get overtime pay and they love it: that's where they make their real money. If a regular police officer is at a siege for eighteen hours, he's happy as can be, because he knows he's going to get paid accordingly. Thus, his bunions don't hurt as much. But if you're paid for eight hours and you're out there for twelve or more, your bunions will be hurting like crazy. And so you get into the mindset of 'Let's do something to finish this and get out of here.'

While I know some individual FBI special agents who I admire and esteem, my experience of the FBI as an organisation has been that it is brilliant at portraying itself as the omnipotent outfit that can get you out of such a fix. The problem is, it often lacks the substance to back that up. It doesn't have the real K&R expertise. Much of the FBI's image is fostered by endless TV shows portraying its agents as daring and chiselled hero-types or forensic science geniuses.

A police officer friend of mine told me a story once about the most difficult negotiating situation any law-enforcement officer can face: when a cop has barricaded himself inside his home with a hostage. Now you're having to deal with one of your own. This occurs more often than we would care to imagine and it's a hugely traumatic experience for the cops involved. When an FBI special agent did the same thing, the first words out of the agent's boss's mouth when they arrived at the scene were 'Can we put a lid on the press coverage of this thing?' In my experience, the FBI is a political and public relations machine more than a law-enforcement outfit, and it behaves accordingly.

None of which stops the FBI or the likes of the CSIS from being viewed as the experts and the go-to guys in a crisis. Westerners – especially Americans – for the most part tend to live in a world that is unsullied by the governmental corruption endemic elsewhere. The justice system works (sort of); the cops aren't corrupt (usually). This makes it possible to have ideals and faith in your government. And one of those acts of faith is that in an extremely bad situation, the government has experts who will step in and sort out whatever mess you happen to find yourself in. Like, say, your husband's a geologist who's had the misfortune to be kidnapped in Afghanistan.

Megan also had other freelance therapists billing her for their sometimes questionable advice. One local therapist recommended she undergo acupuncture treatment. To deal with kidnap trauma. The trauma industry is full of snake-oil merchants who are only too happy to take your money off you and I feared that Megan, for all her intelligence and common sense, might be falling for some of these tricks. When it's your loved one kidnapped on the other side of the world and you haven't had a decent night's sleep in months, it's hard to maintain a balanced judgement. You want to believe people when they say they will make everything better, even when you know deep down that it's not in their power to do so.

Before we could advance negotiations, I felt we needed to have a full and frank conversation with the guys at WS. They were actively preventing a paid resolution to the case, promoting the harebrained scheme that a bunch of their cowboys could ride unnoticed into the middle of Afghanistan and rescue Michael 'any day now'.

They were giving Megan false hope.

'When was the last time you worked at your job?' I asked Megan.

'I stopped . . . I don't know . . . maybe two months after . . . it happened.'

'So four months ago?'

'Something like that.' Her voice was dry and sore, like she'd swallowed sand.

'And you say the kidnappers have called you?'

Megan nodded her head slowly.

'How often is that?'

'Once or twice a month.'

'Same person each time?'

'I'm not sure.'

'Look, I know I've been brought down here to deal with the psychology aspect,' I said. 'And I'm not the type of guy to over-step the mark. But what you're telling me is disturbing. It's like this: if I saw someone lying on the railroad tracks and I saw the train coming, I couldn't stay silent. I would yell. Do you understand?'

'Yes,' Megan said.

'Well, right now I'm yelling.'

Megan stared at the floor and fell into silence as she took in what I was saying. Her breathing was light and shallow. It's hard to hear the truth sometimes. But it needed to be said. I pressed on.

'My experience and my training tell me that this case is being badly managed. This case is endangering Michael's life, and it's torturing you.'

Megan found it hard to take at first. It certainly rattled her cage and I meant it to do that. But in the end this was a good thing. Lives were at stake. Nothing was happening in the negotiations. Nothing sensible was being done to secure Michael's release or that of his Afghan colleague. The only thing happening, I explained to Megan, was that WS was billing for a daily rate, for the special ops team. Having a small army on standby at the cost of a hundred thousand dollars a month was extremely stupid, I explained. If by some miracle WS did find the prison where the al-Hakims were holding Michael, and managed to somehow bribe or neutralise the guards, they'd still need a pretty large plane to drag Michael, the team and their gear out of there. There are plenty of ways and means that are a lot less expensive and wasteful, and more subtle.

At this point I could imagine that the underwriter's butt was puckering like an old lady's lips. The case itself was reaching the point where the fees were amounting to more than the ransom demand.

I said, 'You mentioned that there was a proof-of-life video?'

'It's a couple of months old.'

'May I see it?'

One of my specialities as both a response consultant and a negotiator is to provide a bit of what I call 'kidnap kremlinology' to the case. Sort of like interpreting the runes for the client. The footage from Michael's proof-of-life video confirmed what I had suspected about the kidnappers' mentality.

At first glance it looked like your standard Iraqi or Afghanistan hostage video. Michael was kneeling on the ground. He'd lost some weight compared with the family pictures Megan had shown me earlier, and in place of his square, normally clean-cut jaw he had a straggly beard. His eyes were reddened. An Afghan rug had been draped behind him with some kind of Arabic writing scrawled on it, probably flagging up whatever dubious cause the al-Hakims were pretending to champion. A guy loosely gripped a rusty-looking AK-47 assault rifle while he stood beside Michael and cast long shadows over him.

'This is my proof-of-life video,' Michael sobbed, reading from several sheets of crumpled paper in his hands. 'Hurry up. My life is in danger. Please help me. Please meet their conditions. If you don't help me, I will die.'

He turned the page. I wasn't listening to him. Despite the al-Hakims' intention, my focus wasn't on Michael at all but on all the details around him. I was trying to pick up on any small thing that might indicate to me the mindset of his kidnappers.

'Do you want to kill me or do you want to save me?' Now Michael looked up from the papers and stared straight into the camera. 'Please help me. Please save me. I want to go home. This is my last message.' He paused, then went on, 'I love you all very much. I'm so, so sorry.'

The tape ended. I viewed the footage a second time and made some more notes.

'This is fine,' I told Megan. 'You've got nothing to worry about.'

'How can you say that?' she shouted. 'They're pointing a gun at his head!'

'Sure, but take another look at the guy.'

I rewound the tape. Specifically, I pointed to the foot of the man standing beside Michael and brandishing the AK-47. The man was barefoot. His toes curled up. This small movement told me that the man was relaxed and kind of bored. There was zero tension in his foot. And people who are seriously considering killing someone get very tense. Even the sociopaths. Bottom line, the al-Hakim clan was putting on a display. It wanted to freak out Megan and the employers, and a proof-of-life video

166

where the victim has a gun targeting his head tends to do the trick. If the al-Hakims had any desire to slaughter Michael they wouldn't have requested ransom money. Or they would have sold him on to the Taliban.

Things hadn't gotten off to a good start in Michael's case. But now I had convinced Megan to take control of matters we could focus on getting her husband home alive and well.

First, I had to untangle the mess that had been created around the case.

10

THE EMPEROR'S CLOTHES

Michael Andersen's kidnap was not the first hostage case I had worked in Afghanistan. The previous year, I'd participated in the capture of a Westerner who seemed to have a deathwish. He'd rocked up to the hinterland of Afghanistan with a fixer and a driver. No personal security detail, no convoy, no nothing. If that's how you intend to travel across the most desolate, savage, lawless country in the world, make sure you take out the biggest K&R policy on the planet. Because you are virtually guaranteed to be abducted.

I came to the case relatively late. A buddy of mine called Howard had been handling negotiations up till then. Negotiating is a lonely business but every once in a while you'll be in a hotel some place and meet three or four consultants and security guys working different cases. Sometimes, too, you'll see someone you worked with on a previous case. I knew Howard from a case I'd worked in Mexico that lasted six months. Negotiators can only work for three or four weeks or so before having to take a break because of the mental burnout that results from the lack of sleep and dealing with sociopaths all day. In Mexico I rotated with Howard every three or four weeks.

Remarkably, on this other Afghanistan case I was able to communicate directly with the hostage. His name was Brian Delaney and the kidnappers had left him at the house of a friend. They visited him only infrequently. The friend, Khalid, owned a satellite phone and had given Brian permission to use it to call me. It was clear that Khalid had not sought the kidnappers' approval before allowing this.

By talking to Brian I was able to ascertain that he had not been taken to Waziristan, as he had previously claimed on the phone. The earlier calls had been made under duress, with the kidnappers present, and he had been forced to lie about his whereabouts to put any rescue mission off the scent. It didn't take long before I figured out that Brian was being held hostage by the same guys who would later snatch Michael Andersen: the al-Hakim clan. At times it almost seemed as if these guys had a monopoly on hostage-taking. And yet their lack of professionalism was surprising. No Latin American kidnapper worth his salt would permit the hostage to have free and unsupervised contact with the outside world. In Afghanistan things are often more relaxed. They just let hostages use sat phones. They dump the victims at the houses of friends. This devil-may-care attitude is just as true for the Taliban. Most of these guys are unsophisticated hillbillies. They'll do ridiculous stuff like talk *en clair* (French for 'in clear') on their radios about the precise details of an attack. Not surprisingly, the Coalition forces take advantage of this. The thing about being undisciplined and unruly is that sooner or later, it costs you. Maybe one day you leave a sat phone out. Maybe the next day, a guard falls asleep and your investment escapes into the night.

'I gotta go,' Brian said. His voice was fading in and out. 'The battery on this thing is almost out.'

We secured his release shortly after. The al-Hakim clan got its ransom and we got our man. The next time it wouldn't be so easy.

Two days after I spoke with Megan, I asked her to attend a meeting with Michael's employer's lawyer Dennis Calhoun and myself. Calhoun already struck me as a clued-up and switched-on guy. At a prior meeting he'd mentioned a conversation he'd had with a contact of his who walked in the very highest corridors of government power. The word back from this senior official was that the cowboy approach might be effective in the movies but was '100 per cent fucking useless in the real world and particularly Afghanistan'. I got the impression this had sown the seeds of doubt in the mind of Calhoun about WS's methods. I'd also discovered that a few months prior, Calhoun had tried to take WS off the case. I had high hopes that Calhoun would be sympathetic to my concerns about WS's conduct.

'We really have to get this whole thing back on track,' I told Calhoun as we sat down in his plush office. It was a bubble of quiet amid the throng of corporate noise, the beeps of phones and the tap-tap of fingers on keyboards in the corridor.

'I completely agree,' Calhoun said.

'Glad to hear it, Dennis. Because right now, this emperor's got no clothes.'

Calhoun eased back in his chair. 'What do you suggest?'

'Back to basics,' I said. 'We return to the tried-and-tested method of negotiating a settlement for this guy's release. WS is feeding everyone a bill of goods with its cowboy tactics. Every time Megan speaks to them it's the same old story: "We'll have news for you tomorrow." Tomorrow comes around and they say the same damn thing, "We can't tell you more for security reasons but our source will have something tomorrow." And the day after that and the day after that. It's smoke and mirrors as far as I'm concerned.'

Calhoun sucked in the air-conditioned air and stared out of his window. After what felt like several minutes, he turned back to us.

'Okay. Makes sense to me. What else do you recommend?'

'Streamline the negotiating team.'

There were way too many cooks involved in this, and they weren't just spoiling the broth. They were pissing in it. As well as WS and the CSIS, Barringer had retained some influence in proceedings. I felt that if we wanted to get anywhere with the al-Hakims, we had to put an end to the Chinese whispers and get a single point of reference established. We could also end internal inertia, I felt, by having a crisis management team to vote on major decisions regarding the case.

'I agree. This sounds perfectly sensible, Ben.'

'Also there should be an odd number of people on the team.'

'Why?'

'Because if the team can't agree on a course of action and it comes to a vote, an odd number guarantees it can't be a dead-lock.'

'Okay, Ben.'

'And there's one other thing.'

Calhoun raised an eyebrow. He was a smart guy and saw where I was coming from. 'The story hasn't yet broken in the media,' he said, unfolding his arms. 'We've tried to keep a lid on this whole thing. But if you feel differently . . . '

'No, not at all. You're doing the right thing. The media find out about this thing, it's a catastrophe for us,' I said. 'But we ought to plan for the worst. I suggest we prepare a brief press statement, in case word gets out.'

'Agreed,' Calhoun said, nodding.

Particularly in this case, had word of Michael's kidnapping got out and the al-Hakims found out about it, they would have jacked up the ransom tremendously. Comparatively few North Americans had been kidnapped in Afghanistan. But the Afghans had access to the internet and cable TV and if they saw Michael's face splashed all over CNN.com and the BBC, they'd think, Shit, this guy must be *somebody*. And people who are *somebody* are worth more money. The kidnappers' perceived value of the hostage would go through the roof and probably tack more time on to his captivity.

With my mind at ease on the question of press coverage, I set about trying to create a clear one-to-one communication link between the al-Hakims and our newly formed and focused crisis management team. When Megan explained to me about the three separate offers that had been made, my initial instinct was that this was a direct result of the messy negotiation approach Barringer had started and WS had overseen. People generally like to make important decisions based on facts. When facts are thin on the ground and people are confused, they tend to freeze and not make decisions. They think, I don't have the facts to make a proper decision and I'm not going to be forced into making one. They prefer to do nothing. It's a basic human instinct.

It seemed to me that the opposition were suffering from the same problem here. They were getting conflicting messages from us: on the one hand they had an offer of $424,000 and on the other hand they had the cowboys over at WS trying to stall things while they 'gathered intel'. The kidnappers were not hearing a clear, consistent voice. What they were hearing was many voices saying many different things. Given that they weren't certain where we were at, or the value we attached to Michael, the al-Hakims were inclined to sit and wait. They were home, comfortable in their own backyard, surrounded by food and friends and familiarity. They were in no rush to make a decision. Kidnappers want to get the most amount of money possible for their hostage. If they're unsure of his value, or they're afraid of leaving money on the table by settling on an amount too early, they're going to wait till they're more sure. It's a fact that people are more motivated by what they stand to lose than by what they might gain. The al-Hakims, I'm sure, would be looking at the $424,000 offer and worry that they were undervaluing Michael. They only had one shot at this hostage and they were going to make the best of him. Especially when it seemed to them that the guys at the other end of the negotiating table didn't know their asses from their elbows.

Now that Calhoun was on board, I felt it was time to confront WS. Its guys were still behaving in the same way, still making promises and then pulling up the secrecy barriers whenever Megan pressed for more information. 'We have to protect our sources, it's confidential,' Adam told Megan. 'We're on the verge of a breakthrough and we'll have news for you very soon.' The CIA and its almost paranoid obsession with secrecy have a long history of going hand in hand. While it's understandable and necessary that many of the Agency's activities be clandestine, men like James Jesus Angleton, former chief of counterintelligence at the CIA, handicapped Agency operations for years with his Doctor Strangelove-esque overzealous pursuit of Soviet 'moles'. The point I stressed to Megan, however, was that the bosses at the CIA know exactly what the hell is going on. And Megan, as Michael's wife and the one who had hired WS, was their boss. In my view, these cowboys were pulling the wool over her eyes. That could not be allowed to continue.

I set up a conference call with Adam and Megan and offered to play the role of 'bad cop' and ask WS the uncomfortable questions I'd raised with her prior. I felt that the questions would be better coming from me than Megan. Psychologically she was under a lot of pressure. At the same time I needed to be delicate with WS. I couldn't just storm in there swinging punches when I might need these guys later.

WS claimed that it wasn't practising full disclosure with Barringer because it was afraid of leaks. Now, Barringer had faults but I severely doubted the company was in some way feeding details to the media. They're professional guys, not a leaky organisation. Barringer has been at the K&R game for a long while and added to that I personally knew several people within the company. That notion just did not wash. To me it seemed as if the guys at WS had brought traditional CIA paranoia into the civilian world of K&R.

Although I was circumspect when it came to addressing these concerns, the conversation soon became heated. WS was incredibly defensive and hostile to my line of questioning. I said to Adam, 'You say you have got this person X or Y or Z who has a line to the al-Hakims and yet nothing is happening', framing things in a way that made it very clear this was no simple case of he said, she said.

I pressed on. 'You say you have intelligence assets but what are those assets telling you?'

'We can't say yet,' Adam said.

'Megan is the client. She's paying you for this information. So what is it?'

'We can't tell you yet.'

'But it's our information. We bought it.'

'We can't talk to you in case it compromises our sources—'

'Do you really think anyone in this room is going to talk to the Taliban? And even if you do think that, for whatever reason, right now on the phone, we undertake not to disclose anything to anybody. Deal?'

Silence. I exchanged looks with Megan.

Then, 'No, we can't tell you.'

'And what about the special ops team? Why do you need to burn so much cash keeping them on standby?'

'Because we're going to need them to do the rescue.'

'But when will that be?' I asked. 'Or is this something else that you specifically cannot tell us about?'

The emperor's clothes were coming off faster than a stripper's.

Adam could barely disguise his rage. He and the rest of the WS guys on the call were beside themselves at this outsider coming in and driving a freight train through their cosy little set-up. I had no regrets. At the end of the day, it became very clear – given what I had heard and what I knew about K&R situations – that the guys at WS had nothing. I figured I was the first person actually to question them about the case, the kind of questions that any journalist would fire off. But Megan wasn't a journalist, and by the time I showed up WS had gotten her hopes so high about Michael's imminent release from captivity that she wasn't capable of being tough with them.

One thing we need to be clear on. In the unlikely event that WS did find Michael, there were to be no operations of any kind without express written authorisation from Megan and the crisis management team beforehand. This was vital. I didn't want the WS guys going in half-cocked. My opposition to the rescue idea was simple: the most dangerous part, more dangerous than the abduction and the exchange, the part where the most hostages are injured or killed, is the rescue mission itself. This is exactly what led to the death of Linda Norgrove, the Scottish aid worker taken captive by the Taliban in the Kunar province in September 2010. The following month US special forces launched a pre-dawn raid on the location where Norgrove was being held hostage. She died in the resulting battle. A joint UK–US investigation concluded that Norgrove had died when a hand grenade thrown by one of the rescuers detonated. This was a tragic series of events and I had visions of something similar happening when WS proposed their cowboy rescue plan.

To be fair to WS, Megan was a feisty, independent-thinking woman. Naturally so; I wouldn't expect someone to have the executive job title she had by being shy and compliant. Megan was forced to be in charge of everything but decision-making, and leadership in kidnap cases was not on the curriculum in her MBA course.

I never put it to her like this but essentially I had to make her choose: she could either tell me what to do or she could tell me how to do it, but she couldn't have both ways.

It occurred to me that Michael's employers had given control to Megan on any number of issues. This is the exact opposite of what happened on other cases I worked, where the company assumed total control of the case. In one case, the husband had been kidnapped and he was well-liked within the company and a valuable employee and the wife was simply too cut up to make decisions on what to do. Ceding control to the company worked really well under those circumstances. But Megan was a different type of personality and I could see little point in trying to wrestle decision-making away from her and foisting it on the employers. That would simply multiply Megan's anxiety and distress. I decided that it was in everyone's best interests if Megan helped run the show, but I would give her as much guidance and feedback as possible, and intervene strongly when I felt the need.

WS sent Megan an email regarding a meeting in Dubai with a shadowy businessman calling himself only 'Bilal'. This guy claimed to know the al-Hakims. He looked and sounded a little dodgy, wearing a cheap suit yet sporting a genuine-article Rolex watch and ultra high-end Vertu mobile phone – the ones costing several thousand dollars a pop with the screens made from sapphire and ruby bearings.

The report documented a dialogue exchange with Bilal. He said he wanted to help secure Michael's release. Stating that he had nothing to gain personally from this situation, Bilal was offering to mediate on behalf of WS with the Taliban. Then he produced a flash drive containing a file that turned out to be a new proof of life video.

In a matter of hours, the video got emailed through to Megan. I played the footage. Michael was seated in front of a concrete wall and decked out in traditional Afghan clothing. His condition did not seem to have visibly deteriorated from the previous video. He still had the beard, which had grown to six inches in length. Again he was reading from a script.

'Please try your best to release us. Don't waste time. We are very eager to be with our families again. I want to say to my wife Megan that what you said in your letter still helps me. I am strong because you are strong.'

He finished reading from the script. The camera operator said something unintelligible. The tape stopped and restarted. Michael stayed seated on the floor, except now he had no script. His hands rested on his knees. His eyes bored holes in the camera.

'We can't wait weeks. We need to leave in days. We are in a very difficult situation. Please help us now. Please free us soon. Please.'

The video ended.

Despite the tone of the video, I had reasons to be optimistic. By releasing a second tape, the al-Hakims were demonstrating that they wanted to do business. Nor did Michael's condition seem to have deteriorated. They were feeding him and giving him water – and they had supplied him with fresh clothes. This was a sign that they valued their hostage because he represented a big payday to them.

With the case now gathering a new sense of direction and

purpose, I headed back to the UK and a bunch of other existing situations that needed my urgent attention. I told Megan to keep me posted and call me as soon as anything happened, however small. It was crucial now that, having read WS the riot act and gotten the company on board with our plan of action, we didn't lose this momentum.

I landed at Heathrow after catching the red-eye flight back from Toronto. I wormed my way through the miserable crowds at border control and dragged my carry-on bag to the green exit marked 'Nothing to Declare'. But I did have something to declare. I was exhausted.

I took a cab back to my dark, cold apartment and crashed out the moment I hit the bed. At about seven o'clock the next morning, my iPhone buzzed me awake. It was one of my friends at Barringer.

'Yeah?' I answered.

'Ben, we've got some news.'

The pause filled with me fear. For a moment I worried that the al-Hakim guys had gone completely nuts and executed Michael. Or that maybe WS had staged a rescue attempt and had botched it.

'Michael's escaped.'

I was delighted!

My friend described how Michael and his Afghan colleague seized their chance when the guards were asleep and climbed out of the window, the noise they made drowned out by the loud hum of an electric generator. They made a dash for the highway a couple of hundred metres away. Their determination to escape was due in no small part to the fact that they'd seen a steady stream of military vehicles on this road and realised that they couldn't be far from some kind of base. To the question of why the kidnappers had chosen to operate so close to friendly lines, the answer is that it was a familiar and deliberate ploy on their part to hide in plain sight. They wanted to keep an eye on what the enemy was up to. They also probably figured that by hiding so close to a military base, their location would not be considered when it came to trying to pinpoint where Michael was being held. As in, when you've lost something you look everywhere except under your nose.

Michael and his colleague had no outside assistance in their escape. As I expected, someone from WS tried to claim that the guards had been bribed to look the other way so Michael could make his break for freedom. That's absurd. If WS or the government bribed the guards, that meant that they knew where Michael was being held. And if they knew that, why the hell didn't they spring him loose?

Some days later I had a beer with an ex-SAS guy named Clive. The way the Andersen case had ended was playing on my mind, so I picked Clive's brain about it. Part of me was amazed that the security in both the Andersen and Delaney cases could be so lax. But Clive had worked on the frontlines in Afghanistan combating the Taliban and was not in the least surprised.

'Make no mistake, some of the Taliban are hard as fuck but smart,' he explained in a Mancunian accent thicker than tar, between generous sips of London Pride. 'But you also get the fucking jokers and the chancers. Some of their fighters are undisciplined, amateur, untrained and a lot of these guys couldn't organise a piss-up in a brewery, mate.'

I sank the rest of my rum and weighed up Clive's words. I guess what applied to the Taliban fighters was also true of the kidnappers; they were cut from the same jihadist cloth. The al-Hakims might have had some street smarts and cunning, but without discipline, they were easy to take. There was lots of thinking going on inside certain factions of the clan but little action to follow it up. All the angry posturing and intimidating behaviour in the world counts for little if you can't organise your guards to work in shifts and keep a close eye at all times on the hostages.

This kind of criminal is the most common one: the opportunistic low-life with lofty ambitions but lacking the focus to pay attention to the details. Criminals like this are big on vision but low on attention span, often because the details tend to conflict with the overarching way they see themselves and the situation unfolding. Criminal laziness proved the undoing of the al-Hakims. They had one amateur guard posted on watch at the time Michael and his Afghan colleague escaped. One guard. And he fell asleep! That's pretty much the most basic error a kidnapper can make. The first thing you learn in hostage-taking 101 is always to have at least two guards watching the package, in case one of them is distracted or attacked or simply dozes off. Failing to observe this fundamental rule was not just amateur, it was plain stupid. Setting aside my delight at Michael's release, the al-Hakim clan deserved to have him flee if it was going to make such basic mistakes.

A few days later I flew out to meet Michael. He looked in reasonable health for someone who had been in captivity for over eight months. Michael was six-three, thin and with intelligent, piercing eyes. He did not seem overly traumatised by his experience and his overriding concern was the emotional trauma this had caused Megan and the rest of the family. He was an upstanding, moral guy, more concerned with others' well-being than with his own. Michael's ability to deal with the situation was aided by the fact that he had worked in several war zones before. He had some experience of the way the criminal gangs operated and how these crises usually played themselves out.

I took the opportunity to ask Michael about the ransom videos. Were any of the waterworks put on?

'Absolutely. Most of it,' Michael replied. 'I wasn't worried at all.'

'But the tears—'

Michael shrugged nonchalantly. 'They told me to ham it up and make it look bad. So I did. I wasn't exactly in a position to argue with them.'

The point is that the video was not designed for my trained eye. It was intended for Megan's untrained one, and in that respect, it hit the bullseye. It terrified the crap out of her, as it was designed to do. Few people who see a loved one held captive, the business end of an assault rifle directed at their skull, aren't scared to death. Unless of course, you don't want them back. It's a deeply disturbing image made all the more upsetting by the knowledge that your husband or wife or son or daughter is in danger on the other side of the world and there is nothing you can do to help them. I said earlier that kidnapping someone is a uniquely human crime because it plays on emotion. The movies are terrible at depicting this because in reality, the biggest victim in a K&R situation usually isn't the guy in the ransom video but the distraught and lonely wife at home, making decisions she isn't equipped to make, wringing her hands and wondering if she will ever see her husband alive again.

Case over, I returned to London. WS went its separate way. I was glad to have avoided my nightmare scenario of a rescue attempt for Michael. It just goes to show that sometimes the biggest threat to a hostage's life isn't the guy with the AK-47 to their head, but the guys on the other side holding misguided ideas about how to secure their man's release.

As I write this, Afghanistan remains a K&R hotspot. Things have picked up in the last few years. In July 2007, twenty-three South Korean missionaries were kidnapped by the Taliban in Ghazni province. Two of them were executed. The release of the other twenty-one hostages was secured with a pledge from the South Korean government to withdraw its forces from Afghanistan by the end of the year, and a reported $20 million ransom.

Emboldened by this success, a spate of journalists were snatched by armed gunmen in 2008. Melissa Fung, a Canadian journalist, was seized in October from a refugee camp outside of Kabul. A month later Taliban fighters took Dutch journalist Joanie de Rijke hostage and raped her repeatedly for six days before exchanging her for a ransom of $137,000. The following September, Stephen Farrell, a reporter working for the *New York Times*, was kidnapped in northern Afghanistan. It was a bad time to be a foreigner in-country. The Taliban were hard, unpredictable negotiators, prone to vitriolic outbursts and their daily experiences of violent confrontation both among themselves and with the Coalition had rendered them unafraid of abusing and even killing their hostages. The political situation also presented a challenge, with governments keen not to be seen negotiating with terrorists and in several instances relying on the intervention of special forces to rescue the hostages, with mixed results.

Afghanistan will probably remain a kidnap hotbed as long as the country is flooded with Western armies, aid and dollars and foreigners work within its borders. In earlier conflicts, unarmed civilians were not considered legitimate targets for terrorists. But the ground rules have changed and people have to accept it.

I flew back to the UK with a rare holiday booked up on the south coast. My marriage to Emily was falling apart at the seams and for the sake of the kids we needed to try to work something out. To that end, we decided to go for a rare break, just the two of us, to resolve some of the problems between us. But I also needed some downtime to recharge my batteries.

I had no idea that a major case was about to unfold practically on my doorstep.

Abduction – Captivity – Proof of Life –
Negotiation – **Ransom Drop** – Release

Part Five

BAD BLOOD

'Take me, take me!'

Sienna Ventura

11

UNDER SIEGE

I stood shivering and wet on the cold and dark street corner, surrounded by the bustle and life of people returning home from
work. I was feeling happier than I had been in a long, long time.
Emily had just driven away, loudly crashing over the kerb of the
narrow street as she joined the rushing traffic out of the city. She
was in a fouler mood than the weather. Our so-called reconnec-
tion holiday had proved more like a final disconnect. Three days
on the British south coast with nothing but rain showers and an
angry soon-to-be-ex wife for company, and boy was I glad to get
out of there and back on a case.

The streets were doused in filthy, smudgy blackness. Emily had
dropped me off in a part of town which occupied that uncomfortable space between slum and middle-class gentility. Which
way it would finally turn was hard to tell: the neighbourhood was
a contradiction of trendy estate agents and boutique fashion

emporiums, and depressing warrens of terraced houses that looked like rotting teeth. The smell of kebab sauces mingled in the air with the stench from overflowing rubbish dumpsters and urine-soaked pavements.

The streets surrounding the siege location had been cordoned off. Police patrolled up and down the cordon line. A large crowd of onlookers had gathered around the cordon, rubbernecking the drama going down inside.

I was glad to get some feeling back into my legs after a cramped ride. Cold winds blew sheets of rain into my face, each frozen drop like a hard pellet hitting my face. A warm welcome. Christ, I thought. Why do hostage situations always happen in the shittiest places in the world? Nobody does ever get kidnapped in Hawaii.

As Emily sped off I waited sheepishly for the black-helmeted police officer to approach me. He walked at a regal pace, a look of disgust etched on his face, his helmet glistening in the rain as the stripes on his fluorescent high-visibility jacket flickered on and off, reflecting the lights of the passing cars.

He lifted up the yellow plastic police cordon separating the crime scene area from the throng of onlookers.

'Ben Lopez,' I said. 'The psychologist.'

He checked my name against a clipboard, then nodded and lifted the tape.

'Step this way, sir.'

As I ducked underneath the cordon, I overheard people in the crowd asking, 'Who's that? What's he doing here?'

A six-five guy like me, decked out in civilian clothes, breaching the police lines and having been dropped off in style, well, I guess I stood out a little.

I walked around the dark mass of the City Hall building. The car park was empty. I passed a silent apartment complex. Terrace houses flanked the road. All I could hear was the distinct clip-clop of my shoes against the cobblestone paving. But although I couldn't see or hear anyone, I knew there were several sets of eyes trained on me, hidden behind nearby trees, the curtains of living room windows and parked cars. I crossed a stretch of deserted, rain-slicked tarmac and made my way towards the mobile command centre, which amounted to a converted van at the end of the street basking in the sulphur glow of floodlights.

I entered. Inside the van looked like a motor home. A few desks, some phones, carpet on the walls. It was kind of cheesy looking. It's not like in the movies, with banks of hi-tech equipment and monitors. There was a chair at the far end reserved for the incident commander. It wasn't glamorous, but there was no need for it to be. The command centre isn't designed to be hooked up to spy satellites. Its proper function is to provide a place for people working on the case to meet away from the public eye. Bottom line, in a crisis scenario, communication and coordination are everything. If you don't have that, you've got nothing.

Training is the backbone of every skilled hostage negotiator. A lot of the time you're going into negotiations with no idea of who you'll be working with. Sometimes you get good folk alongside you, stand-up guys who know what they're talking about. Sometimes you're not so lucky. On this case I was reassured by the fact that I'd be dealing with people who came from the same tribe and held the same ideals as me. I had worked alongside them at the national negotiators' course, held four times a year at the Peel Centre and inspired by the sister course at the NYPD.

In the history of negotiation, New York City is where it all began; it's where the first hostage team in the world was formed. In the same way that all special forces units follow the SAS playbook, all top-class hostage negotiation teams have followed the

NYPD model in terms of technique and philosophy. This includes the Hendon course.

Another advantage of having similar courses is that everyone knows what the drill is. So when I turned up at the scene on a miserable, arctic night, I had total confidence that the guys I would be working with had the skills and the know-how to manage this crisis effectively.

Exiting the mobile command centre, I paced down the street, the sound of my footsteps echoing around the empty space. The rain had settled into shallow puddles along the potholed, uneven road. Surrounding homes had been evacuated. Their dull, black windows, like empty eyeball sockets, glared at me suspiciously as I approached the building housing the negotiator cell. Generators hummed. Dozens of SO19 firearms officers were huddled to one side. They were silent for the most part and stared out at me from underneath Kevlar helmets, their faces obscured by ski-masks. Their blue fire-resistant overalls were covered in Kevlar body armour and their assault vests held an array of stun grenades, tear-gas canisters and spare magazines. They were packing Heckler & Koch MP5K sub-machine guns with torches fixed to the end of the barrels. Jet-black Glock 17 pistols nestled in holster straps around their thighs.

I felt a little underdressed.

In law-enforcement cases, the negotiator cell is the room where the negotiator talks to the kidnapper and where the key decisions among the negotiation team are made. Ideally the cell should be situated separately from the inner security cordon but near to the forward commander's position. The rulebook states that the cell must be able to house six people and it should be selected with a long-term occupation in mind. In simple terms, the cell is where it all happens. It's the negotiating nerve centre. In any given incident, the team will invariably spend most of their waking hours in the cell. It becomes like a second home.

In this case, the cell was the second floor of a dilapidated council block on the corner of the opposite end of the street to the siege location and flanked by decrepit post-war terrace houses. Police floodlights soaked the place in hot light and a dark-blue tarp shielded the entrance.

I pulled back the tarp and was confronted by an officer jerking his chin towards the second floor. The stairwell was filthy. The linoleum floor was layered in cigarette butts and crushed plastic coffee cups. Muddy footprints were imprinted on the lino. Police sign. Anywhere cops have been, practically two seconds later the space will be overflowing with coffee cups, cigarettes and the trample of dirty boots.

It wasn't hard to spot the cell. The front door of the apartment was missing. Splinters lay scattered around the hallway from where officers had kicked the door in. The apartment itself was in a shitty state of disrepair. By the time I arrived on the scene the siege was already more than a day and a half old, and it showed. There wasn't a lot of furniture. Linoleum floor in the kitchen, the cream colour worked into a dirty brown wash by police shoes, and an old-fashioned stove layered with grease. Heinous green carpet in the bedrooms. The flat was a prime candidate for the wrecking ball.

The bathroom window overlooked the stronghold from a right angle. I looked out and studied the surrounding area. It looked like a ghost town. Nobody was allowed to stand in the direct line of fire. I could see the left side of the terrace. Fast-food signs were fixed to the ground floor, the neon lights dead. A billboard hung from the left-facing wall. A sparkling-toothed, blonde-haired woman was advertising Moet champagne. I looked at the stronghold and thought about the guy holed up inside. Tried to imagine what was going through his mind.

I left the bathroom and headed towards the living room. The negotiators' cell. From beneath the door I heard the crackle of radio static and the steady but tensed-up voice of another negotiator on the team trying to keep the perp talking. I felt a nervous energy spread through my system. Like electricity.

I was home. The sanctum sanctorum, the holy of holies. This is where I belong.

I knew this day was going to be different the moment I received a voicemail from Luke Diamond that began, 'Sorry to bother you on your holiday, Ben . . . '

12

THE CELL

At the time of this siege, more than two decades had passed since the last major hostage crisis in the UK.

In 1980, six terrorists stormed the Iranian embassy in Prince's Gate, South Kensington in London and took twenty-six people hostage. Among those captured were BBC journalist Chris Cramer and soundman Sim Harris, and police constable Trevor Lock. The gunmen threatened to execute all the hostages and blow up the embassy unless ninety-one of their comrades, whom they alleged to be political prisoners of the Iranian government, were freed immediately. This wasn't as unrealistic as their initial demand – the creation of an independent 'Arabistan' in southern Iran – but nonetheless doomed to be rejected by both the Iranians and the British.

Trained police negotiators arrived and promptly used every trick in the book to calm the terrorists down and defuse the situation. At the same time they were gathering intelligence and trying to figure out a way of ending the siege peacefully. Every negotiator is the same. They don't like people getting hurt, regardless of which side they're on.

On the sixth day, the gunmen killed a press attaché and dumped his body out on the street. This changed the game. Negotiators, police officers and soldiers all operate on a central, key assumption: if a kidnapper kills one hostage, the chances of them killing a second, then a third are much greater. It's like getting your girl-friend pregnant. You can't un-screw her. The Prime Minister, Margaret Thatcher, responded to the killing by green-lighting Operation Nimrod.

The SAS were called in.

At 7.23 p.m. on 5 May 1980, the SAS launched their assault on the embassy. A frame charge was placed on the skylight on the second floor at the rear of the building, shattering the glass. Millions of viewers around the world watched on TV as the SAS detonated stun grenades to disorientate the terrorists. Five of the gunmen died in the ensuing battle. The sixth posed as a hostage and walked out the front door, only for one of the real hostages to quickly identify him. The siege was over.

The resolution to the Iranian embassy crisis had played out like a James Bond movie. To the millions of people watching the dramatic footage of the assault, the SAS became a byword for courage. A mindset developed that this was the right way to deal with hostage crises. With the murder of a hostage, the British government had little choice but to launch a violent, lethal intervention. But the perception would put a lot of pressure and expectation on future sieges to be ended with a gunshot.

So when I received the voicemail early that morning and Luke Diamond explained the bare bones of the situation to me, it became apparent that we were dealing with something that had the potential to explode like the Iranian embassy siege, if handled incorrectly.

Diamond was a leading psychologist who sometimes worked with the police. When they had a crisis, Luke was the man they consulted. So I was intrigued. And excited. There is nothing in the world that beats the drama and tension of hostage negotiations.

I had called Luke right back.

'Got your message,' I said. 'What's going on?'

Luke had cut straight to the chase. 'Look, Ben, there's a bit of a drama developing. I'm afraid I'm already on my way out of the country and I can't be there. It's quite serious. The chap in question appears to have barricaded himself into a flat. I believe he's also holding a hostage. Says he has enough guns and ammo to fill a bathtub.'

That was all I knew about the case as I approached the negotiators' cell. Things were about to get seriously interesting.

The door to the master bedroom in the flat was closed. I figured that was where the surveillance team was based. Only guys with the highest security level clearance were granted access to that room.

I opened the living room door and entered the Holy of Holies. Goosebumps popped up and down my arms. I was excited by the work lying ahead of me. This, truly, was what I was born to do.

Police negotiator cells can be anywhere with enough room for five or six people to sit in peace and quiet. Sometimes it's an anonymous meeting room with the sterile atmosphere of a transatlantic business conference call. That's if you're lucky. If you're bang out of luck, they take place in dingy, threadbare council estates on the wrong side of town. On that cold and wet evening, I was out of luck. The cell was a shithole.

Dirty-white net curtains had been draped over the windows and a musty smell crawled up my nostrils. A crappy electric heater was fixed to one of the walls. There was a table in the middle of the room and a bunch of chairs positioned around it in a semi-circle for the negotiating team. On the table stood the rescue phone.

The rescue phone is the first and often only vital piece of equipment of any negotiating team. One end of the rescue phone is the throw phone. A throw phone comes in a unit roughly the dimensions of a lunch box, with a handle and a long wire streaming out of the end of it. This is what the cops will chuck into the place where the kidnapper is holed up, giving them a secure and unbreakable line direct to the kidnappers. Mobiles are less desirable. The last thing you want is for the battery on the subject's BlackBerry to die suddenly while you're trying to talk them out of committing suicide.

The other end of the rescue phone sits with the negotiators and is the size of the suitcase. You open it up and there are all the jacks for headphones and a control panel to manage the various connections. The negotiators will each have a set of headphones because they prefer to listen in that way – it cuts out unnecessary background noise and helps them to focus. Only the negotiator – the one actually speaking to the perp – has a boom mike attached to his headset.

A woman by the name of Rebecca was sitting at the table with the negotiating team. She stood at five-five but carried herself like she was twice that height. She had a slim, athletic figure and a freckled, soft face. Her eyes, though, were the colour of gunmetal and told of a woman who had a steely resolve. Rebecca wouldn't back down if she felt she was in the right. Despite appearances, she was anything but a soft touch.

As the coordinator, Rebecca sat above all the negotiators. It was her job to oversee the work of the negotiations team. She had to liaise with the incident commander, or whoever the commander has designated to deal with the coordinator, and in addition she had to have overall care of the cell – making sure it's properly equipped and sited and that the team is given drinks and food.

While they have to be good negotiators, coordinators also need to be meticulous organisers and courageous leaders. Their job requires a different skill set from negotiation. Coordinators are more of a manager type; they're obligated to deal with the burdens of power that come with the role. Rebecca was a first-rate negotiator and an even better coordinator.

I counted five people in the room. Six, including me. The roles of each member of a hostage negotiations team vary from case to case, but fundamentally the team works on the principle of a single key negotiator, the Number One. This is the man or woman who is actually on the phone talking to the kidnappers, backed up by Numbers Two, Three, Four and so on, who provide support to the Number One.

When I arrived the Number One was a guy by the name of Aaron. A cop by trade, Aaron hailed from Northern Ireland. He wasn't the tallest or biggest guy in the world, but he wasn't the smallest either. He was a good-looking guy in a rough, streetwise kind of way. He had a greying, weather-beaten complexion and spoke in a Belfast brogue so thick you could bottle it up. Being Irish, Aaron also had the gift of the gab. Helpful, I'd say, if you're planning a career in hostage negotiations.

Aaron was joined by Linda, the Number Two. This is the person who sits closest to the negotiator and is charged with helping the Number One interpret and support the incident commander's overall strategy through the use of negotiating tactics. In face-to-face scenarios, when the negotiator is speaking directly to the kidnapper rather than on the phone (say, in a domestic siege where the husband is in a bedroom and the team are on the stairs, and the guy pops his head out of the door), the Number Two is also responsible for the negotiator's safety.

Also present was a guy named Doug. He was the Number Three. This guy provides a communication link between the negotiators and the rest of the police command structure. He or she will also be involved in intelligence-gathering: assessing the number of weapons or hostages involved in the event. They will also jot down notes in a logbook of key events as they unfold. Doug was a sound, switched-on kind of guy with the slight build of a middle-distance runner and a smooth, calm voice that could suddenly shift to a much more commanding tone when the need arose. He hailed from Glasgow. Twenty years of living south of the border had done nothing to dampen the edges of his hard Scottish lilt.

The role of Number Four went to Jon. He was a grizzly bear of a guy, the exact opposite of Doug, with big hands and a burly manner that disguised a sharp mind. Four's main task is to provide a visual outline of the information relevant to the negotiators, so that it is easily accessible at any time when they're on the line to the kidnapper. This information is usually written clearly on large sheets of butcher paper hung around the cell and could include stuff like deadlines, ransom demands and coming-out plans.

By the time I arrived the team in the negotiator cell had already made contact with the perp. I needed an update, and fast. It was kind of cramped in the room and the negotiating team was conversing with the perp, so Rebecca and I shuttled down the hallway to the kitchen and stood at the window. The counter was covered in generations of dust. There was a rotten smell in the air, like gone-off milk.

'So,' I said, 'what's going on?'

'It's been going on for three days.' Rebecca ran a hand through her hair. 'And to an extent we're still playing catch up. I mean, we didn't know we even had a hostage until yesterday.'

'Kidding me.'

Rebecca shrugged and gave me the lowdown.

The perp was a guy called Shelton Sunday. Of African-Caribbean heritage, Shelton came from a badly damaged family which, in various ways, had fallen foul of the law. Shelton had a rap sheet as long as his arm.

Despite the fact that drugs and violence had exacted a terrible toll on his family, Shelton fancied himself a Yardie. But the truth was he was too incompetent even for the Yardies. He thought he was a bad guy but really he was a twenty-six-year-old with the emotional age of a twelve-year-old.

By the time of the siege Shelton had already served time in prison. Several days before, his car had been identified in connection to a murder enquiry. The police put surveillance on the car and waited. For six days nothing happened. On the seventh day, the police decided to tow the car away for forensic testing. As they hooked the vehicle up to the tow truck, Shelton popped his head out of the window and started firing at the cops.

'Get the fuck away from my car,' he shouted.

The officers ran for cover. Shelton retreated back inside and holed himself up. In less than the time it takes to make a cup of coffee, he'd instigated a siege. Now he was engaged in a one-man war against British police, and apparently he had enough ammo to kill a lot of people.

We were in for a hell of a ride.

13

SOLDIER OF JAH

Aside from the incarceration of practically his entire family, I had very little background on Shelton himself. This was my first evening at the crisis, case day one, and I wanted to get an insight into his character so I could start planning a negotiating strategy. I pressed Rebecca for more intel.

'Who's the hostage?'

Rebecca said, 'His name is Samuel.'

'Any relation to Shelton?'

'None that we know of,' she said. 'He lives in another room in the property.'

Samuel Koram was a student from Ghana. The place Shelton lived was a bedsit in a block that had twelve or thirteen rooms to it in total. Everyone else was out at the moment the shit started hitting the fan. The only one left was Samuel.

On the day the siege began, Samuel had been laid low with a

hangover. He happened to glance out of his window and spotted the cops trying to tow away Shelton's car. Then he went back to bed to sleep off the effects of the night before's partying. Not for long: Shelton's gunfire exchange with the cops terrified Samuel, forcing him to hit the deck in case a stray round tore through the window. From inside his bedsit Samuel could hear furniture being pushed around and more gunshots from the toilet window right next to his room.

A while later, Samuel emerged from his bedsit to find Shelton hunched up in the corridor with a revolver in one hand and a semi-automatic pistol in his other, his pockets bulging with ammo. Shocked and a little confused, Samuel had quizzed Shelton about what had happened outside. Shelton said he'd fired at the cops. Fearful that Samuel might try to leave, Shelton said that the cops had the building surrounded and if Samuel went out the front door, they might mistake him for Shelton and pump him full of lead.

Samuel decided to try and sweat it out in his bedroom, laying low in the hope that the situation would go away. In my opinion, alarm bells should have been ringing inside Samuel Koram's head.

While Shelton busied himself with turning the flats into a kill zone, Samuel returned to his room and used the landline installed there to call Scotland Yard. Eventually, after trying several different numbers, he got put through to the local emergency team and explained that he was inside the building with no way out. In other words, that he was a hostage. Samuel claimed to have called on the second day of the siege but word didn't filter down to the negotiating team until the third day. Whatever the time factor, it was already too late to intervene and rescue Samuel: the police had by this point erected a cordon around the stronghold.

'You know something?' I said.

'What's that?'

'We could be here for a while.'

Rebecca screwed up her face like she'd sucked on a lemon. 'What do you mean?'

'There's food in the rooms, right? Booze too, I'll bet. Lots of water and fresh clothes. He's in his own house. This guy is all set.'

'That's about the size of it,' Rebecca said.

'Okay, I'm getting the picture,' I said, turning the information over in my head. 'It looks like you guys are set up here, right? So tell me what you want from me.'

Rebecca gestured to the cell. 'Why don't you go sit with the negotiators and pitch in.'

I paced back into the cell, pulled up a chair at the table and slipped on a pair of headphones just in time to hear Shelton coming on the line.

Aaron had established a rapport with Shelton. The perp's warmth towards Aaron had its roots in the fact that he believed they shared a common past as being under the boot of 'imperial Britain', something that Shelton referenced several times on the phone.

'You and me, we're both fucking oppressed,' he told Aaron. 'We've been through the same thing, brother.'

This might not sound like a good thing but Shelton viewing Aaron as a 'fellow sufferer' was definitely an improvement on the first Number One. She was an excellent negotiator but Shelton was sexist and abused her relentlessly. He'd said some vile shit to her, so the incident commander decided to pull her off the detail. This was no reflection on the negotiator's abilities – from a purely pragmatic point of view it didn't help since she was clearly aggravating Shelton and making him twitchier.

Aaron had been brought in to calm things down. Like every Irish guy ever born, he could talk on pretty much any subject for hours, in a soothing Gaelic lilt. His approach certainly worked in terms of calming Shelton down some, but there's always the danger that a Number One can get sucked into the mind games and crazy world of the perp. Which is where Linda, the Number Two, came in.

Linda was seated in such a way that her knee was resting against Aaron's thigh. Physical contact is designed to keep the negotiator from 'falling in'. This is when the negotiator falls into the black hole of the perp's crazy world. Falling in can happen to the best negotiators because everything is happening inside their head. There's no one there to pull you out if you fall in. By touching the negotiator, you're keeping them physically rooted in the real world. Linda's job was to stop Aaron from getting sucked into the web of Shelton's twisted thoughts. It sounds crazy but in our line of work it happens every day. And when it does, it can have potentially disastrous consequences.

Falling in happens to everybody, especially early on in your career. And I was no exception. Back when I was grad student I did some work in a rehab clinic up in the Bronx, in the shadow of Yankee Stadium. The Bronx was a legendarily shitty neighbourhood, host to some of the lowest of New York's low life. I was assessing a guy named Harold. Now, Harold was a physically intimidating presence. He towered over me at six-eight and was built like a Greek god, walking around in a wife-beater T-shirt parading his biceps the size of cannonballs.

Harold was also a stone-cold psychopath. He was selfish and completely self-interested. Harold's thing was to go to Times Square and beat the crap out of people with a hammer. Day or night, men or women, it was all the same to Harold. There was no pattern to the people he chose to assault remorselessly. But when I was in the consulting room with him, before long I found myself conversing over the relative merits of a ball-peen hammer versus a claw hammer for beating the crap out of somebody. I found myself agreeing that, as every schoolboy knows, a ball-peen hammer is better because it doesn't get stuck in the victim's hair or clothes and you get more whacks per minute out of it than with the claw hammer. I sat there immersed in Harold's world. His magnetic aura was messing up my own compass.

Then I came out of the consulting room and thought, Jesus, that guy was talking about beating people up with a hammer! But at the time it seemed completely normal.

That's what happens when someone falls in.

Doug was writing things down, making notes and observations that could prove helpful when deciding how to play things with Shelton, and also to use as reminders to the team about important points with regards to Shelton. These scribbles would later be transferred to the big rolls of butcher paper, and the sheets would be hung from boards, listing the important information like the list of requests that the police had fulfilled.

It's the job of the Number Two to decide whether to pass messages on to the Number One. If he or she doesn't think it's a good idea, they won't do it. Linda, the Number Two, effectively acted as that gatekeeper between the negotiator and the rest of the team.

That first night I worked all the way through with the negotiating team. I had a pair of headphones on, perched on the edge of my seat, listening in to the back-and-forth between Aaron and Shelton.

My initial thought was that Shelton hadn't planned the siege. It had been a spur-of-the-moment decision. He didn't get out of bed that morning and say, 'Fuck it, I'm gonna kidnap someone today and start a siege.' Few people do. In the same way that relatively few people get up and say, 'Today I'm gonna stalk someone' or 'I'm gonna saw somebody's head off today.' His violent actions were a completely unplanned response to the police towing away his car.

This type of siege is one of the two most common types.

Criminal, or law-enforcement, sieges tend to happen when the cops or federal agents in the US knock on a suspected criminal's front door and the guy decides he's not going to go with them. Unlike K&R, which has a clearly defined structure of abduction, ransom, release, the criminal siege is chaotic and potentially much more difficult to diffuse. It's not simply a case of offering money in exchange for the hostages. When they're cornered, perps don't want cash. They want the law off their back.

Since he hadn't planned the siege, I knew Shelton would be a hell of a lot more volatile. My first mission was to help him relax a little.

My shift lasted from 6.30 p.m. to 8.30 a.m. on case day two. We'd spent most of those hours on the phone to Shelton. He didn't sleep much. The stress of the situation was feeding his adrenalin and keeping him hyped up. The whole negotiating team was huddled in the cell, the negotiator talking with Shelton, listening in to his dialogue and trying to keep him talking. Nancy popped in and out as she liaised with the incident commander and the firearms guys in SO19.

Aaron kept Shelton busy on the phone. When someone is getting along well with the perp, you really don't change negotiators unless you absolutely have to, for the plain and simple reason that if a negotiator is keeping the perp on the phone, he isn't doing anything else. By chatting to Aaron, Shelton wasn't shooting cops or threatening Samuel or trying to kill himself. And there was one of him and four of us in the cell, so we could keep him talking twenty-four-seven if we had to, until he finally fell asleep from sheer exhaustion. We could, in theory, wear Shelton down to the point where he was left with no choice but to come out with his hands up in the air.

I wasn't assigned a role as a Number One, Two or Three – but my task was to observe and advise where necessary, speaking as the qualified psychologist among the negotiators. That I was even welcomed into the cell as a civilian, outside the law-enforcement magic circle, was a major coup.

I have to wind back a little here. At this time, psychologists weren't exactly welcome in the inner sanctum of law enforcement. Someone told me that I was the first psychologist Scotland Yard had used since the Rachel Nickell case. Nickell was a twenty-three-year-old model from Tooting in south-west London who was stabbed 49 times in a daylight attack on Wimbledon Common. Her son Alex, who was two at the time, was found clinging to his dead mother, covered in her blood and pleading for her to wake up. The case made national headlines.

Despite a lack of forensic evidence, the police were convinced that a man from Roehampton by the name of Colin Stagg was guilty of the murder. He had been known to walk his dog on the common. A psychologist was drafted in by the police to assist in a covert operation to find out whether Stagg was in fact the killer. The resulting operation was openly criticised by the trial judge, Mr Justice Ognall, who labelled it a honeytrap and called it 'wholly reprehensible'. In the end the Crown Prosecution Service withdrew the case and fourteen months after he was charged with the murder, Stagg was acquitted.

Shelton said he was a soldier for Jah, the Rastafarian god. This was significant for me because soldiers, combat and the Yardie tradition were issues of deep insecurity to Shelton. In his head our guy identified with the Yardies and wanted to be part of the Yardie 'crew', but he lacked the nous and mentality to be a successful gangster.

I spent those early hours trying to get a handle on the context of the crisis. I pulled Aaron aside at one point.

'What's the guy wearing?'

'I'm not sure,' Aaron replied. 'Want me to ask him?'

'Please.'

Why do I care what the perp's wearing? Because the small details about a person can dramatically change the meaning and impact of what's going on in their head. If you have a guy talking shit and he's dressed in combat fatigues, military boots and an army vest, that's telling you one thing. If he's wearing a bathrobe, that's telling you something else. As it happened, Shelton was just wearing the standard outfit of jeans and a T-shirt with a hoodie on top. Nothing unusual. Nothing that made me worry unduly.

At the same time that I was working the case I had other cases and projects to manage for LCG. After my shift at the negotiators' cell had ended I dragged myself to the local Holiday Inn to grab a few hours' disrupted sleep. It was hard with all the damn sunlight pouring through the windows. I got no more than two or three hours' shut-eye before it was time to wake up again, fire up the laptop and my phone and take care of my own business. Then it was back to the cell.

On case day three I reviewed the heaps of notes I had made that first night, in order to build up a picture of Shelton in my head and work out what angle to take with him. I decided we ought to be using an incremental approach.

You use the incremental approach in all kinds of situations. Like, for example, seducing a woman. If a guy sees a woman he likes, normally he wouldn't just walk straight up to her and say 'Fancy a shag?', because ninety-nine times out of a hundred, the answer is going to be 'No, go away.' Instead he'll introduce himself, chat to her for a while, buy her a drink, take the woman out to dinner, hold hands, kiss and then, if he's lucky, he might get laid at the end of it. He might not but his chances are a hell of a lot better than the direct approach.

It's true for everybody but especially for someone as avoidant as Shelton. He was so afraid of everything that a gentle approach would be much more effective than something confrontational and in-your-face. After you have established a rapport with someone like that, you can be more direct with them. He had to be convinced to jump through a lot of small hoops in order to get him to jump through the big one. Saying 'Just come out' to a guy like Shelton wouldn't work.

Shelton displayed all the characteristics of an inadequate, avoidant personality. In other words, he was essentially a loser, overly sensitive to rejection and with a natural feeling of inferiority to others. The kind of guy who snatches defeat out of the jaws of victory. This type of person might have been unemployed since for ever even though it's probably killing them inside not to have a job. Then they'll get a fantastic job interview at last – and show up late. This is what these personalities do. And I definitely got that vibe from Shelton.

Avoidant personalities have difficulty maintaining relationships with other people because they're desperately sensitive to criticism and to being rejected. They can't trust people. They can also be suspicious of other people so they often end up avoiding social situations. The central question of their life is 'Why would anyone want to be friendly to me?' They turn second-guessing into a kind of vocation. So much so that they won't pay attention to or enjoy the social interaction itself.

Negotiators encounter a lot of avoidant, inadequate personality types in our line of work. There's a movie starring Al Pacino called *Dog Day Afternoon*. Inspired by true events, the film vividly depicts an avoidant-personality kidnapper. This movie is used by every hostage-negotiation training course I'm aware of – as an example of *what not to do*. Pacino plays Sonny Wortzik, a budding crook who robs a bank in Brooklyn in the seventies. The robbery goes wrong, but of more interest in the movie, from the perspective of hostage negotiation candidates, is the very public way in which the siege played out and the firestorm of criticism that followed. The botched police negotiations led to a rethink about how to handle negotiations in the future, and played an important part in informing the philosophy and approach of the NYPD negotiating team.

Valuable lessons were learned from Brooklyn 1972. Such as, never let commanders negotiate. They can easily be manipulated. If the negotiator is a detective or someone lower down the chain of command, they can use a stalling tactic when the kidnapper makes requests, whether reasonable or otherwise: 'I'm sorry, I can't give you that because I have to ask my boss first.'

Shelton's aggressive tendencies, combined with his lack of education and poor impulse control, made it hard for him to foresee the consequences of his behaviour. If he'd been able to see what would happen when he pulled a gun on a police officer outside the front of his home, I doubt he would ever had done it. But the deed had been done and there was no turning back the clock. This time he would have to face up to the consequences of his actions.

On the other hand, Shelton was shy and tended to steer clear of conflict. Anything that caused him anxiety, Shelton avoided like the plague. I felt that the guy was out of his depth in his role as a kidnapper. He'd acted impulsively when the police tried to tow his car away and quickly found himself in a situation he couldn't control.

On case day two, Aaron implored Shelton to come out.

He refused. 'I'm a pussy if I walk out of that door,' he said. 'You're not taking me alive.'

Over the next few hours we went to great efforts to convince Shelton that this wasn't true. Convincing people that the obvious is in fact false is a skill all good negotiators possess. One NYPD negotiator famously told a kidnapper who worried that he would be charged with possession of an illegal firearm that 'this is Brooklyn, a gun is practically a fashion accessory round here'.

'No one's going to judge you for coming out,' Aaron said to Shelton. 'It takes a brave man to walk out that door. Your friends would respect you.'

Only Shelton didn't have any friends or social contacts to speak of. He was the archetypal loner. He rejected Aaron's pleas. His mood hardened. He started talking about committing suicide. 'I'm a put a gun to my head', that kind of thing. I didn't think he was particularly suicidal at this time. People who are genuinely about to kill themselves no longer care about the future. Shelton did. He made constant references to life after the siege. But he was becoming obsessed with the idea of being a soldier of Jah.

'I'm a soldier, I gotta defend my territory,' he said.

The key was to turn Shelton's head and get him off the politics stuff. We had to refocus his mind on the fact that it wasn't about Irish and Jamaicans but about him and us. Politics is an easy way for people to distance themselves from the real nature of events. We wanted Shelton to forget about politics and to get him focused on the main thing: surrendering to the police.

One technique we employed was to ask, 'How can I leave you alone if you won't let Samuel go?' This puts the onus back on the perp to be realistic. There's an irrefutable logic about this argument that even a severely crazed individual can't fail to understand.

Aaron would say, 'How can we send food up to you if you keep shooting out the window? Who's gonna deliver it?'

And Shelton had no comeback.

We had to stop Shelton threatening to use his weapon because as long as he felt threatened enough to make threats, there was an outside chance he'd use it.

Of course, firearms are only really dangerous when they're pointing directly at you. Bullets don't go around corners and they don't bend around curves. That's why they call it a *line of fire*.

Don't step directly into it and you're pretty safe. We were out of harm's way in the cell. But on my second day at the siege I happened to leave the apartment and go out into the street. I was standing around and checking my phone when I heard shouting behind.

'Hey you! Get the fuck back here!'

I spun around. An armed officer was frantically gesturing at me. What's this guy's problem? I wondered. Then it clicked: I was in the middle of the street. Shelton had an easy shot. If he'd wanted to, he could've popped his head out of the window and taken me out. I scrambled back to cover, grateful but embarrassed.

On case day four, two hours before I was due back at the negotiators' cell, I happened to be meeting with a guy I knew from the SAS for a lunch meeting on unrelated business at the Michelin-starred restaurant in a nearby five-star hotel. He was footing the bill.

As we tucked into our main courses the conversation inevitably turned to the siege. The guy, who I'll call Phil, was desperate for details; I was equally keen on a resolution to the whole thing.

'What would you guys do?' I asked, picking at my plate of scallop carpaccio, peas and artichoke vinaigrette. The food looked powerful delicious but the lack of sleep and the stress of the case were playing havoc with my appetite. I pushed my plate to one side and motioned to the waiter for another cup of coffee.

'Simple,' Phil replied as he cut into his rare sirloin steak. 'Put a couple of guys behind a ballistic shield, bust into the flat and corner him. Just walk the bastard down.'

The waiter poured me a third cup of coffee. 'That's it? That simple?'

'That simple, Ben.'

Now, I've done a lot of work in the US and depending on the jurisdiction, that's probably what would happen there too. A police response here in the UK is different. They have health and safety issues, to begin with. Shelton had a violent streak and had been linked to previous incidents of shooting at police officers, which made it more difficult to justify knocking down the front door.

There is no gun culture in the UK. The use of firearms is essentially foreign. When they are used to deadly, chilling effect in cases such as Derrick Bird's massacre or the fugitive Raoul Moat, they tend to dominate the news agenda in a frenzied manner that doesn't happen in the US. In a country where firearms are freely available, like America, if a guy walks into a coffee shop and blows away a few cops with a semi-automatic, it might make state headlines but it won't be the number-one item on the national news.

Shelton seemed perfectly content to sit tight and wait for us to make the next move. Sitting in the cell and surrounded by coffee cups and empty takeaway boxes, by the evening of case day four we started to realise that we were going to have to work new angles to end the siege.

'This guy's enjoying himself too much. Just by sitting there and doing nothing, he's on national television,' I said to the team. 'We're reinforcing his inaction. This is the most attention Shelton's ever gotten in his entire life.'

'So what do you think we should do?' Nancy asked.

'Just keep him talking,' I said. 'We could be shooting the breeze about anything. Sports, sex, the fucking weather. Anything at all. As long as he's talking, the situation's under control.'

At the back of my head, I allowed myself a dark thought: If Shelton ever decides to stop talking, that's when the trouble will really start.

14

BREAKTHROUGH

The impasse with Shelton Sunday continued. We were into case day five now and he steadfastly refused to come out. We kept on talking to him, knowing that we were containing him and keeping the public safe. But we were no closer to the magic moment of surrender. I felt it was time to up the ante a little bit. Apply some pressure. Although I'm a psychologist, I don't think it is okay to accept people's bad behaviours and I have a relatively hard attitude towards cases like Shelton Sunday. So I was the one who, from early on in the siege, argued that we should be making life inside the stronghold increasingly difficult for Shelton.

'Well shit, let's turn off the juice,' I said at one meeting. 'Don't let him have electricity. Don't let him have water or heat. Let's freeze this guy out.'

But we had to take account of the Human Rights Act. The

procedure asserted that the overriding principle guiding negotiations was Article 2 of the Human Rights Act, i.e., the right to life. That made it extremely hard for us to argue that Shelton should be denied fresh water or electricity. Though you could argue that other parts of the act were being violated by keeping people from their homes.

The police also had to deal with a bunch of political considerations that a military outfit wouldn't need to worry about. I was conscious throughout the siege that there was a strong racial angle to what was going on. We had a black hostage, a black perp in a predominantly black neighbourhood. This became a major factor when the news outlets started focusing on the siege. It's a sad fact – but still a fact – that in a highly publicised crisis, whether the police do everything right or wrong, the furious media-driven indignation and armchair generalling (led by a chorus of 'security experts' airing their views on TV) often leads to the dismissal of whoever is unfortunate enough to be in charge.

My guess is that in the back of each commander's head was the burning question: 'What if Shelton dies or kills himself?' Each commander I was aware of was highly qualified, skilled and experienced at the job. But they must all have been conscious of the career-limiting prospects of Shelton dying while they were in command.

I don't blame them. If I was in the same position, and knowing the political realities and the way the media would portray a tragic outcome, I would probably do the same thing.

Another development within the stronghold actually worked in our favour. Shelton had began striking up a special bond with his hostage, Samuel.

'He's got my back,' Shelton would tell Aaron on the phone. 'We're brothers.'

And Samuel would reply, 'I'm your friend.'

Over the next two days we heard Shelton talking away to Samuel. And to listen to Shelton and Samuel talk, you'd think they were having a 'bromance'. This was all the more remarkable to me given that, in my experience, Africans and Caribbean people often resent each other. At one point Samuel and Shelton were literally comparing the size of their respective brothers' penises. Here we had a hostage situation where the kidnapper and victim were male-bonding.

Apparently, both had very impressive brothers.

By case day eight Shelton had begun confiding some of his fears to Samuel.

'I've lived by myself since the age of twelve,' Shelton told Samuel. 'No fucking Christmas presents since I was twelve. No help. No fucking nothing. But you know what, I never signed on the dole. Nah, not for me that shit. I never took the Queen's shilling. Never will, neither.'

Samuel listened silently to Shelton's rant.

'And you know what else?' Shelton went on. 'That fucking megaphone they use. It's embarrassing, brother. I wish they'd stop using it.'

The cops used a megaphone to tell Shelton to get on the phone when we were trying to get hold of him. This megaphone must have been a million watts because it boomed through the air and blotted out every other sound in the vicinity.

The bond between Samuel and Shelton strengthened over the next forty-eight hours. Samuel told Shelton he hailed from a village where, according to him, there was a high concentration of healers and a lot of juju medicine still got practised among his people. Shelton found this agreeable.

'Yeah, yeah, maybe that's it, man. Juju. That's what I should be doing. Fuck all this Western oppressor shit, you know?'

From a negotiator's point of view, Shelton's growing friendship with Samuel was a good thing. It would help humanise Samuel in Shelton's mind, making it harder for him to hurt Samuel. He was being forced to confront and deal with Samuel as something other than a mere pawn in his twisted game. Even something as simple as needing to go to the bathroom or having to feed him would force Shelton to confront the fact that he was dealing with a fellow human being held against their will.

However, there was a flipside to the bond between the pair. Shelton came to see Samuel as his companion. For most of his adult life, Shelton had been a loner with no close friends or social contacts. The admiring attention from Samuel was more than anyone had ever paid him in his life. Shelton had suffered from people abandoning him. Any further abandonment could push him over the edge.

I was proved right when, later on case day eight, Shelton told the relief negotiator, Colin, that he didn't want Samuel to leave him. Shortly thereafter, we heard two gunshots coming from inside the stronghold. I exchanged a nervous glance with Colin. We were both thinking the same thing.

Has Shelton just shot Samuel and then himself?

The entire negotiating team stood frozen to the spot in the kitchen, anxiously waiting for news from the police commanders about the situation inside the stronghold. Time passed like kidney stones. Eventually, the phone rang. It was Shelton. He said Samuel was fine. He had fired a couple of shots in frustration at the wall.

When he wasn't building up his relationship with Samuel, Shelton was constantly fretting about his media image: how he was seen and portrayed by the newspapers and television reporters.

'Bob Marley says that every man has the right to choose his own destiny,' Shelton told Samuel, settling into his rhythm. 'I can sit this out. I'm comfortable here. This is my place, after all. Fuck giving myself up to the police. Yeah, they're all nice now but that'll change the moment I step out that door and they put the cuffs on me.'

For once, Shelton was on the money.

On day nine Shelton told Samuel he had a dream. 'It was weird,' he said. 'I was with the Queen. Round her place. I was dressed just like I am now. She kissed my hand. And it was . . . it was, you know. Fucking weird.'

While Shelton was fantasising about chilling with Elizabeth and Co., we were desperately trying to get Samuel out of the stronghold. This proved easier said than done.

We spent hour upon hour trying to convince Shelton to release Samuel. Finally Shelton then tried to turn the issue of Samuel's captivity into a potential trade-off.

'Here's the deal,' Shelton said to Aaron down the phone. 'I'll release Samuel, if you get my brother out of prison. Like a swap deal, innit.'

There was more chance of Elvis bringing me lunch than the incident commander agreeing to that outrageous demand, so we worked on alternative ways of springing Samuel free – without Shelton's consent.

When Shelton dozed off, the team took the opportunity to talk to Samuel alone. Aaron did the talking and the rest of us listened in. Some wise guy wondered why the cops didn't just storm the stronghold while Shelton was asleep. It was considered too dangerous. Police don't do silent entries. They'd make a lot of noise, which would wake Shelton up, then maybe he'd start shooting.

But although the cops couldn't take Shelton down, we believed that Samuel could simply wait until Shelton was asleep and then sneak out the front door.

'There's a couple of problems with that,' Samuel said on the phone.

'Such as?' Aaron asked.

THE NEGOTIATOR

'I can't just walk out the front door.'

His problem was that the bedsit was three storeys high and Shelton had chucked a bunch of furniture against the main door to block the entrance. If he made his big break for freedom, the noise would alert Shelton. No, if Samuel wanted to escape, he would have to jump out of a window. That wasn't necessarily a problem and in fact we had one escape plan set up for Samuel involving a trampoline to break his fall. Even when Shelton was awake, sometimes he and Samuel would be on separate floors of the building. Shelton would be upstairs, leaving Samuel completely to his own devices on the floor below. And yet still, for whatever reasons going on inside his head, Samuel refused to make the break for freedom. For the life of me, I couldn't understand why.

I spent the evening of case day nine huddled up inside the cell with nothing but a pair of headphones, a notepad and a cold pizza and cup of coffee for company, both of them tasty as old leather. But my spirits were lifted when that same evening I finally won my first personal battle of the siege.

I had managed to convince the incident commander to turn off the juice. This is one of the difficulties of being a negotiator; you're the ones liaising directly with the perp but you don't hold the power to make any executive decisions around the case. That power resides solely with the incident commander. All we can do is make recommendations until we're blue in the face. I'd been up front about cutting the juice from the start. Why? Simply, I didn't think we – negotiators and police – ought to be making it easy for Shelton to maintain his stand-off. Given the rancid weather, the kind of cold that makes you feel like your skin's been peeled off, it made sense to deprive the guy of heat. He might give himself up if he could no longer feel his fingers or toes. People have surrendered for less.

Every decision a negotiating team takes is like a high-stakes poker game. Fold, or play. While I was in favour of cutting off the juice, others in the team expressed their doubts about depriving Shelton of the TV. They felt we might inflame the situation. I guess on one level, they were right. If Shelton was watching TV, we knew what he was doing. He was watching Second World War documentaries. He wasn't hanging out of the window and shooting people because Jah told him to. Maybe if he had no TV, he'd be more inclined to take potshots at the cops.

'Okay,' I said. 'I see your point. But if the TV stays on, Shelton can rest up and take it easy. There's no incentive for him to come out.'

'And there's no reason for him to go killing people either,' Jon said. 'He's unstable.'

'But from where I'm standing, I see him in his own living room. In his own home. In his goddamned slippers. He's watching whatever the hell he wants and getting all the food he needs.'

Eventually we agreed that no TV was better than TV, given how long this thing had already gone on.

Turning off the electricity supply prevented Shelton from getting a kick out of the extensive media coverage. But the guy did have a battery-powered transistor radio that allowed him to listen in to the news bulletins of the drama going on in his bedsit.

I remember hearing one report in which the siege was the lead item on the national news. The newsreader said excitedly, 'We're now entering day ten of what has become the longest-ever standoff in British history – longer than even the Iranian embassy siege.'

The reports wanted to sensationalise the story as much as possible. But what they perhaps didn't take into account was how their reports were feeding Shelton's ego.

Shelton came on the line a while after the report.

'Are you hearing this?' he said.

'Yes, Shelton,' Aaron replied. 'We're listening to it.' Me and Aaron swapped grudging looks. Both of us knew what was coming next.

'This is fucking great! I'm gonna be a record breaker!'

For a guy whose life so far had been a monumental failure, breaking a record represented a big achievement. After all, how many guys do you know who've broken records? It's a small group of people and Shelton had just joined the club. The news only made him more determined to hang on in there. Our efforts at the negotiating table were badly disrupted.

We took a time-out in the kitchen. By this point, the place was overflowing with garbage. There were so many crushed coffee cups on the floor, you couldn't see the linoleum any more. I considered the new decor an improvement.

'This is messed up,' I said. 'He's getting a big boost out of all the media reports. Can't we block them somehow?'

'What do you mean?' Linda asked, rubbing her eyes. She, like the rest of us, was looking exhausted after so many caffeine-fuelled days working without a break.

'They must have jammers in there, right?' I thumbed the room next to the negotiating cell. The one that had been commandeered by the surveillance team. God only knows what hi-tech kit they had in there; I lacked the clearance to enter. 'I mean, can't we stop Shelton from listening in to the reports?'

Linda shrugged. She was aware that the kind of technology I was talking about existed. I wasn't entirely sure whether they were able to direct it in such a way that it only jammed the signal in Shelton's bedsit or whether they would have had to knock out the whole neighbourhood. If it was the latter, then it was best not to use it; the locals were getting increasingly irate, moaning openly to the media about the inconvenience of the siege. My favourite was one guy who said, 'People are having to walk around the houses to get anywhere.'

I had a lot of sympathy for the residents, which is one of the reasons I pressed early on to deprive Shelton of electricity and water. At the same time, others argued that the main pressure came not from the locals but from the national media. I understood that there was a lot of media pressure on the police to resolve the situation quickly. Me personally, I didn't experience that pressure. I'm pretty sure none of the negotiating team did. We were protected in our cell – in a bubble, if you like – by Nancy and were so deeply entrenched in our dialogue with Shelton, and then going straight home to bed, that we really didn't get exposed much to what the TV or newspapers said.

It was a different story for the police brass. They had to deal with the very vocal gripes of local residents. Some had been evacuated at the outset. Others had been confined to their homes since Shelton fired his first shot. These people needed things. Armed officers delivered groceries. I remember looking out of the window and seeing big, burly cops in bulletproof vests with riot helmets and ballistic shields delivering Tesco bags to old ladies, the Moet woman smiling down at them from the poster. This can't get any more crazy, I thought.

I was soon proved wrong.

When Shelton realised he was stuck in the bedsit with no way out, he began to make ever-more ridiculous demands that he deluded himself into thinking might allow him to avoid imprisonment. Shelton feared jail. He said so several times on the phone to Aaron.

'All right,' he said. 'This is how it's going down, yeah? I want a letter saying that I'm not going to go to jail.'

I can't remember what Aaron's response to such a ludicrous demand was, but there was no way the cops would ever agree to such a thing. The fear of incarceration was driving Shelton's actions, as opposed to any coherent agenda.

Later that same day he came back on the line to Aaron.

'Man, I'm fucking hungry.'

'Okay, Shelton, I'll see about getting up some food. Pizza?'

'Nah man, I'm wanting some chicken, you feel? There's a KFC up the road.'

'I'll see what I can do,' Aaron replied.

'And I want my bredrin to bring it up.'

We agreed to let Shelton's associates fetch him some fried chicken wings, plus a Diet Coke and large fries. But we would never allow them to deliver the chicken to Shelton directly. Instead we agreed that they would bring the chicken to the cops, who would then take it up to the bedsit, and Shelton would appreciate the extra trust we'd placed in him. So his friends showed up at the KFC joint up the road from the stronghold on the tatty thoroughfare that passed for a high street in this dumpy part of town. They collected this big bucket of chicken.

As they approached the bedsit, the police sniffer dogs went crazy. They'd picked up a scent. The cops confiscated the bucket and looked inside. They found packets of marijuana hiding underneath the breaded skin.

When I heard about this, I looked around the cell and waved my arms in amazement.

'Are you kidding me?' I asked.

No one answered.

Needless to say, Shelton didn't get his chicken. He wasn't happy about it and wasted no time in getting on the phone to shout at Aaron.

'I want my weed, man.'

'I'm afraid we can't do that, Shelton.'

'Why the fuck not?'

Aaron looked at me, exasperation etched into his face. 'Come on, Shelton, we can't give you *marijuana*. It's *illegal*. We're the *police*! If we bring you drugs, we're gonna have to arrest ourselves.'

The longer the siege drifted on, the more we focused on busting Samuel free. We felt that, without a human life to barter, Shelton would be in a weaker bargaining position and our chances of ending the siege quickly would increase.

On the night of case day ten we managed to speak to Samuel on the phone while Shelton was asleep in a separate part of the building. Samuel seemed ready to mount an escape attempt. He'd clearly had enough. This was it, we decided. Samuel had a real shot at getting out of there and we were determined to make it happen.

'Here's what you're going to do,' Aaron said. 'You come out of the window. There will be a ladder waiting for you. Climb down the ladder and make your way to the wall in the back garden. An officer will be waiting there to cover you.'

'Got it, got it,' Samuel said.

'It's really important we get this right. No one wants anything to go wrong.'

'Yeah, yeah, I know.'

For four hours we sat round the negotiating table and listened to Aaron running through the plan over and over with Samuel, stalling for time while SO19 covertly manoeuvred into position.

I was starting to feel confident that we could pull this off. Once Samuel was out of the picture, Shelton's bargaining position would be monumentally screwed. The only person he could threaten to kill was himself.

You have to be careful with these plans for getting hostages out of harm's way. The main reason being that you want to avoid the situation of tense armed police officers shooting the hostage by mistake. Not that this was likely to happen – all the armed cops present had received proper firearms training and siege drills specifically to prevent that type of disaster unfolding – but no one wants to be the guy who made a mistake and accidentally killed an innocent person.

'Okay, Samuel, are you listening?' Aaron said.

'Yeah, yeah,' he whispered.

'When you come out, I want you to wear a green shirt. Do you hear me? What did I just say?'

'A green shirt, yeah,' Samuel replied.

Getting the person on the other end of the line to repeat stuff was a good way of making them remember what had just been said. It sounds stupid but in the tension of the moment, people can forget incredibly important details. By asking him to wear a certain shirt, we could ensure that everyone around the stronghold would know that it was Samuel coming out – and not Shelton intent on a murderous rampage.

'All right Samuel, one more time before I put down the phone. Tell me the plan. I want to know every detail because when we finally do this, there's no going back.'

There was a nervous atmosphere in the cell. The number of people in the flat had swelled to twenty, but everyone was so knotted up with tension that nobody said a damn thing. After the exhausting negotiations of the previous few days, when it felt like we had been pushing a rock uphill, this seemed like the breakthrough everyone had been waiting for. We felt like we were on the verge of finally pushing the stand-off towards closure.

Samuel repeated the plan word for word.

We're almost home and dry, I allowed myself to think. Which is a dangerous thought. I recall my negotiator friend from the NYPD, Tanya Watkins, working on a case where the perp, a Latino in Brooklyn by the name of Jorge Martinez, toyed for several hours with the idea of giving himself up. He had a firearm and a ten-year-old boy hostage. But Martinez ummed and ahhed and tested Tanya and the other negotiators' patience to the limit. Every time he seemed ready to surrender he stepped back from the precipice. Martinez only gave himself up several tortuous hours later. So I didn't want to start celebrating until we had Samuel out of that door and behind the police cordon.

'That's great, Samuel, really great,' said Aaron, now breathing a heavy sigh of relief. 'I'm going to hang up the phone now. This is it. When you hear me hang up, that's the sign for you to start the plan and do exactly as we discussed. Does that sound good?'

'Okay . . .' said Samuel, his voice sounding uneasy about something.

'Here I go. I'm hanging up on a count of three.'

'Wait, wait,' Samuel said.

Aaron shot me a puzzled look. Said down the phone, 'What is it?'

'Wait a minute. I wanna take a bath first.'

Everyone in the cell did a double-take. I didn't know whether to scream or laugh. I couldn't believe what I was hearing. From the next room we could hear the frantic exchanges of chatter over the police radios. 'Did he just say he's taking a bath?'

Yes, I told myself, he did.

'I cannot believe this shit,' I said to Aaron.

Aaron just shrugged as if to say, *nothing surprises me any more.*

'Are you fucking kidding me?' someone said as the sound of the bathtub being filled came down the line.

'Maybe he wants to make a clean getaway,' I said.

The siege dragged on.

15

JAW-JAW

All hostage negotiators operate according to Winston Churchill's advice that 'to jaw-jaw is always better than to war-war'. As long as the perp is talking, they aren't killing anybody.

On the morning of case day eleven Shelton discharged several apparently random shots from the guns he had in his possession. No one was killed or seriously injured as a result. We felt the shots were deliberately intended not to hit anybody. They seemed to be signs that Shelton was scared.

We felt sure, as a negotiating team, that we were on the right track in our approach with Shelton. The real stronghold, we knew, was between his ears. We wanted to know what was going on in there so we could do something to help him come out. Progress had been painfully slow. But on the plus side, a highly combustible situation had been contained. Who knows what might have happened if the cops had stormed the building?

Maybe a sniper would have taken down Shelton with a single well-placed bullet. Or maybe the assault team would have been stuck inside the flat while Shelton opened fire from above, determined to go down in a suicide-by-cop blaze of glory. To anyone who thinks that negotiating with kidnappers is somehow 'soft' or politically correct, I can point out the countless number of assaults – called 'immediate actions' – that have resulted in needless loss of life. In Moscow in 2002, Chechen rebels took over a theatre with more than eight hundred people hostage. Anaesthetic gases were piped into the stronghold to disable the rebels ahead of an assault. Yet more than a hundred hostages died, not because of bullets fired by the terrorists but at the hands of the very gas intended to save them. A similar thing happened in Waco in Texas in 1993.

I performed a risk analysis of Shelton and concluded that he had a high potential for sudden surrender. Meaning, the guy might decide right there, on the spot, 'Fuck it, I'm coming out.' And because it's unplanned and because he's not the sharpest knife in the drawer, he might come out the front door with a gun in his hand. At which point, he would force us to shoot him. The only alternative Shelton would consider would be suicide by cop.

Or he might set fire to the damn place.

In the afternoon of the eleventh day of the siege, Samuel finally escaped.

He left spontaneously, without informing the police, and he was wearing the green T-shirt when he came out. Nevertheless, with no advance warning and no time to coordinate the armed response units, he could easily have been mistaken for Shelton and fired upon. What happened was, Samuel had been cooking a stew and asked Shelton if he could go and fetch some ingredients from another bedsit in the building. Shelton said, 'Okay', and went upstairs, leaving Samuel alone on the lower floor.

Samuel rushed towards the barricade at the front door, tore away the furniture and bricks and sprinted out the main door.

However lucky he had been, I was just glad that Samuel was out of there. Basically it was one less person for Shelton to potentially hurt. But on another level I was worried about the effect Samuel's sudden exit would have on Shelton. My worry was that now that he was alone, Shelton would be more likely to do something drastic, like lashing out at the police.

Sadly, I was to be proved right.

By case day fourteen Shelton's mood had worsened significantly. The negotiators had last spoken to him at two o'clock that afternoon, before I came on at six o'clock. After that conversation he spoke to his aunt. Then he refused our pleas to get on the phone again. The police got on the megaphone. He ignored them. I sensed something was up and asked to listen to the recording of Shelton's earlier conversation with his aunt. Listening with me was a guy called Dominic, a cop from out of town who had been drafted in because they'd run out of local negotiators and had to resort to pulling people in from all across the country.

Shelton had no electricity or utilities. He ought to have been feeling the effects of living inside a cold, wet place with no food. Yet he made no mention of his physical hardship to the negotiating team. He was, however, speaking with an overwhelming majority of negative verbs.

'I wanna shoot after one of them,' he said, referring to the cops. 'I'm gonna get one of them, yeah. I'm gonna fucking die and I'm gonna fuck them up. Shoot them in the face, you feel? These are the last days, yeah. I'm just waiting for those fuckers to come. Could be soon. Could be today, could be tomorrow. Yeah, it's coming.'

He went on: 'If I feel like I'm gonna collapse or I can't cope, I'll blow my motherfucking brains out. Man, fuck it. After this,

I'm not answering no phone. I'm meditating.' He paused. 'And when I come out of this place, I ain't coming out alive. I feel suicidal.'

I suspect that with Samuel's escape, Shelton knew deep down that we were in the end game. It was inevitable that he'd lose his battle with the police. Justice was coming but his avoidant personality meant he refused to face it. For Shelton, there seemed to be only one way out. His sense of entitlement and inability to reflect on his own behaviour made it unlikely that he would weaken in his resolve not to surrender.

He seemed totally detached from the reality of his situation. I felt he was unemotional and verging on autistic. These were all red flags that Shelton had reached some kind of breaking point. And when a kidnapper reaches that point, it's very difficult for the negotiator to reel them back in. It seemed to me that Shelton was planning suicide by cop.

If someone is bound and determined to kill themselves, there is very little anyone can do to stop it. Eventually they'll succeed. At one point, I turned to Dominic and said, 'Are we listening to a dead guy?'

'We might well be,' Dominic replied.

Shelton refused to talk to us, despite repeated pleas on the loudspeaker. This wasn't good. I made a note that he seemed to be on a downward spiral: the verbal threats, the collapse in communication between the negotiators and Shelton, and the warnings about shooting up the police, all pointed to a guy who was actively preparing for his own death. As morning broke, it was time for me to end my shift. I didn't want to leave. No negotiator does. It's that base instinct of wanting to be there when something major happens. Reluctantly I accepted that I was in need of a break.

I drove back to the Holiday Inn in a daze. The siege had taken it out of me. I sloshed freezing cold water on my face in the bathroom. I hadn't shaved, my hair was a mess and my eyes had dark crescents beneath them. I looked like crap warmed up for breakfast. I stumbled into bed, closed my eyes and didn't sleep a wink.

What the hell is he going to do next? I asked myself.

I didn't have to wait long to find out.

A couple of hours later my phone sparked into life. It was Aaron calling me. The moment I saw his caller ID flash on the screen, I knew something was up.

'Yeah,' I said, hack-coughing to clear my throat.

'Shelton's dead,' Aaron said.

I closed my eyes and lay slumped on the bed. That's it, I thought. It's over. *It's really all over.*

Partly I was relieved that it was finally over. But another part of me was sorry that a human life had been lost – one that I, along with the rest of the negotiating team, had been trying to save. After a long pause I asked, 'What happened?'

'Details are a bit sketchy,' Aaron said. But he'd heard from someone else about the final moments of Shelton's life.

Apparently Shelton tried to flush the toilet only to discover that the cistern under the roof had finally run dry. Pissed off, Shelton stuck his head out the window and spotted an armed officer to the right manning his post. Shelton shot at the officer. He missed. The officer returned fire. His bullet struck Shelton in the lower lip. Later ballistics tests would show that the round struck his lip, burrowed beneath the flesh, skirted around the inside of his scalp and came out the back of his head without ever penetrating his skull. A pathologist's report determined that the bullet didn't kill Shelton.

Wounded but conscious, Shelton retreated inside the house and for the next hour no one knew what he was doing inside. He was making a hell of a noise, the sounds of furniture being clattered suggesting that he was trying to bolster the barricade in anticipation of a police raid. The incident commander then gave the order to fire tear gas through the windows to disorientate and disable Shelton. But Shelton had set fire to the house and at some point before the fumes or the gas got to him, he shot himself.

Several hours later, after the tear gas had evaporated and the firefighters had extinguished the flames licking at the tarred-black brickwork, the police finally broke into the bedsit.

They found Shelton's body and with that, the siege was over. It had been a bloody end to a fraught and tense negotiating process. With the kind of guy we were talking to, there was always a chance Shelton wouldn't give in and instead choose to go out guns blazing. The coroner's verdict was a self-inflicted gunshot wound to the head.

From a negotiator's perspective, it's hard to argue that the siege was a victory. I considered it a draw. It's not a loss because Shelton failed to kill his hostage or any of the police or residents. At the same time, the news of his death left me deeply unsatisfied. I wanted Shelton to do what I wanted him to do, which was to come out and face justice. We all did, in that negotiator cell. We wanted to end the siege on our terms, not his. As a negotiator, I don't consider to have 'won' a case unless I've gotten the guy to do what I want him to do.

I didn't go back to the scene of the siege. I had no reason to. There was a burned building and a dead guy and a bunch of cops and journalists. There was nothing left for me to do there. I felt sad. Partly because I didn't want Shelton to die; I had no interest in him losing his life. But also because I would be moving on again. And moving on meant losing the camaraderie that I'd built up with Aaron, Linda, Jon and Doug. A psychologist doesn't often have the chance to work as part of a tight-knit team and it's something that I really value when I get the chance to do it. In the negotiators' cell in a squat apartment block in a rundown city neighbourhood, I found it with these guys.

16

WANT YOU BACK

January 2009 and I was back in Latin America and facing a messy and costly divorce from Emily now that our marriage was officially dead in the water. As usual, I had consumed myself with work to take my mind off my personal relationship woes. However, Carlos Guillermo Font was about to show me a whole new level of bad blood between a couple. Font was a self-made man who had built his wealth from nothing to become one of the most respected businessmen in Argentina. He enjoyed all the trappings his multi-million-dollar fortune afforded him: a mansion with panoramic views overlooking Buenos Aires, a beautiful wife, three kids and a fleet of luxury cars that most people will only ever see through a showroom window.

And then one day Font's wife got kidnapped.

Elizabeta Font was on her way to work in her Lexus on a crisp

Monday morning when the abductors pounced. Boxing her in at a busy downtown intersection, four guys in ski masks and wielding machine guns ordered her out of the car. No shots were fired. That is your typical Latin American kidnap. The abductors will usually try to avoid violence, instead relying on shock and surprise to carry out their mission. It worked. Elizabeta was terrified and bundled into the back of the kidnappers' BMW. They raced off, leaving Elizabeta's Lexus abandoned in the middle of the road.

Just like that, a dream family life had been shattered.

Though he'd refused the services of the insurer's British security company, I had been called in by my contacts at the company because of my expertise in the psychological and emotional aspects of K&R, with a brief to assess Font and help his son Sergio, aged ten, and twin daughters Lucymar and Marisol, aged fourteen, cope with the ordeal. While it initially concerned me that Font had refused the assistance of the security company provided by the insurers to deal with negotiations, I put my concerns aside and got on with the work at hand. Font wanted to conduct the whole process himself. That seemed a little odd to me – why wouldn't you want to benefit from the experience of professional help? But I didn't think too much about it because I figured that Font was a man used to doing things his own way. He liked to be in control, he'd been through many tough business negotiations and he saw no reason why negotiating with kidnappers should be any different. It was a business after all. But the thought kept nagging away at the back of my brain: why would Font refuse the help of a negotiator but agree to my help as a psychologist?

In hindsight, Font's bizarre decision should have been a warning sign that all was not right with the case.

I hopped on a Delta flight from Heathrow to Atlanta and caught a connecting flight to Buenos Aires. Departing at seven o'clock in the morning, I finally touched down at Ministro Pistarini Airport just outside Buenos Aires at close to five o'clock in the evening local time, with bags under my eyes the size of mail sacks and enough coffee in my bloodstream to fuel a fighter jet. But there was no time to sleep off fourteen hours of jet lag. I dumped my bags at the three-star Monasterio Hotel set in an old Spanish colonial building. Buenos Aires had its own charms, a cosmopolitan, almost European city with modern steel and glass skyscrapers and baroque government buildings and churches lining the Rio de la Plata that runs through the city and connects Argentina and Uruguay. Like the city's name, the air was cool and the sky a perfect blue tint.

I headed straight to Font's compound.

At my briefing before I flew out, the security company had offered me some discreet advice. Font was rumoured to be a tough customer. The word was that Font could be a real pain in the ass when it came to getting what he wanted. He thought he knew what he was doing. Fine, I said. I can get along with most people. I have an approachable, easy-going manner that others seem to find agreeable. And having worked with sociopaths and terrorists, I figured that Font couldn't be as bad as the security company guys were making out.

Font lived in an exclusive neighbourhood in the suburbs. The mansion was gated at the front with an elaborate electronic security system. Beyond the gate I spotted a guy tending to the exotic plants in the front garden. A strange voice barked at me through the intercom. Not Font's voice. Someone else. I said my name and that Font was expecting me. The guy muttered something unintelligible down the intercom and the gates clicked and whirred open. I paced along a driveway bigger than my entire street in London. If anything, the Font residence looked a bit like the security compound in Karachi. The main building had probably been whitewashed but I couldn't tell as it was surrounded by plant life: Andean lupine flowers, flor de mayo orchids, yellow-petalled frailejon plants and blooming moriche palm trees. It had a Spanish-tiled roof and a mock-colonial look with beam windows and Venetian blinds. The air smelled of jasmine and mango.

I rang the doorbell and was greeted at the solid oak front door by a tiny old man, the house porter. He led me down a marble-floored hallway. The walls were lined with fine art, most of it abstract. My footsteps echoed around the place. Cool air stroked my face. Outside the temperature was in the mid-forties and beneath my jacket I could feel my shirt clinging to my back, the sweat acting like a kind of glue between fabric and skin. Inside it was a cool mid-twenties. The porter directed me to a living area. The furniture was all antique. Font had gone for the Spanish landed gentry look. I thought to myself, Christ, this guy clearly has big money.

A voice at my back said, 'So glad you could make it.'

I did a one-eighty and sized up my client. Carlos Font was in his late forties or early fifties with a prominent paunch. He stood at around five-five, a good foot shorter than me. He wasn't exactly from the Fernando Lamas school of handsome Latino men. Font was 90 per cent bald on top, with just a few sad traces of what had once been a thick head of hair, and his body type was dumpy. He appeared to have some Native American Indian ancestry, with his dark skin and flat nose.

Font was also very direct. From the get-go I could see why he had been so successful. At a basic level, all business people are busy and get straight to the point. They don't like to pussyfoot around. Likewise Font. He wasted little time on small talk or asking me how my flight was, any of that stuff.

'Please, take a seat,' he said, shaking my hand. Firm handshake, brief. I sat myself down at one of the two L-shaped leather sofas in the room. Font placed himself at the other and faced me at a ninety-degree angle.

'Thank you for coming at such short notice,' he said, crossing his legs.

'That's my job,' I said.

As Font gave me the lowdown, I got the distinct impression that he was spending an inordinate amount of time telling me about how he'd been conducting the case. In other words, he wasn't exhibiting the rambling emotional distress that I would typically expect of someone whose wife had been abducted. Instead he appeared to be treating the case in a clinical, businesslike manner. He had a problem and this was what he intended to do about it.

No alarm bells were ringing in my head at this point. It isn't wildly unusual for a husband or wife to hold it together during a kidnap drama. Some people are programmed to respond differently to this kind of shocking event. They have the emotional equipment and make-up that allows them to stay level-headed even when the love of their life and the bosom of their family has been ripped away from them. Then they fall apart afterwards. Or they don't. Everyone is different. In addition, Font seemed to me a guy whose approach to life was defined by his success in business and overcoming adversity. His background hadn't been one of privilege. He was a bright and ambitious boy from an impoverished family who got to the top the hard way. It was only natural that he would seek to apply the same approach that had worked so well for him when it came to the kidnapping.

I listened to Font talk about how he wanted to manage the case himself, careful not to interrupt him. When he was done, I said, 'Mr Font, I understand what you are saying. But you still haven't explained why you don't want the professionals to take control of the situation.'

'I don't want them, end of story. They're no good. I can do better.'

'You don't believe they can add any value here?'

Font shook his head. 'No, I do not.'

I got the sense that there was something a little hinky going on. Trouble is, I couldn't quite place my finger on it. Two things occurred to me as I listened to Font. One, the guy simply did not grasp how qualified the security company was to assist him in the safe return of Elizabeta. Two, he didn't recognise that he was drastically overestimating how useful his business nous would be in negotiating with vicious, hardened criminals.

Only later did a third reason for Font's approach reveal itself to me.

'So right now you are the sole person negotiating with the kidnappers? There's no team to assist you?'

Font said, 'That is correct.'

I said, 'Tell me how the negotiations are going.'

Font informed me that the case was four days old. The kidnappers had called him several times using different mediums. The first call had been made from Elizabeta's mobile. The second from an unknown number that I presumed was a payphone. I figured they were paranoid about Elizabeta's mobile signal being traced and had taken the battery out. They also contacted Font using burners. They never stayed on the phone for longer than a minute; again, the fear of the call being traced dominated their thinking.

Each call followed the same pattern: Font answered, the kidnappers outlined their demands, Font responded aggressively and argued with them. As Font described his 'negotiating' strategy, my eyes damn near fell out of their sockets.

Are you kidding? I thought. But I said, 'You can't just argue with these people. You have to do business with them.'

Font wouldn't listen. He seemed adamant that he wanted confrontation with the kidnappers and saw nothing wrong in saying to them, 'Fuck you, I'm not giving you one red cent, you bring my wife back home right the fuck now!'

Later that evening, and not long before I was to leave, Font introduced me to his children. Sergio, Lucymar and Marisol had been told that their mother was seriously ill, hence her absence. The dad had elected to shelter them from the grim reality of her kidnapping, and at his request I had to maintain this fiction while assessing them. Even so, they were scared to death that they might lose their mother. They asked me many questions about her and it took all of my professional experience and discipline not to tell them the truth. Fundamentally, however, they seemed to be okay. I seriously doubt they would have been scarred for life had they known the truth. But all things considered, I felt they were coping as well or better than could be expected.

Oddly, Font did not appear to care much for me asking about the welfare of his kids – which was the main reason I had been engaged on the case in the first place. To speak to him, you would think that Font was not at all concerned with the welfare of his wife and only vaguely interested in that of his children. He was much more engaged with the notion of arguing with the kidnappers. It seemed like he relished the heated conversations he was having with them, from a perspective of winning, not from that of getting his wife back home.

As with the Toronto case, over the next several days I began to think that the case was being managed badly. In this instance, however, the guy doing everything wrong happened to be the hostage's spouse.

After a few days, a pattern started to emerge. If the kidnappers told him to do this, he would do that. If they made what, from a K&R perspective, was a perfectly reasonable request for him to go left, he would go right.

I went back to the hotel and collapsed on the bed. I awoke the next morning with the alarm clock not yet hitting the 5 a.m. mark. I was overdosing on jet lag by this point and the east-west time difference was playing havoc with my body clock. My body didn't know what time it was and I was losing IQ points that I couldn't afford to lose. I hailed a cab to Font's mansion. The same old guy welcomed me inside and a few minutes later Font appeared.

'How are the children?' I asked.

'Gone to school,' Font replied. 'Best thing for them.'

'The kidnappers call you since yesterday?'

Font nodded. 'From a payphone. They wanted me to put an ad in one of the newspapers.'

The ad was to be placed in the personals section of the paper and it would be written in coded language. It was to read, 'Rosita wants Juan to give her a nice present.'

In the old days, negotiations weren't carried out via mobile or satellite phones as they are today, but through less conventional means. CB radios, for example, or newspaper or radio ads. The ads could be a coded way of discussing the ransom figure. So if the kidnappers wanted a ransom of $200,000, they might place an ad in the paper saying, 'Romeo wishes to give Juliet 200,000 roses.' Or the ad might say, 'Large blue house for sale for $200,000.' And the negotiator would get the message that the kidnapper was looking to up the ransom. The kidnappers might then respond in another ad with their counter offer. This process continued until the final settlement was reached. However, this is a long drawn-out process that taxes everyone's patience and resilience. Yet many kidnappers will still demand the use of this method of communication because they're afraid of being located through their mobile phone signal or phone line traces.

Font had been instructed by the kidnappers to place an ad in the previous day's edition. He had blatantly disregarded this order, only putting it in the edition of the newspaper I was holding in my hands. I couldn't wrap my head around why Font would screw up something as important as this. He was an intelligent businessman and he was perfectly capable of putting an ad in the newspaper. How could he possibly profit from ignoring the kidnappers' demands? What was he getting out of it?

Although to all appearances Font appeared to be keeping his composure, I worried that under the surface he might be losing the plot. I decided to observe him more closely over the next few days in order to shepherd him through the crisis if necessary. But as I shadowed Font, and his behaviour became more and more counterproductive and puzzling, a sinister thought arose in my mind. I had assumed that Font wanted his wife back home. Which made his behaviour entirely illogical. But what if that assumption was wrong? What if the truth was much darker?

What if Font didn't want her to come back at all?

On the morning of case day three, Font told me that the kidnappers had asked him to make an announcement on a local radio station that played pop songs and had a sizeable number of listeners. This seemed to me to be a pretty standard request. Radio announcements have been used in various sieges and abductions and can serve a variety of purposes. Sometimes, like the newspaper ads, it's a coded message regarding the ransom. Or it can simply be used to broadcast the kidnappers' political or religious message. During one prison siege in the US, a correctional officer being held hostage was released by inmates after prison officials allowed an Aryan Nations inmate to make a live broadcast via a local radio network.

'Did you make the announcement?' I asked him the following day.

'No,' said Font, waving his hand dismissively. 'I put an ad in the paper instead.'

You have got to be kidding me, I thought. The kidnappers specifically mentioned the radio. That meant they'd be huddled around a set waiting for the announcement. They might not read the newspaper that day. It's one thing to get the message wrong or to mix up the dates. To get the medium wrong suggested that there was something else going on.

To me the discrepancy between what the kidnappers wanted Font to do and what he actually did seemed wilful. Anyone can screw things up once, especially when that person is dealing with the emotional turmoil of having a loved one snatched away from them. But I was seeing here a consistent pattern of disregard and disruption. The only logical explanation was that Font did not want his wife back home alive. He would rather she died at the hands of the kidnappers. And why? I racked my brains over that one. He didn't need the insurance money from her death. Not with his wealth. In any case, lots of policies won't pay out in the case of murder. I considered the possibility that Font might have a mistress. It's common in Latin America for a rich and successful man to have a girlfriend or two on the side of his marriage. But I hadn't seen a mistress around the place.

I had no proof to back up my theory. I decided I would test it out by doing a scientific experiment. This test took the shape of making a very precisely worded suggestion to Font and then carefully observing his response. I wrote down my hypothesis: 'When I tell Mister Font that I have information about the possible whereabouts of his wife that I have sourced through my "unofficial" contacts in the local police department, I predict that he will react with the marked surprise, anxiety, anger and defensiveness characteristic of someone who's been confronted with their own guilt.'

When I told him the 'news', he responded entirely predictably. First he pretended not to have heard me, despite my having made a point of speaking clearly and loudly enough. Then he said, 'That's great! Where is she?' But it was too late. I'd seen the microexpressions on his face. He was lying.

Microexpressions are non-verbal expressions of emotion described by American psychologist Dr Paul Ekman. He codified and inter-preted the minute facial expressions people make to reveal what they mean versus what they're saying. 'Yes' sometimes means 'No' and the microexpressions can tell us this. Microexpressions last as briefly as one twenty-fifth of a second and most human beings don't realise they have seen them. But if you look for them, you can see what's really going on inside someone's head. Microexpressions can reveal disgust, anger, fear, sadness, happi-ness, surprise or contempt. Try as he might, Font couldn't fully conceal his guilt and shame.

Despite Font messing up the communication with the kid-nappers, he had not yet fully poisoned relations with them. They told him to put another ad in the newspaper making a money offer. These ads were less about the negotiating of an actual ransom fee, than an invitation from the kidnappers for Font to show willing. They were an opportunity to demonstrate that he would comply with them and was prepared to do business. I duly forecast that Font would alter both the wording of the ad and the timing of it too.

Twenty-four hours later, he did just that.

I doubted that Font had engineered the abduction or had started out with the intention of not bringing his wife back home. I didn't think he was a killer. I suspect that like any good businessman, he spotted an opportunity that he could turn to his advantage.

I stiffened up, put some psychological distance between myself and Font. It had taken a couple of days to convince myself but despite the small amount of good work that I'd been doing with Sergio, Lucymar and Marisol, as soon as the penny dropped I had to pull out. I found the idea of a man doing that to his wife, the mother of his children, distasteful. If you don't want to be with your wife any more, just divorce her. Don't engineer her death through your action or lack of it. I had gotten to know Font pretty well in the few days I had spent in-country. As I've said, you tend to get very close to people very quickly in K&R situations. They're emotionally intense episodes and everyone is usually willing to work together to get their loved ones back home. Here I did the opposite. I retreated from Font psychologically and became more of a neutral observer of his behaviour.

One afternoon in his office, I brought up the wife-killing thing as a joke. I said, 'Jesus, Carlos. Every time I advise you to do something, you do the exact opposite. If I didn't know any better, it would seem like you're trying to get rid of Elizabeta.'

Font chuckled and slapped his thighs. As if he thought this was the best joke ever. 'Woo, yeah! That's a good one, Ben. That's a really good one!'

His exaggerated response struck me as strange.

In the beginning, Font had also asked me to call up the newspapers and put in the ads. The reason he had given for delegating this task was that it would look suspicious for a powerful CEO such as himself to put obscure messages in the personals and word would get out that his wife had been kidnapped. I kind of understood where he was coming from but I declined and suggested he place the ads himself as he wanted to be in control of the negotiations. Now I considered myself fortunate to have turned Font down. If Font was caught by the authorities, I would have been implicated in the whole thing. And that would really have sucked.

The case reminded me of another incident I worked on in Caracas. The husband was kidnapped and the wife subsequently learned that he had a mistress. The police couldn't rule out the possibility that the girlfriend had set up the husband's abduction in order to get money from his family. To that end, they decided to bug the hotel room where she was holed up while she received treatment from her psychiatrist. I could see why the cops were suspicious: middle-aged, rich husband looking for some fun, a twenty-something girl with a pert ass and dollar signs in her eyes. Throw in the fact that she had a scheming brother and a boyfriend also keen to make some fast bucks and boom – you've got yourself a classic honeytrap. You always play the odds in any K&R case. Like a murder case, the first people you look at are those closest to the hostage. So they put the girlfriend under surveillance and tapped her phones.

Watching the video, one thing became clear immediately: the psychiatrist was very definitely giving the girlfriend 'the treatment'. He was screwing her brains out. This is why clients and security firms prefer the experts to come from abroad. I've been around long enough that I am no longer shocked by the amount of corruption that exists in most countries in the developing world. Even if they call themselves democracies, most of these places are run by and for the benefit of the people at the top who have all the financial, political and military power. And this situation was a good example of how it isn't just the people at the very top who are corrupt.

A doctor like that, in a country like Venezuela, will never get busted for having sex with his patient. Myself, I come from a background that expects and demands much higher standards of professionalism and self-discipline from its practitioners. The consequences are also much higher. A psychologist who sleeps with a client in the US will be barred from the profession, become jobless and will likely face criminal prosecution and maybe even jail time.

I began to suspect that Font encouraged my presence precisely for that reason. I was the incorruptible foreigner who could provide cover for him should his wife die and the police name him as a suspect. He could point to me and say, 'This is the guy who advised me.'

On my fifth and final day with Font, I sat down with him and had coffee over my final briefing notes. I told him his kids were okay and that I didn't think they were going to have any long-term issues as long as they eventually learned the truth about their mother. They may, I added, experience some short-term trauma symptoms and I told him how to manage them. I handed him my contact details and said he could reach me any time he wanted. Font thanked me for my help and I went back to the airport.

I was stuck between a rock and a hard place in terms of the case. I had no rock-solid evidence to back up my suspicions. Though it was my duty to report my concerns back to the security firm that had contracted me, I was concerned that these suspicions would only make it harder for them to help Elizabeta. They were still hopeful of convincing Font to cede control of negotiations to them. More than anything, though, I felt sorry for the kids. They had no idea what was going on with their dad and mum and they were suffering for it.

As the cab shuttled me back to the airport, I was thankful to be leaving the case behind. I had trust in the security firm's ability to get a negotiator on-board and from a purely selfish perspective, I had never lost a hostage and I had no intention of starting now. As far as I was concerned, the best outcome would be for the response consultants to take centre stage and help negotiate Elizabeta's safe release.

On the flight back I had trouble sleeping. I read through my case notes and was reminded of a condition known as Darby and Joan Syndrome. People with Darby and Joan Syndrome tend to follow a similar broad trajectory: they excel at school, go to a prestigious university, run a successful business and make a lot of money, marry the girl of their dreams, pay their taxes, go to church, never break the law – and then one day in their retirement, they brutally murder their spouse. We're talking the kind of overkill violence where a man beats his wife with a cricket bat repeatedly, long after she's dead, or stabs someone seventy times.

This sudden, unexpected episode of rage is probably the result of year upon year of pent-up frustration about being married to the same person.

Font seemed to be in a similar situation. Here was a guy who had it all and yet he seemed willing to be complicit in his wife's murder. He didn't necessarily have to have a mistress to want her dead. His motive could just as easily have been to get rid of her simply because he was pissed off with being married to her. He'd been with Elizabeta for at least fifteen years. And fifteen years is a long time to be around someone that you can no longer tolerate. That is not a justification for such an extreme and violent response – there is no justification for that action – but merely to look at the scenario from the psycho-logic, distorted world-view of someone who probably wants his wife dead.

I later learned that Elizabeta had been returned safely home after the kidnappers received a ransom payment. Sometimes bad stories have good endings, I guess.

17

HIGH-VALUE TARGET

On a balmy Saturday night in Palermo in southern Italy in April 2009, forty-year-old sculptor and celebrated artist Sienna Ventura was leaving an opening of her work. Sienna was already well known in arts and media circles, and she was happy that the great and the good and the glitterati of the Italian arts establishment had finally begun to recognise her work. It had been a good night for the Ventura family. Good but tiring. Sienna was looking forward to getting home and going to bed. Accompanying her out of the building was her younger sister. Thirty-six-year-old Renata worked as an art director for a publishing house. Renata walked over to Sienna's car, a silver Mercedes CLK Coupe, so Sienna wouldn't have to drive home alone. They were joined by Alessandro Scotti, Sienna's assistant, and Pippo Conte, a friend of the family.

As they prepared to leave, a removal van stopped in front of the Mercedes. A navy-blue BMW 3 Series then accelerated and pulled up behind the Mercedes, boxing them into the parking space.

Four men jumped out of the removal van. They were wearing black jeans, black hooded jumpers and ski masks. Sienna, Renata and Scotti immediately realised what was going on: they were being ambushed and maybe abducted. But the speed of the attack was such that they had no time to react. Wedged in between the removal van and the BMW, there was nowhere to run and no place to hide.

The men in the ski masks immediately converged on the Mercedes, smashing in the tinted windows with hammers and hauling the sisters out. They put up a valiant fight, screaming and flailing as the men dragged them free of the car. Eventually two men grabbed Sienna, one taking her arms and the other her legs. They dumped her in the back seat of the BMW. Renata was next. As two ski-masked men grabbed her arms, Conte tried to intervene. The gang fired two warning shots at him, forcing Conte to run for cover. He was unharmed but badly shaken. The gang then made Conte and Scotti sit on the curb at the side of the road and put their hands behind their heads and stare at the pavement. The men heard the *clunk* of car doors being slammed, followed by the screech of tyres against hot tarmac. When they looked around, Conte and Scotti spotted the BMW as it sped off into the distance, the licence plate too far away to read as it shimmered in the heat waves coming off the road.

It had been a professionally executed abduction. From start to finish, the kidnap had lasted a total of forty seconds.

Professional to a point. Amazingly, Conte and Scotti discovered that the kidnappers had left the Mercedes key fob in the ignition. The two men wasted no time. They hopped into the Mercedes and Scotti gunned the motor, taking off after the

BMW, which by now was a glittering dot on the horizon. But Scotti was a skilled driver and the CLK Coupe has got some serious horsepower on it. He managed to catch up with the BMW. Then one of the kidnappers rolled down his rear window and stuck the muzzle of an AK-47 assault rifle out. He fired a pray-and-spray burst in the direction of the Mercedes. Bullets starred the windscreen and skated off the hood. Scotti slammed on the brakes, his hot pursuit abruptly over. He and Conte were forced to watch helplessly as the BMW careened off into the distance.

Three hours later the cops discovered the BMW in a rundown neighbourhood several miles to the north. Broken glass littered the leather seats. There were spots of blood on the asphalt.

In some ways the abduction of Sienna and Renata was a disaster waiting to happen. They came from a celebrated family in which almost every single relative was a personality in the media or entertainment industry, and they sought out and revelled in the attention. In doing so, they committed a cardinal sin and broke the first rule when you're a famous person in the spotlight in a country prone to kidnappings: don't be high profile. Or if you're in a business that requires a high profile – like being an artist – then have security. If you're famous, people automatically assume that you have money. Kidnap gangs don't understand things like mortgages.

But the abduction is only the beginning of the problem. Plenty of things can go wrong in the aftermath, as this gang was about to discover.

The first problem they had – and by far their biggest one – was the hostages themselves. It had been the kidnappers' original intention to kidnap only Sienna. From their perspective, it made sense to target her. She was the celebrity figure – so that's where they figured the money would be. Renata, by comparison, had a sporadic income stream. Abducting her didn't have any immediate financial benefit. It later transpired that taking Renata had been a spur-of-the-moment decision. The kidnappers spotted her inside the Mercedes and figured she was simply Sienna's friend. Maybe a rich one, they hoped. But their greed in taking both Sienna and Renata hostage would later come back to haunt them.

Sienna might have been famous and successful in her own right but in celebrity terms she had nothing on Grazia. Their talented, beautiful little sister had once been the ugly duckling of the siblings but had now carved out a career as a glamorous actress. She had a sultry voice and an alluring, sensual, photogenic face. To top it all off she had recently become engaged to Antonin Rodimov, a Russian businessman who was now in the process of raising her profile across Eastern Europe, where he believed she could be a superstar with her own perfume and clothing range. Grazia had the money, the looks and the lifestyle. Her imminent wedding to Rodimov had seen her relocate to Moscow, where Rodimov was based. Their big day was big news: the wedding was announced in all the major glamour magazines. This was why the kidnappers had targeted Sienna and Renata: they figured they could tap the money trail all the way back to Rodimov.

Their plan had *cojones*. High net-worth individuals are often surrounded by a lot of bodyguards. Both Rodimov and Grazia were out of the gang's reach. But the relatives were legitimate targets and getting to them would be a damn sight easier. Yet targeting the Ventura family was a big mistake. Because by any standards, this was one seriously dysfunctional family.

Almost immediately after the abduction, the kidnappers called Grazia. They'd obtained her number from Renata's mobile phone. They put in a second call to Sienna's home, where it was answered by one of her teenage children. The initial ransom demand was €10 million, to be paid in used notes, a demand that

I believed was clearly directed at Rodimov. The amount the kidnappers were talking about was far beyond the means of all but a handful of people.

Along with the ransom, the first-contact call contained the typical threats of violence against the victims. They came out with all kinds of stuff. 'We've got Sienna and Renata, we're going to cut their faces unless you pay the fucking money!'

Such threats are designed to put pressure on the family, the logic being that the family will panic, then quickly cave in to the kidnappers' demands. Despite the violent language, I felt the threats were all pretty standard and nothing I hadn't heard a hundred times before.

For the first three days, before I arrived on the scene, negotiations with the kidnappers were handled by Sienna's ex-husband, Massimo. However, he appeared to favour what could be called the 'Seth Rogen' style of communication. He was so laid back he was almost horizontal. Eventually he was replaced by another of the sisters, Isabella. She was an academic and a committed Catholic.

No sooner had Isabella taken control of negotiations than she dispensed with the services of a local lawyer by the name of David Lucarelli, who had been hired by Massimo and Marco, Renata's ex-husband. Lucarelli wasn't exactly from the school of hot lawyers. I never met the guy but the security director at Rodimov's company described Lucarelli to me as 'an unprofessional, pompous, little short-assed Italian lawyer'. He had failed even to provide a tape recorder for incoming calls from the kidnappers. This is crisis management 101, standard operating procedure for any negotiator. You show up in a room and the first thing you do, before you shake anybody's hand, is whip out the tape recorder. You want to record the calls so you can review them and dissect them later. Figure out the kidnappers' weak points and ways to manipulate them.

For this dubious service, Lucarelli had charged the family an extortionate fee. I have no idea why Massimo and Marco thought it was a smart move to hire this guy in the first place, but I had to respect Isabella for elbowing Lucarelli out of the picture.

The K&R industry attracts plenty of snake-oil salesmen because you are dealing with a situation where people are desperate and will do literally anything to get their loved ones home. One of the staple actions of desperate people is to throw money in every direction in an effort to find a solution to their problem. It's like if your car breaks down and you take it to a garage and the guy repairs the brakes. Then it breaks down again and you go to another garage where the mechanic swears on his mother's grave that the problem is with the engine. And suddenly you don't know who to trust. You don't know who's trying to rip you off and who genuinely wants to help and knows what they're talking about. You end up with a car that doesn't work and an empty wallet.

I've worked on cases where the relatives have engaged the services of clairvoyants and astrologers in the hope that they will provide a breakthrough in negotiations. In all my experience in the world of hostage negotiating, I've seen some pretty messed-up stuff. But I have yet to see a situation that has been helped by the presence of a clairvoyant. In one case I worked, the clairvoyant scheduled a meeting but cancelled it due to unforeseen events.

Sorry, I couldn't help it.

At the same time, I sympathise with the victims. What I call a job, they call the worst period of their lives. Ever. If they're religious, then perhaps that person is more likely to turn to God and the advice of a local priest. The fact the priest knows nothing about hostage negotiation is irrelevant. The person is looking for answers and the priest – or the clairvoyant or whoever – promises them.

If my wife or brother has been abducted and I have no experience in how K&R works or who the experts are, I'm liable to go through every single name in my contacts book asking for help. That is exactly what people do and the result is that a case can quickly become surrounded by so-called professionals and experts promising the earth.

Sadly, the truth is that many of these people are looking to make a quick buck out of other people's misery and the K&R industry is unregulated. In fact, many countries have laws that prohibit or limit what K&R insurers and consultants like me can do. In Colombia, for example, it's illegal to act as an intermediary between kidnappers and victims' families. In Mexico, Article 366 of their Criminal Code makes it a felony for any outsider to profit from a kidnap. That means that any consultant who charges a fee for his services is liable to arrest and prosecution. Adding insult to injury, bail can't be granted for this offence. Some politicians in these countries argue that K&R policies encourage kidnapping – even though they have more kidnappings than anywhere else in the world. Insurance helps you out in a time of need. It doesn't cause the problem.

This is when I stepped in.

I took a direct flight on British Airways from Heathrow to Sheremetyevo International Airport in Moscow. Four hours later I touched down and took a cab to the Rodimov residence in Moscow's prestigious Ostozhenka neighbourhood, otherwise known as the Golden Mile. A statue of Friedrich Engels, co-author of *The Communist Manifesto*, gazed down across Ostozhenka from outside the local metro station. He had quite a view. Art Nouveau apartment blocks overlooked fancy-looking restaurants and fashion outlets.

Rodimov and Grazia lived in a neo-gothic house down a quaint side street. It had its own discreet security presence out front. Inside, you could smell the money. Because this case was a big deal to the security company that had hired me, they had a back-up response consultant stationed in Moscow named Dan Somers. He was also present at this meeting.

Rodimov was a no-nonsense guy. He was born and raised in Moscow during the Cold War and had a kind of hard-nosed, straight-talking way about him. We got along from the start. We shared a common vision about how to manage the case, which was to let the professionals do what they need to do. Things were complicated by the fact that Grazia's relatives didn't have any money. Their actual finances were not in line with their celebrity status and there was no way they could pay what the kidnappers were asking for. Sienna's earnings as a sculptor were not vast, despite the celebrated nature of her works. Renata had little to no money to hand. Neither of their ex-husbands was willing to help. As for the parents, they mostly relied on handouts from Grazia.

By default this placed the burden of the case squarely on husband-to-be Rodimov's shoulders. The kidnappers assumed that the Russian side of the family would behave exactly like a traditional Italian family, where distant relatives dig into their pockets for the ransom. Blood is thicker in southern Europe than the east, however, and Rodimov had an acute understanding of what would happen if he caved in and paid up. The kidnappers, or similar groups, would come back again and again tapping up his wealth. They'd never leave him alone.

Adopting a hardline stance is all well and good but Rodimov and Grazia both realised that refusing to negotiate with the kidnappers could endanger the sisters and be a huge PR disaster for them. The couple would have to walk a tightrope throughout the case, balancing their private stance with public declarations. Rodimov seemed to me like he was thinking three or four steps ahead and considering the fallout from a media circus. At the very least, the kidnapping had the potential to derail Grazia's acting career and potential future earnings in Italy.

Rodimov was also vague when I pressed him for details about the case. I don't think he really trusted anyone enough to confide in them, and certainly not the professional he'd met only five minutes ago. I didn't have a problem with that. I was sure I'd win their trust in due course, once I had a handle on the situation.

At the outset of a case, you always fear the worst. You fear that the kidnapper is no mere tough looking to make money but a bona fide psychopath. In Mexico in the 1990s, the famous *mochaorejas* (ear cutter) Diego Arizmendi Lopez, another pathology in search of a cause, triggered widespread panic when it was reported that he cut the ears off his captives with a pair of scissors, then posted the severed object to relatives or left them in public places for the families to find. Other victims were left with mutilated fingers. Between 1995 and 1998 Arizmendi and his associates kidnapped more than twenty people. They murdered three of those hostages. When business executives – the natural target for Arizmendi's group – heard about the fate of his hostages, they pressed for police action. The president at the time, Ernesto Zedillo, issued a direct order to catch Arizmendi using whatever means possible. He was finally detained in 1998 and sentenced to 393 years in prison for his crimes. But there is always the fear that the guy who's kidnapped you might turn out to be the next Diego Arizmendi Lopez.

After pressing the flesh with Rodimov and Grazia, I returned to my hotel room and waited for the green light to fly down to Palermo and meet the family.

18

THE COVEN

I touched down at Falcone-Borsellino Airport in the early afternoon. The airport was situated twenty miles west of Palermo in Punta Raisi. The airport was named after a couple of judges, Giovanni Falcone and Paolo Borsellino, who had been assassinated by the mafia in the early nineties. The mafia presence in Palermo was sizeable, dating back to the city's construction boom in the post-war period, when the Cosa Nostra took control of the Office of Public Works in the city. Between 1959 and 1963 around 80 per cent of building permits were allocated to just five people, all of whom were suspected of acting as frontmen for the mafia. By the time I showed up in Palermo, the city was estimated to be home to half of the four-thousand-strong mafia clans based in western Sicily.

I met my handholder in the arrivals lounge. In a few cases a handholder is needed because either the consultant can't get there for a few days or there is some uncertainty about the case. They're necessary to sit with the client and to relay my suggestions to the family and tread water until I get there. Handholders are usually local, or at least work in the local office of the company. They are often ex-pats who have ingrained themselves in the local culture and landscape over a period of time. Handholders are assigned to cases ahead of response consultants, first of all to ascertain whether they have a genuine kidnap on their hands, and if they do, to manage the introduction of the negotiator/consultant into the equation.

My handholder's name was Frank Calvini. He spoke Italian and was a former US Special Forces Green Beret who held a degree from the University of Michigan. Frank's job was complicated by the fact that the family had advisers – and bad advice – coming out of their ears. Getting the family to listen to me was not going to be easy.

I arrived at the house in the late afternoon, when the sun was ceding ground to the encroaching night. The moon was already out, full and bright as a spotlight framed in the sky. The family lived in a well-heeled place in an exclusive suburb just outside of the city proper, the kind of place that upper-middle classes everywhere retire to when they have kids. I was introduced to the mother Flavia, the oldest sister Isabella and the rest of the family. My impression was that it was the classic artistic family. Very disorganised, one or two probably crazy, with a lot of expressed emotion. Lots of screaming and crying, followed by smiling and hugging, followed by more crying and screaming. With that much expressed emotion it makes for a volatile and highly combustible atmosphere where things can change in an instant.

It also made my job twice as hard. At one point I pulled Isabella to one side during a pause in the discussions with the intention of prepping her for the next call. I could see she was under a lot of stress and wanted to put across a few brief, salient points to make to the kidnappers on the phone. As I ran through my list, I realised I was wasting my time. I could see her mind was elsewhere. Everything I said to Isabella went in one ear and straight out the other. The febrile atmosphere put a big dent in the family's ability to be clear and level-headed.

Still, my priority was to try to help organise things. Up to that point the case hadn't been flowing smoothly and I felt if I could inject some order into this chaos and perhaps calm the relatives down, we could bring the sisters home sooner rather than later.

I was wary of adding to what was already an emotionally charged atmosphere. Adding my voice to the mix wouldn't do much except make things noisier. I decided to adopt a quieter, back-seat role. By separating myself from the din, I could project an air of calm authority. Over time I could win the trust of Isabella and the rest of the family, allowing me to influence the case positively.

An initial offer of €70,000 was made to the kidnappers. Unsurprisingly, they rejected that offer out of hand. No one anticipated any different. The offer was a long way short of their original ransom figure, and with their eyes on Rodimov, the gang felt they could do a hell of a lot better.

But not everything was going to plan for the kidnappers. Pretty soon they realised they had bitten off more than they could chew by abducting both sisters. It's hard work keeping one human in captivity. You have to guard them, feed them, clothe them and escort them to the toilet every few hours. They might complain, scream and shout and generally make a nuisance of themselves. Looking after two hostages creates twice the workload and requires twice the manpower – hence why gangs tend to kidnap one person at a time. The kidnappers hadn't budgeted for two hostages. They had limited resources and sooner or later, something would have to give.

I spent some time with Isabella, listening to her concerns. She had many. She was critical of the security firm introduced to the case by Zirikov, the security director at Rodimov's company. I didn't read too much into her criticism. It's a common occurrence for the relatives to rail against the very individuals and organisations who are doing their best to help them. People are highly stressed and in fight-or-flight mode. Fight-or-flight floods the system with adrenalin, which in turn triggers two reactions in a person: it activates your body – not your mind – to either fight what is attacking you or run away from it.

One of the outcomes of fight-or-flight, at the emotional level, is that people who are under a great deal of stress are often overly hostile or aggressive. Why? Because if you're fixing to have a fight, it sure helps if you're hostile or aggressive. People don't generally win fights by being relaxed and friendly towards their opponent. However, when there is an excessive outpouring of aggression, as happens in a highly tense situation like a kidnapping, it is common for that person to then become hostile towards everybody – including the people trying to aid them.

Hence Isabella's criticism of the security firm. She argued that the first consultant who showed up on the case, before my arrival, was too laid back and did not sufficiently engage the family or the kidnappers. The first nine calls made by the kidnappers also went unrecorded. The consultant didn't speak Italian, which was certainly a hindrance, but a negotiator can still perform many tasks when faced with a language barrier.

The lack of engagement on the part of the negotiator was damning. Whenever the kidnappers made contact, this guy made no effort to communicate on a meaningful level with them or to establish any semblance of a relationship. As a matter of fact, he acted more like a personal answering machine – a very expensive answering machine. He'd take a message from the kidnappers, hang up and relay it to the family. I was taken aback by this.

Every negotiator appreciates that a phone call from the kidnapper is a golden opportunity to engage. And to engage means to open the door to the criminal's psyche and to expose their weaknesses. Simply saying 'Hi' and 'We'll get back to you', and ending it with 'Bye', wasn't good enough. This guy didn't even put across the standard line of 'We'll pay but you gotta give us proof of life first.' Nothing at all.

Nine wasted calls in the space of three days. Nine missed opportunities.

Apart from issues with the original negotiator, Isabella directed her venom every which way. No one escaped criticism. Everyone, it seemed, was somehow to blame for her sisters' kidnapping.

In my opinion Isabella was simply stressed and drained from the case and responded in a way that is entirely natural for a person in her position. This is also a question of experience and what kind of angle you, as the negotiator, should be pursuing with the kidnappers. In my experience, the client always believes you should be aggressive. Sometimes that's the right approach. On other occasions, you need to rein in the hard line and opt for a more cautious, less confrontational line. It all depends on the psychological make-up of the kidnappers and the specific details of the case. But this is something that can be hard for relatives of the victim to appreciate.

At the end of day seven, Isabella sought out help from another security company. Let's call them Dynamo Security. This is the right of the client; it's like seeking out a medical second opinion. Dynamo had been formed directly in response to the increasing number of kidnap cases in southern and central Europe. As a result, these guys had acquired a reputation as being incorruptible, supposedly having significant expertise in kidnap cases. I couldn't personally vouch for their credibility. I suppose it was better than calling the cops.

Whether to involve law-enforcement agencies in a K&R case is a difficult question. There are pros and cons. My advice to families differs from case to case. It depends on the country and the standard of the local cops: how well the victim's family knows them, how endemic is corruption inside the force, and so on. In most cases where it is decided to involve the authorities, I recommend that they be approached through an intermediary who can protect the family's identity. This is because an approach to a corrupt official can lead to catastrophe if they are connected to the kidnappers.

As far as apprehension is concerned, the rate in a country like Colombia is alarmingly low. I would say less than 10 per cent of kidnaps are reported to the police, so an even smaller number are apprehended and prosecuted. I also ask families to bear in mind that cops have two agendas: getting the hostages out and arresting the perps. Whereas me, I don't care about apprehension. My sole objective is to secure the safe release of the hostage.

When it came to the Ventura case, for many reasons I felt very strongly that the family shouldn't be ceding primary control of matters to the authorities. Their advice would be coloured by the fact that their interest wasn't simply in returning Sienna and Renata. At best, they might want to apprehend the kidnappers and maybe launch a rescue attempt without the knowledge or authorisation of the family. At worst, they might be corrupt and in cahoots with the kidnappers themselves. When it came to Dynamo things were different and I struggled to convince them of my point of view. These guys clearly had Isabella's ear. She was accepting their advice over mine.

When I had a free moment, I asked Isabella why she had approached them for case guidance. To me it seemed a little nuts to have faith in an agency that you didn't fully trust. When you factor in her experience with Lucarelli, it made even less sense. Why, I wanted to know, did she do it?

'I asked God what to do that day,' Isabella said. 'He told me He had put an offer from the Dynamo people in front of me. So I accepted it. It was His will.'

I only found out later that Isabella was a born-again Christian who had spent years preaching in local jails. Thinking about it now, it's possible that one of her 'flock' set her family up for the kidnap.

After being kidnapped, the sisters had been taken to a house on the outskirts of town. Although she was blindfolded for much of her captivity, Renata believed the house belonged to a woman. At the times when the blindfold was off, she noted an abundance of trinkets, jewellery and female clothes draped over chairs and sofas. The TV was on permanently and the volume was set to the max, a common tactic for kidnappers – a loud radio or TV masks the sound of beating the hostage. Nobody will hear their screams. At night Renata could hear the gang in the room next door and the relentless *clack-clack* of assault rifles being stripped, cleaned and reloaded.

Around this time Sienna started becoming paranoid. She panicked that the world had forgotten about her, that no one was coming to rescue her by paying the ransom. To varying degrees, every hostage experiences the same thing at some point in their captivity. When someone is isolated from other people and days pass without any signs of progress, people tend to lose faith. Sienna suffered from this times a hundred. She started engaging with the kidnappers, even psychologically stroking them and soothing them.

One of the first rules of hostage survival is not to negotiate for yourself. It interferes with the work others are doing for you and usually results in longer captivity and a higher ransom.

Incredibly, Sienna managed to interfere with negotiations while still held in captivity. At one point she overheard one of her guards discussing our latest ransom offer. He misspoke and referred to the offer as one million Russian roubles. Upon hearing this, she bellowed: 'One million *roubles*? I'm worth much more than that! You must have misheard them, I'm worth one million *euros*!'

You can't make this stuff up.

One million roubles translated to around $35,000. Sienna's self-worth was so inflated that she couldn't believe anyone would make what she regarded as a pitifully low offer for her return. And note that she was saying 'I' not 'we' – despite the fact that she was holed up with her sister Renata!

Forty-eight hours later, right on cue, came the next call. The caller – there were several members of the gang speaking with the family – said, 'Listen carefully, *zoccola*, whore. We are not interested in Sienna or Renata. We are not interested in Grazia. We are only interested in Rodimov.'

This stance told me the kidnappers were streetwise. They knew where the real money was: in Rodimov's bank account.

To counter this, a lie was constructed that would derail the kidnappers' logic. 'I'm sorry,' they were told, 'but Rodimov is calling off the wedding with Grazia. He couldn't give a shit about her, nor for her bitch sisters.'

This wasn't true but the lie had the effect of making the kidnappers think Rodimov didn't give a damn about the sisters and would rather hang himself than cough up a red cent in ransom. For two days Isabella relayed the same message to the kidnappers. She hammered it home in the face of their protestations.

'*Afungu!* Fuck you! We don't believe you,' one of the gang members said.

We responded, 'The rest of the family won't have anything to do with Grazia because they told her that Rodimov was a dickhead. She didn't listen and now they are right, but she is too proud to admit it.'

'No. It is not possible that Mr Rodimov wouldn't want anything to do with the family. Even if he is not married to Grazia, he was engaged to her.'

'You don't know how things work in Russia. Things are different there.'

The story was repeated several times on the phone. The wedding is off; Rodimov doesn't care. Get over it. On the second day, after exhausting their options, the kidnappers finally bought it. They stopped talking about Rodimov.

The lie worked because of an age-old truth about lying: people are far more likely to believe a lie when you tune into their worldview and you use their language. *Of course*, this fiction implied, the cold-hearted Russian was jilting the pretty Italian girl; *of course* he wanted nothing more to do with her family; *of course* he didn't care what happened to Grazia's sisters.

The lie was also credible because the kidnappers had experienced the sisters up close and personal. They'd witnessed what a nightmare they both were, especially Sienna. I doubt any of the gang had expected Sienna to shout and berate them over the original ransom offer. Sienna's behaviour brought to my mind the movie *Ruthless People*, where Bette Midler's character is such a pain in the ass that the kidnappers become desperate to get rid of her. So the idea that Rodimov would want to wash his hands of the whole family was one the kidnappers were able to assimilate.

After the gang bought the fiction about Grazia and Rodimov's separation, the negotiations became a lot more realistic.

Unable – and perhaps unwilling – to keep both sisters hostage for a long period of time, the kidnappers eventually decided to let one of them go. They knocked on the door, a signal that the sisters should put on blindfolds, then walked into the cell. The sisters were conscious of several men in the room. A musty smell of bad cologne and body odour lingered in the air.

'Good news!' the leader of the gang said. 'One of you is to be released today. The question is, which one?'

'Take me, take me, take me!' Sienna shouted without a moment's hesitation.

Leaving her sister Renata in the cell.

The experience of being in captivity affected the sisters in different ways. Of the two, Renata handled herself much more capably. By contrast, Sienna was very clingy to her sister and refused even to go to the bathroom on her own. Sienna was the diva of the two. Partly I guess that was because she was an artist, and to be successful in that field you need to be a little narcissistic.

When Sienna returned home she promptly took control of negotiations herself, on the recommendation of Dynamo. I wondered how good she would be but Dynamo's people claimed, 'There are no better negotiators than the family.'

Taken at face value, this statement isn't wrong. The theory goes something like this: Sienna had spoken with several members of the gang. She knew their names and had an idea of how each would respond. As I said, I don't disagree with this idea. When I'm consulting a family in a situation where there is no company involved, I will sometimes recommend that one of the relatives conducts the dialogue with the kidnapper, someone who is briefed by me and has notes that I have prepared for them. It's usually better, in my experience, to have a trusted family friend or work colleague handle the dialogue, but I have worked on cases where the company doesn't consider itself to have a duty of care towards the employee taken captive, and after effectively washing its hands of them, the immediate family has to step into the breach. Negotiators often use this line as a ruse when trying to lower the ransom, as I did on the Karachi case.

But making a call on directly involving family members in the negotiations can only be made in the context of the people involved. And for me, asking a woman as volatile as Sienna to handle the negotiations was like steering the *Titanic* straight towards the iceberg. It was asking – no, begging – for trouble.

At first Sienna appeared to conduct herself reasonably well on the phone. Soon enough, however, my worst fears began to be realised. Sienna became a difficult negotiator and increasingly displayed a bad temper towards the kidnappers. She ignored the script I prepared for her. Another of the sisters, Mistico, was on lithium prescribed for manic depression and was drinking heavily.

Worse, the sisters at home were feeding off each other's bad vibes. At times the Ventura household felt like a coven.

I have friends who are corrections professionals and they tell me that it is a well-known fact that female-only prisons are much more crazy, dangerous and toxic than male-only prisons. The Ventura house was worse.

There was no respect for intimacy or personal space and Sienna and her other sisters would denigrate the mother in front of everyone, causing great friction between them. Reading between the lines, it was clear that Isabella and Sienna were jealous of Grazia's success.

Despite wanting their money and help, the family cold-shouldered Grazia and Rodimov. They were unhappy that their most famous daughter and her husband hadn't stumped up the ransom money at the start, arguing that they had ducked their responsibilities. Never mind the fact that this would have been a monumentally stupid decision and would have resulted in the sisters being targeted again in the future!

Isabella spoke of using the power of God and faith towards 'stopping the hate and resentment' that existed between Grazia and her sisters. And there was sure as hell a lot of both boiling under the surface. Their mother, Flavia, didn't bother showing up until the end of day seven. Grazia did not attend the house at all, knowing that her family was more *War of the Roses* than *The Golden Girls*, and happily stayed away. Most families, when faced with a desperate situation, such as the death of a parent, come closer. They pull together for the sake of their kin. But these people were so dysfunctional they made the Simpsons look like a model family.

Through my observation of the various family members, I soon realised that Renata could be the unifying element. Often social groups or families will have a unifier: a person who brings the others together. It made sense that this would be Renata; she was level-headed, well balanced and most definitely *not* a diva, unlike her siblings. Unfortunately for me, Renata was the one who remained captive. Getting her out wasn't just a concern for her own well-being; it could stop the rest of her family going nuts.

As we approached the second week of the abduction, Sienna was authorised to make a new offer to the kidnappers of €215,000.

'We will come back to you in two days,' one of the gang said.

By now we were able to conduct negotiations without press interference. Early on in the case media leaks had been a major problem. Isabella told me she suspected the leaks were coming from Marco, Renata's ex. He had a background in media and still moved in those circles. He may not have been deliberately leaking stuff to the media. More often than not, leaks occur because someone is careless as opposed to wilful. All it takes is a few cocktails at a party, a loosened tongue and a conversation with the wrong person. Either way, the media coverage was proving intrusive and problematic. I felt it would be impossible to conduct negotiations while the kidnappers gleaned so much attention from the press. As a matter of urgency, these leaks had to be stopped.

Once Marco was removed from the magic circle, the leaks swiftly ended. This didn't stem the coverage entirely, of course.

If you're dealing with high-profile victims, or relatives of the victims, a certain amount of media coverage is perhaps unavoidable. However, there is a difference between having the occasional statement or development fed to media outlets and the wholesale real-time leaking of every single thing going on with the case. This type of leak is extremely detrimental to the negotiating process and I was relieved that Marco had been excluded from the team. Now we had wrestled back control over the leaks, we could focus on the more important task of getting Renata back home.

Eventually a ransom of €325,000 was agreed with the kidnappers, or 3.25 per cent of the original demand of €10 million. In my opinion the settlement figure was reasonable. Given the precarious state of the Ventura family finances, the cash payment had to be supplied by Rodimov. However, we had to manufacture a way of getting the money to the kidnappers without having Rodimov's fingerprints all over it – otherwise the gang would suss out that we'd been lying to them about his 'separation' from Grazia, and the whole deal would go up in smoke. It was agreed that Rodimov would pass the money to Isabella via bank transfer. She would then make a withdrawal from her bank in dollars and deliver it to the kidnappers at a predetermined exchange location.

Rodimov ponied up the ransom cash in the knowledge that he would get it back from the insurers, but this is one of the most stressful things about negotiations – the insurers will only pay out after the event. First someone has to come up with the cash. Unless there is a generous benefactor like Rodimov on hand, or a company with plentiful cash reserves, raising the ransom can be difficult. A family might have to sell their car, remortgage their home or drain their 401k pension plan. The fact they can claim back from the insurers does nothing to ease the stress of getting a stockpile of cash in the first place.

With the ransom paid out, Renata was released and reunited with her family. I found some time to talk to both Renata and Sienna afterwards. As I debriefed Renata, I found her to be the polar opposite of Sienna. She was calm, level-headed and reasonable. She spoke frankly of her time in captivity.

'Did the kidnappers hurt you in any way?' I asked.

'Not once,' she replied.

I asked Renata how she felt about her sister voting for herself to be released first. She shrugged her shoulders and rolled her eyes. It was clear to me exactly what she thought about it, that similar selfishness had happened before and that it would happen again.

All I can add to that is this: if I was held with my brother and he begged to be released before me, he'd be off my Christmas card list sharpish.

I slipped out of there the next day. I didn't get the feeling that the family would even notice I'd gone. Most of the time families are too busy reuniting to know that I'm out of there and in any case, I'm just an unpleasant reminder of a horrible time. I quietly faded away, which is just how I like it. Dealing with the Ventura clan had been stressful enough anyhow.

I jetted north to Moscow and paid a whistlestop visit to Rodimov at his home to review the case and prepare my report for the Box back in London.

In order for Rodimov to be reimbursed for the money he'd already laid out, I had to prepare that report for the Box. Before they pay anything, the underwriter has to know that the case isn't fraud. I can usually establish whether it is or not pretty quickly. Lots of times you can smell it; most people, no matter how intelligent or successful, aren't slick enough to pull off a major scam like this. There are telltale signs I look for in fraudulent K&R cases. Although I won't tell you what they are, for obvious reasons, things such as scant information from the victim's family, accompanied by a lack of cooperation, usually raises my suspicions.

Rodimov welcomed me into his home for the second time. On this occasion he ushered me into a large, antique-furnished office. He was in good spirits, like an anchor weight had been lifted from his shoulders. I'm sure both he and Grazia were looking forward to resuming their normal lives once more.

As we chatted it became apparent that a huge rift had torn open between the Russian and Italian branches of the prospective family. Though problems had been festering beneath the surface for some time prior to the abduction, the kidnap had simply accelerated and intensified them. During the case, Rodimov had used all his substantial PR powers to stop Renata and Sienna's plight from being extensively featured in the Russian and Italian press in the latter stages of the case. Since Marco had been removed from the inner circle, there had been nuggets here and there but nothing really damaging.

'Now the case is over, it's open season with those guys,' Rodimov said. 'The sisters are basically in prison in one of the family homes down there. Whole bloody army of paps and straight media are camped outside the front door. And yesterday Grazia and I are heading over to a restaurant for lunch, when guess what? I got a damn photographer on my doorstep as we're walking out. Guy tails us the whole trip. Him and his camera-crew friends.'

'Jesus.'

'It could have gotten very ugly.'

I sipped my glass of water and noticed that Rodimov had a plasma TV hanging from the wall. It was tuned into an Italian cable TV channel the whole time I was there. The volume was muted. While we were talking a news programme started and up flashed a live feed from outside the apartment where the sisters Sienna and Renata were hiding, though not very successfully.

The coverage had been round-the-clock. Rodimov picked up an Italian newspaper lying on his desk. He unfolded it and presented it to me. On the front page was an article about the case. Sienna was quoted extensively. 'This was a family matter,' she was quoted as saying. 'We did not have any help from the outside. We resolved this as a family and no more.'

Implying that Rodimov and Grazia were unhelpful didn't hurt Rodimov's feelings. He didn't become a major businessman by worrying about stuff like that and he clearly recognised that his participation in the case had to be kept on the down-low. The reason? No one associated with the case wanted to reveal that Russian money had subsidised the sisters' release. The local government in particular would look like assholes.

But the downside to hushing up the payout was that Grazia's public image was taking a beating. The media twisted Sienna's words and came up with headlines like 'Grazia and Mr Moneybags Didn't Give Us a Brass Farthing', garbage like that. This was painful for Grazia. She'd cultivated an image as a caring, innocent, fun, happy-go-lucky type. Now she was engaged to someone perceived as a heartless monster.

'Why don't you use some of that PR influence to put an end to the speculation?' I asked.

Rodimov shook his head. '*Niet*. I called in all my favours months ago. To be fair, they played ball. They didn't fuck me over. But it's payback time now. And even if I could put a block on it, you think that *blyad* Sienna gives a shit? She's loving it.'

He was right. Sienna had kudos as a sculptor but only within artistic circles. The kidnap had suddenly projected her on to the public eye in a way she had never experienced before. She loved all this attention being fostered upon her. There was no way she'd let Rodimov silence the media on this one. She probably felt this was her chance at grabbing fame and riches, like her sister Grazia.

I thought about other ways to counteract this. I put an idea to Rodimov.

'Why don't you offer Sienna a part in a movie about the kidnap? Fund it yourself. You have the money. Say you're filming it here in Russia. You'd have control of the script. And maybe Sienna gets uncomfortable with it and you cancel the film by means of a contractually bought-out silence. It'd be far cheaper and more flattering for all concerned than a nasty all-out PR war.'

Rodimov said he'd give it some thought. I had a plane to catch back to London. I did not hold out much hope that the various factions of the family would put aside their rancour. Certainly there would be a line drawn through more than a few names on the wedding invite list. The fallout from the kidnapping had poisoned relations perhaps permanently. For the Ventura family, for Grazia, for Rodimov – things would never be the same again.

Abduction – Captivity – Proof of Life –
Negotiation – Ransom Drop – **Release**

Part Six

PIRATES

'Hello, I will have eight million dollars please.'

Mr Farhan, Somali pirate

19

THE WOLF

In June 2009 I was in the process of moving offices again and packing my rubber chicken into a removal box when my iPhone sparked into life. The iridescent blue screen told me I had a new message. I tapped in my passcode and opened up the text. It had been sent by a negotiator friend of mine, Patrick. He was working on the case of a European tanker that had been captured six months before by pirates off the coast of Somalia. Patrick and his colleagues had flown into the shipowners' country to talk to them about ransom. 'Bumped into the Archbishop of Canterbury and his party this morning,' read the message. 'Says he is on official visit to the local Church. Asked him to put in a good word for us with the Man upstairs in relation to Somali case.'

I don't think Patrick believes in God. But when dealing with pirates, a negotiator needs all the help he can get.

That summer I was called out to Somalia for a case involving a European vessel seized off the Puntland coast by pirates. It was gone midnight on a mild but muggy July evening and I was sitting in my new office struggling to catch up with some paperwork when my phone lit up. I eagerly took the call, since anything is better than paperwork, and swigged from a can of Red Bull. Second of the day.

'Mr Lopez, I need your help.'

The voice on the other end of the line was heavy like lead, rough as sandpaper and hard like a fist. I've known enough Greeks in my time to recognise the accent. I had this guy down as Greek from the moment he said 'Mr Lopez'.

His name was Giorgios Venkis and he was the owner of a dry-bulk carrier ship that had been making its way out of the Kenyan port of Mombasa into the Gulf of Aden when a Somali raiding party boarded it. The Gulf of Aden is some 1.1 million square miles. The ship had a crew of nine. Four Eastern European officers and five Filipino crew. The cargo of grain was from Canada. The ship had been built in Germany and was registered in Liberia. This is par for the course in the shipping industry but it adds a thick layer of complication to the negotiating and insurance end of things. As in, who's responsible for the vessel itself? Who's responsible for the crew? The cargo? Usually the people chartering the vessel assume control because all of the people working under them are employed by them. In this case, it was Giorgios Venkis.

While my brother Tony hooked me up with a flight to Athens, I recited to Venkis the standard holding instructions. When the pirates call, tell them we will do business but do not enter into any dialogue with them. Take a message and say you'll pass it on. Don't start cooperating with them yet. Remember they're judging you from the first second of the first call.

Negotiations with Somali pirates usually take place via the ship's satellite phone to a phone in a conference room in the offices of whichever company owns or chartered the vessel. The sat phone was practical, maybe they got a better signal than they did from ashore. Or more likely, they just didn't want to burn up the credit on their mobiles.

I popped two ProPlus pills in my mouth and washed them down with more Red Bull. My head was buzzing. Like someone had attached a couple of jumper cables to my ears. Another case beckoned. And this was going to be a harder negotiation than anything I had done before.

In 2011 it's almost impossible to pick up a newspaper or turn on the TV without seeing a report on piracy. Somalia has received the bulk of media attention because of the high-profile nature of many of the kidnappings: middle-class white Anglo couples kidnapped while on their round-the-world retirement cruise are newsworthy; unfortunately crews of twenty or thirty Filipinos are not. The rise of the global economy has seen a concomitant increase in sea travel as international trade, commercialised fishing and fresh oil deposits become ever more important. For many years the hotspots of maritime piracy were centred on the seas outside Lagos in Nigeria, Chittagong in Bangladesh, the Strait of Malacca and Singapore. Each of these three regions shares two common traits: they are vital transit routes for international commercial vessels and the surrounding nations lack the naval power to exert any authority. Activity was restricted to for-profit strikes: the pirates would assault cargo vessels and oil tankers while they were anchored at shore and rob the crew at gunpoint and perhaps siphon off the ship's goods too. The pirates were just plain thieves.

All that changed in the mid-1990s.

After Siad Barre's government collapsed, Somalia sank into a period of extreme chaos and poverty from which it is yet to emerge. An estimated two-thirds of Somali citizens rely on food aid to survive. Per capita GDP is around $600 a year. It stands to reason that any thrusting young guy is going to want to make a better life for himself. In Somalia, the path to riches is through piracy.

A lack of opportunity, combined with a rich fishing heritage and the strategic importance of the shipping route around the Horn of Africa, created the perfect conditions in which a new kind of piracy could thrive. Early successes emboldened the pirates, encouraging them to hijack all types of vessel, from large tankers to small fishing trawlers. Now they can attack ships miles off the coast using speedboats equipped with souped-up outboard motors. As they near the vessel, the pirates will employ grappling hooks and rocket-propelled irons to scale the side of the hull. You might wonder why ships don't open fire upon the invaders. The truth is that despite the risk they are taking, most vessels don't carry the necessary security. It's expensive, and since thousands of vessels sail through the area each year, but only a few are hijacked, many companies just cross their fingers. Also, the Somalis are armed with assault rifles and machine guns and aren't afraid to use them. If security personnel aboard an oil tanker open fire, they will only succeed in encouraging the Somalis to return fire, further endangering the lives of the crew and cargo. There have also been several cases of pirates launching RPGs (rocket-propelled grenades) and setting fire to the decks. Some captured ships are anchored at the pirate town of Eyl in the northern Puntland region, for safekeeping until negotiations have been concluded. Eyl is a safe haven. Special forces operators consider it virtually impenetrable.

As the pirates get richer, their equipment gets better. The consequence of these daring raids is that some assaults have occurred more than two thousand kilometres from the Somali coastline. The area of attacks covers almost a quarter of the Indian Ocean. That's equivalent to 17.5 million square miles. Factor in the vast number of vessels that must navigate its waters each year, amounting to 20 per cent of the world's commercial shipping fleet, and you begin to see how policing the Horn of Africa is impossible. In 2008 a multinational naval task force was dispatched to the region to curtail the number of pirate attacks. The fleet concentrated its efforts on three international shipping corridors. While there was a slight drop in attacks, pirates were still capturing boats in the double figures each year.

In my opinion, the political will to prevent Somali piracy attacks is lacking. Despite the presence of the task force, Somali pirates continue to operate with impunity. Ships and crews continue to be captured every week. Of course the lawyers are involved. So there is confusion over the legal definition of piracy, which contributes to the failure to intervene. A friend of mine told me that the rules of engagement for the naval task force are so stringent that even if a cargo ship or trawler is being pursued by pirates, the task force might not be able to come to their assistance. They have the right and ability to stop and search suspected pirate ships. But when the pirates see them coming, they dump their weapons overboard. Then they are released since legally, only armed ships and crews can be seized. The pirates are well aware of these rules. Armed guards aboard the ships could fire at the pirates. But this doesn't usually discourage the pirates from their attack.

The thing is that once a ship is seized, the pirates have won. The ships, cargos and crews are far too valuable for their owners to risk. It is better and 'cheaper' to pay a $20 million ransom than to risk a $200 million loss. Everybody – the owners, lenders and insurers – understands these facts of life. So do the pirates.

The frequency of piracy attacks reached a sort of tipping point in April 2010, when US President Barack Obama issued an executive order authorising the Treasury Department to freeze the assets of US individuals or companies (or international companies with US interests) who have dealings with Somali individuals or organisations found on the Specially Designated Nationals (SDN) list. The order was designed to block funding to the pirates. It was interpreted in some quarters as a ban on ransom payments. Because if you're paying a ransom to pirates linked to a guy on the SDN list, that effectively means you're financially supporting the pirates and potentially even Somali-based terrorist groups like al-Shabaab.

Another old idea is now being used with some success by the Chinese Navy. They have a large presence in the region and instead of wasting fuel patrolling for pirates, they are organising large convoys of ships that they then escort back to China. As a result, very few of these vessels have been attacked. Not surprisingly, the Chinese are now offering to escort non-Chinese vessels to safe waters – for a large fee, payable in advance, of course.

The main problem with this approach is that it's very expensive in time and money, and in shipping, time is money.

Tony dropped me off at Heathrow Airport. I hadn't eaten for twenty-four hours so I grabbed a quarterpounder with cheese and large fries from the bar in departures. Both tasted like plastic doused in salt. I washed the meal down with Diet Coke. I trawled the bookstore for a travel guide to Somalia. Surprisingly there wasn't one. Finally the call came for my Aegean flight and I was headed towards the gate to catch the Airbus A321 when my iPhone started ringing.

I took one look at the name flashing on the display and thought, Aw, crap.

Freshly divorced and back on the dating scene, I'd arranged a dinner date with a stunningly beautiful Canadian woman named Dana I'd been introduced to through mutual friends. Sadly, in the rush to head out to Athens and begin work on the pirates case, I'd completely forgotten about our dinner date. Pacing double-quick towards the gate, I hit the answer button and pressed the iPhone close to my ear.

'Hey, I'm just checking we're still on for tonight,' Dana said, sounding chirpish.

'I'm really sorry,' I said, getting my excuse in early. 'I'm gonna have to cancel.'

Silence. Then, 'Oh. Can I ask why?'

'I'm about to jump on a plane to Greece.'

More silence. 'Oh. I see. So are you a pilot or something?'

'No. I'm a hostage negotiator.'

The nature of my job means I've had to cancel more than my fair share of dates. The usual response is either an expression of sympathy or more often disbelief. I think the majority of them think I'm some kind of Walter Mitty fantasist feeding them a line of bullshit. This woman did neither.

'Will you pay a ransom?' she asked.

'That's generally what happens.'

'Oh,' she said.

As I neared my gate Dana launched into a scathing attack on me and the role of negotiators generally. According to her, negotiators were single-handedly responsible for the proliferation of kidnaps worldwide and the K&R industry was flourishing by paying out blood money.

'We should never, ever pay ransoms,' she said. 'I mean, by doing so you're encouraging these criminals to take more hostages. You're practically as bad as the kidnappers.'

Dana was a highly intelligent individual with a successful career. She was well-read, sensible, pragmatic. And yet her opposition to ransom payments, which is mirrored in numerous political circles, was devoid of logic. Arguing that negotiators promote kidnapping is as stupid as arguing that car insurance promotes motor accidents.

We live in a world where some people are extraordinarily rich and others are desperately poor. Opportunity is there for many; it is transparently absent in the lives of others. As long as people continue to need money, they will continue to abduct others and demand money for their release.

This is not a justification for kidnapping. I find kidnap abhorrent and though I make my living in it, I honestly wish it didn't happen. But it does. My job is to make sure that people are returned home safe and sound. Any other strategy, be it armed intervention or a refusal to negotiate, does not assure the hostage's release.

I hung up on Dana. I had a plane to catch and a case to prepare for and I didn't have the time to pick apart her flimsy arguments. Needless to say, I didn't rearrange our date.

I landed at Eleftherios Venizelos International Airport three and a half hours later. I'd hoped to grab some shut-eye on the plane but the urgent need to familiarise myself with the case and formulate a plan of action meant that, as usual, rest had to take a back seat. I collected my go bag from the overhead locker and hitched a taxi straight to the shipping company's offices. After pressing the flesh with Venkis, I described a few of the standard negotiating tactics the Somali pirates were likely to employ.

It's impossible to predict how long the pirates will wait before calling you back. Could be an hour, could be a day. Could be a week or longer. It depends on whether they were in a good or bad mood when they got out of bed that morning, that kind of stuff. I've already explained how the Wait can be frustrating for a hostage negotiator. In general, clients feel it even more. He's got a ton of money on the line, plus the cargo, plus the lives of his hostages. While the lives of the hostages are important to the owner, the scale of the numbers mean that it's more like a headache to these guys, as if there were a strike or a natural disaster. Obviously a kidnap has bigger implications but it's still a headache that has to be managed.

In a separate case, the negotiators didn't hear back from the pirates for more than a week. You can't assume that the pirates are using deliberate delaying tactics. Sometimes they're doing things as mundane as attending weddings or funerals, or they simply don't feel like working that day. If they don't answer the phone, it's crucial that the negotiating team doesn't take it personally.

As I spoke with Venkis, I carefully observed his body language. I was looking for telltale signs of whether the guy was really listening to me. When it comes to dealing with pirates, a lot depends on the shipowner absorbing the briefing material and sticking to it like glue. I've briefed certain businessmen and women who have clearly not been listening to a thing I've said. Their minds are elsewhere, focusing on their dry cleaning or how they got laid last night. Or they think, This is important shit, but the minute they walk out of the door they forget everything.

Then a week passes and the client calls you and says, 'We haven't heard a word from the pirates. You screwed up. The crew are obviously dead. You've cost me the lives of my men and my ship.'

Of course, if they'd paid attention during the briefing, they would realise that the only reason the pirates haven't picked up the sat phone is that Asad, Korfa and Taban are sitting under a shade tree chewing khat.

It's not unusual for clients to lash out at me as the negotiator. In a way, I'm like Winston Wolf, the character played by Harvey Keitel in the movie *Pulp Fiction*. The Wolf is an underworld 'cleaner' who helps dispose of dead bodies and incriminating evidence at murder scenes. Some people are pissed at the Wolf, other characters adopt the attitude of 'Who the fuck are you to tell me what to do?' But through his polite manners, his professionalism and his will of iron, the guy ends up getting a lot of respect from those same characters. That's the ideal. In real life some people end up lashing out at you. Sometimes they harbour lingering resentments or they're just highly strung and lash out at everybody. Other people are more phlegmatic. That's just the way it goes.

My sleeping pattern is never great when I'm on a case but in Athens I found it especially bad. I had a room in a crappy hotel in the shipping district. Not a bad place but I was on the outskirts of town surrounded by shipping containers and industrial buildings and even if I wanted to check out the Acropolis, I simply didn't have the time.

The pirates made contact at last. They called Venkis on his mobile. A young-sounding man said, simply, 'Hello, my name is Mr Farhan and I will have eight million dollars please.'

I particularly liked the 'please'. You can't accuse Somali pirates of lacking manners.

One quality marks them out as particularly tough cookies: they are prepared to play the long game. Somali kidnappers will sit on their hostages for months, sometimes even years. The Chandlers, the British couple, were in captivity for thirteen months. A long time, by Somali standards.

Part of the problem is the pirates' skewed perception of the Western world. While they have street smarts in abundance, they also harbour some pretty distorted and plain wrong ideas about us. In the case of the Chandlers, the kidnappers demanded a ransom of $7 million. Their justification for such an extortionate payment? I think it's because they simply could not believe that a retired white British couple sailing around the world didn't have any money. They see a white couple on a yacht and think they must be multi-millionaires.

It's a different story when the item in question is a cargo vessel costing tens of millions of dollars to build. A kidnapper takes a hostage and a car, no one gives a crap about what happens to the vehicle. But a ship is a company's livelihood. They and the insurance company are going to want that ship back. Building a new ship from scratch is much more time-consuming and expensive than repairing a captured vessel that has suffered some minor damage. The pirates know this, so they rack up the price to eye-watering levels. They know the value of the ships.

The ship my buddy Patrick was involved with had a low freeboard. The freeboard is the distance from the waterline to the upper deck. Pirates like low freeboards because they can easily use them as motherships, effortlessly loading and unloading cargo and launching further attacks on nearby vessels using their motorboats. It's a cosy set-up and means the pirates have no reason to give the vessel back. Even as they were negotiating with Patrick, the kidnappers on the case he was working were using the vessel as a mothership.

On my case, however, Mr Farhan and his gang were never going to keep the ship. But they were interested in the cargo. Very interested. Cars were of no interest to them because serial numbers can be traced. If the pirates are lucky enough to have stolen a fully laden oil tanker, they've hit the jackpot. Unlike meat or grain, for example, oil isn't perishable. And unlike vehicles, it's unidentifiable and can be sold anywhere in the world.

They're very adaptable and extremely pragmatic. Somalis are good at languages. And many pirates, like Mr Farhan, are fluent in English. Physically and psychologically they are hard as nails. They're hard because there are no weak Somalis left. They died in the desert. It's a tough environment that breeds tough people. And they live in a failed state – one that exists in a state of permanent anarchy. You cannot be fragile and sensitive in such a place and expect to survive. And they bring this attitude to the negotiating table.

Somalis are not like other Africans. They're born with self-regard.

They see themselves as a warrior race. They're often quite courageous. They're obsessed with clan hierarchy. They're very proud and arrogant and self-confident.

Like other warriors, they're also romantic. They like to read poems about war and camels. They like to resolve problems. Because they live in a place where if you don't resolve problems, you end up dead. The kidnap groups are loosely arranged along clan lines but they are not clan-based. In any gang there might be two or three guys from the Smith clan but there's also going to be a couple of guys from the Jones clan and one or two from the Doe clan. And while the gangs will rely on the main clan for protection, they are independent of them. It's not like the pirates are somehow 'authorised' by the clans. They just happen to be from the same clan in the same way that if I'm going to do a project, I'm going to choose people to help me who speak English and whose frame of reference is similar to mine. It's just easier that way.

Defined by their circumstances and the harsh environment in which they live, Somali pirates are Muslim in the technical sense, just as most Britons are Anglican by name only. They're businessmen. Their primary goal is to make money. Everything is secondary to that objective. And they won't settle for a piss-ant payday. They want millions. From the kidnappers' angle it requires an enormous upfront investment. Ships, time, financial investment in terms of paying people and buying guns, supplies to feed and hydrate everybody.

But business is a social activity. You can't do business on a desert island. To thrive, to function, a business needs clients and suppliers and an income. For the pirates, their suppliers are the gangs that sell them assault rifles, RPG rocket launchers, grenades, ammo and food.

Somalis are individualists by nature. Groups tend to equate to conflict. A regular Joe in a pirate gang has almost as much say in kidnappings and negotiations as the leader. Funnily enough, this is similar to how pirates operated in the seventeenth and eighteenth centuries. They were unusual in that they modelled themselves on democracies, where everyone has a relatively equal voice, which was radical at the time. They were the opposite of the rest of the world at the time, which operated on a very rigid up-and-down hierarchy. There were no dictators in pirate gangs. Then, or now. In Somalia, the pirate leader is voted in by the men he commands. Below him will be an executive committee of maybe four pirate commanders.

One consequence of a flat hierarchy is that when one of the pirates disagrees with the leader's tactics, he will often refuse to back down. The yelling can escalate until leader and dissident start shooting at each other. It seems this happens on pretty much every single case. Certainly that was the case here.

Farhan and one of the pirates had a beef over the size of the ransom they were demanding. We heard plenty of raised voices and threats that the men were going to shoot each other. But relations never soured sufficiently for me to be able to drive a wedge between the warring factions. Eventually, Farhan and his subordinate resolved their differences and the negotiations continued.

Business is business, after all.

That's the thing about K&R. When the phone goes and I'm briefed on a kidnap-for-ransom case, I breathe a sigh of relief. At the opposite end of the scale, politico-religious kidnaps give me nightmares. They're scary because you're essentially dealing with someone who holds a fixed and rigid belief that strongly persists despite evidence to the contrary. A cynic might argue that's pretty much true of all religions. Whether any kidnapping is purely religious is debatable: to the best of my knowledge, there is not a single religion out there that urges its disciples to go forth and kidnap people or chop their heads off. Pseudo-religious groups like the Taliban are populated by individuals who latch on to religion like a leech does to human flesh. It's the *political aspect* of religion that converts human behaviour into a model where criminal enterprise is acceptable. Even admirable. The Marxist guerrilla armies that have plagued Latin America for so many years provide the same 'believer'-type outlet for their extremes of human behaviour.

Doing business with the Somalis isn't easier but it's certainly more rational. Both parties are operating on the principle that each has something of value. The negotiating team has the money. The pirate gang has human lives and a vessel. Both sides wish to exchange one thing for the other. You might be miles apart in terms of valuation, and there are plenty of other hurdles to overcome, but the will to do business is there. I might be on the line to a politico-religious kidnapper and he'll suddenly throw me a curveball and say, 'My reward is in heaven.'

Now the goalposts have shifted. I no longer have anything of value to exchange with the kidnapper. Money is meaningless if all he really wants is to get a ringside seat to the big show upstairs. What negotiating tactics are going to work with someone who thinks they have a direct line to God?

This absence of rationality informed many of the kidnappings that took place in the aftermath of the Iraq War. Margaret Hassan, the Irish NGO official who was shot by her captors in November 2004, worked for the humanitarian relief organisation CARE International. Now, CARE has done much commendable work in Iraq in the areas of health, sanitation and nutrition. Many thousands of lives have been saved and dramatically improved and Hassan herself has been credited with contributing significantly to these achievements. But what could CARE do about fulfilling the kidnappers' demand that British troops unilaterally withdraw from Iraq? Nothing, is the answer. Hassan was doomed from the moment she was taken hostage. Had they targeted a soldier then they may have had a stronger case for achieving some political concessions. Hamas has held the Israeli soldier Gilad Shalit captive for more than three years; my gut instinct is that eventually the Israeli government will come to some arrangement for his safe return. Nothing will be made public but some time later, once the public brouhaha has died down and the media focus is elsewhere, the most logical scenario suggests a number of Palestinian prisoners will be quietly released and sent across the border.

Seen from that perspective, haggling with Somali pirates is a walk in the park. But any negotiator dealing with these guys has to bring their A-game to the plate because the Somalis are masters at exploiting weakness. I define weak negotiating tactics as paying up too early, increasing offers too easily or putting pressure on them with weak statements like 'We've got to get our guy back this week.' Projecting a rushed and anxious demeanour only hardens the pirates' attitude.

Negotiators have to be on-point when it comes to detecting the subtle nuances of the English language. If the guy on the end of the line comes from, say, France, he might come unstuck with the Somalis and become stressed as a result. The pirates like to parry verbally. You have to be quick of tongue and sharp of mind to understand what they're really saying and come back with a decisive line of your own. Even the bad English-language speakers among the pirates have a good feel for language and its subtleties. I liken them to jailhouse lawyers.

They also like to convey an excessive concern for the welfare of the hostages. As though they're guests rather than innocent civilians held against their will. To some degree the pirates treat hostages with more grace than, say, Colombian kidnappers might. If I knew I was going to be kidnapped tomorrow, I'd catch a plane to Somalia tonight. In general the pirates don't beat up their hostages, they give them bottled water and feed them. Even the Somalis' death threats lacked credibility.

That's the pirates in a nutshell. They can be extremely polite and friendly one minute, and the next they're yelling and pointing machine guns at each other. In psychology this is known as being affectively labile. Their mood swings one way then the other. When you're negotiating with the pirates, you never know what kind of mood they're going to be in from one conversation to the next.

After tortuous, drawn-out and heated talks, we finally reached a settlement of $4 million. In general K&R terms this is an extraordinarily large sum but in the high-stakes environment of Somali piracy it's by no means the biggest ransom anyone has paid. You might think that Farhan and his buddies were rich as Croesus at the end of all this but you'd be wrong. The case took four months to resolve. Their pay equals $1 million per month. But the gang had a burn rate of hundreds of thousands of dollars each month too. Groceries eat up a lot of money. Don't forget that in a failed state like Somalia, everything costs twice as much. Then they've also got to pay for the fuel for the light motorboats that have to make repeat trips from the shore to the cargo ship. Minus all those costs, plus having to divide the profits between the gang, and you might be looking at only $50,000 a head.

The involvement of governments in Somali negotiations is a sticking point. In one recent case, the Spanish government allegedly paid a ransom, rumoured to be £2 million, to Somali pirates for the release of a fishing trawler carrying a crew of thirty-six. The Spanish Prime Minister Jose Luis Zapatero said in a news conference, 'The government did what it had to do. The first obligation of a country is to save the lives of its countrymen.' When questioned, he refused to deny reports that the government had paid the ransom directly. This does not surprise me. Latino governments tend to have a macho 'Let me fix it now' culture and have been known to pay, in contrast with the stricter states to the north – France, Germany, the UK.

Governments that do pay, pay fast. Politics is a time game and senior ministers and officials can find themselves under intense media pressure to act and set the hostages free. Panic sets in. The government ends up paying the initial asking price. Which leads to the kidnappers thinking, Holy shit, we can tap these guys up. They've got money and they pay up quick. No kidnapper is going to leave money on the table – that leads to situations where a ransom is paid but the hostages aren't released. The kidnappers hold out for a further ransom payment until they're sure the well is truly dry. But the problem for governments is that – in the mind of the kidnapper at least – money is unlimited. Kidnappers love that.

Once we had agreed a ransom amount, we drew up a list of commitments that Farhan verbally agreed to on the sat phone. I will say this: these pirates took their promises seriously. Once they agree to do something, and if you can get them to tell you the name of the clan, they will keep their word. These guys typed out the list of commitments and emailed it through to us via a free Hushmail account as a symbol that they would honour their promises. It's an idiot-proof way of conducting business. There are no grey areas – there's a contract that both parties can refer to in the event someone breaks the agreement, and no one's going to track down a Somali IP address to convict anybody. When we were both satisfied with the terms, Farhan printed out the email document, signed it and faxed it back to us in the negotiating room in Athens. Just like any other business deal.

The ransom drop was made via a Britten-Norman Trislander utility aircraft flown by an ex-Royal Air Force pilot, who came in low beside the cargo ship and then released the ransom into the sea inside a waterproof canister under a parachute. The pirates sent one of their motorboats out to collect it.

Conducting business this way gets around the problem of where and how to meet in a lawless country. It's as much a pain in the kidnappers' necks to go to land for an exchange as it is for the negotiators. They're comfortable aboard the asset. They can control who comes and who goes. Why risk going ashore, where a special forces team might be lying in wait to ambush them?

Once the ransom drop has been made, the pirates usually honour their side of the bargain and release both the ship and crew. Sometimes the crew continue their original voyage, depending on the fuel state at the time of the drop. In other cases, the vessel is taken to a safe port in Yemen, to Mombasa or to Colombo in Sri Lanka. Ships are always returned.

After all, where can the pirates hide a two-hundred-metre ship?

After the case I met up with a friend of mine who also works in the K&R game and he told me that right now his inbox is overflowing with cases featuring vessels captured by Somali pirates. This type of crime has become so prevalent that several companies, such as Compass Risk Management, now specialise in maritime piracy. My friend has been doing kidnap cases for longer than me, and his view is that negotiations are taking longer and that ransoms are increasing. Eventually things will reach a head and Western governments will be forced to do something about it. But we're not there yet.

Thirty thousand ships sail along the Horn of Africa each year; seen from that perspective, thirty-odd ships captured represents a tiny percentage. I figure that many shipowners probably look at those odds and reckon it's worth taking a chance, on the basis that 'It won't happen to me.' Like soldiers on the frontline: every guy is getting ready to go into battle and knows people will die. But nobody ever thinks it will be them. If they did, we wouldn't have wars.

Six months later, in January 2010, I was contacted by my old SAS friend John. Like every other guy on the Circuit he was very busy with Somalian cases and he needed my help here. Two local NGO managers, Dutchman Rob Kampen and his Brazilian colleague Ricardo Alves were in-country. After two weeks of dodging bullets and sorting out logistical operations on the ground, it was time to fly home.

That morning Kampen and Alves were packing their bags and carrying out a last-minute check of their functional hotel room when their local fixer rang on Kampen's mobile to say that something urgent had cropped up and he was very sorry but he couldn't work that day. However, his cousin would fill in for him and escort the two men to the airport. The pickup truck accompanying Kampen and Alves's beat-up BMW carried a security detail of eight men, all armed with AK-47s. That ought to have been a strong enough deterrent to any local criminals planning an abduction – unless the security detail happened to be the gang itself.

Then the pickup truck raced ahead of the BMW and both observers got a bad feeling in their guts.

Their worst fears were realised when the BMW driver hit the brakes, stopping a couple of metres from the pickup truck. They watched in horror as the gunmen debussed from the pickup and quickly swarmed over their car, pointing AK-47s at the two men and shouting at them to get out. Both men were bundled into the pickup truck and had their jackets wrapped around their heads to blindfold them. They were then driven from the town they had been staying in towards the mountain valleys at break-neck speed. For the next twelve hours both Kampen and Alves had to endure a torturous ascent up a mountain range in brutalising heat.

Their ordeal was a terrible one but at least negotiations had been opened up very quickly with the kidnappers and I was confident that both men would be released soon, especially because the response consultant was a good buddy of mine, Alex.

He was reaching the end of his three-week rotation and we overlapped a day for the handover. I reported to the open-plan, dingy building that housed the NGO. I noticed that someone had tacked photographs of the actors Colin Firth and Johnny Depp to the wall in the conference room that Alex and his team had requisitioned for the purposes of negotiations. Alex bears more than a passing resemblance to Colin Firth – big, tall, good-looking guy who carries an air of authority about him. Another guy on the team looked like Johnny Depp. Not me, I have to say.

Both Kampen and Alves handled their time in captivity well. They were never really afraid for their lives. On one occasion bullets were fired outside the cave they were being kept in. The men believed a rival group was attempting to steal them. Other than that, they were fed spaghetti and pancakes and roasted goat, received cigarettes and even played chess to keep their minds active.

Not that the men weren't distraught and angry at being separated from their loved ones. Once in a while Alves got pissed off. He was anxious about the health of his father. That's natural. Hostages have a lot of downtime. There's nothing to read, no TV and if they're alone there's nobody to speak to. So they spend a lot of their time thinking. Invariably their thoughts turn to their relatives and partners. How much they miss them, how much they wish they could turn back the clock. How much they regret getting kidnapped in the first place.

Knowing that news of his kidnap would seriously stress his father, Alves became irritable and angry while in captivity. On a few occasions he shouted at and went chest-to-chest with one of his guards. I would never advocate hostages being confrontational with their kidnappers but sometimes it's hard to control your temper and frustrations boil over. That's part of human nature. Fortunately for Alves, the pirates come from a culture where yelling is part of everyday conversation. He berated them. They dismissed his words with a jerk of their shoulders. They had assault rifles and RPGs. What threat did the unarmed, exhausted, terrified Alves pose, in the eyes of the kidnappers? None.

I was, however, very concerned about the welfare of Alves's immediate family back in Lisbon. I travelled to see them at their family home in the historical Alfama district, a warren of winding cobblestoned streets and baroque houses and cafés. They lived in a whitewashed, clay-roofed place with an excellent vantage point over the rest of Lisbon.

The father wasn't talking about the case, he wasn't sleeping and he had a history of heart problems that I feared might be triggered again by the stress of knowing that his son was being held captive in Africa. He stubbornly refused to undergo any kind of psychotherapy. I wasn't offering that; I felt that I could be of more help to the family by guiding them through the likely sequence of events leading up to release, and the subsequent readjustment hostages and victims make to ordinary life. I also tried to explain that whatever responses they had to the kidnapping were a perfectly normal part of the healing process, and that I could help them regain a sense of control and mastery over the situation.

It was up to the mother to hold the family together and she had to do it in the face of a media frenzy. The paparazzi camped outside the parents' house and news channels covered the story from every angle imaginable. Had the men been journalists, for example, there would have been a media blackout because since the second Iraq war and the many journalists who've been captured and killed, there's an unwritten agreement among all the media outlets that they won't report on kidnaps if the company believes it will jeopardise their hostage. Not only that but journalists tend to be sympathetic to the plight of their peers and they appreciate how media intervention can severely screw up a case.

I also had to work on calming down Alves's brother-in-law. The worst thing you can do is take power away from a man. It goes double for Latin men. And in kidnappings you have no power. You have no information. You're fighting a whirlwind. As I explained the likely sequence of events to the family, the brother-in-law began arguing with me.

'Look,' I replied in a steady tone of voice, not rising to the bait, 'I'm not here to argue with you. I'm telling you how it is, based on what you've told me and my experience in working this type of case. You can either listen or not listen but don't attack me just because this situation is out of your hands.'

A ransom was eventually negotiated with the kidnappers and both men were released unharmed. Upon their release Kampen and Alves were flown to a neighbouring African country. Alves, who happened to be a good writer, immediately began penning an article about his time in captivity. I thought this was a good thing. In the same vein, journalists who are kidnapped tend to cope quite well with dealing with their return to normality. They're open and they like to talk and analyse, perhaps more so than other people who don't communicate for a living. The emotions someone feels on release vary from guilt to ecstasy to depression and he or she has more ups and downs than a Wall Street stock market graph. Alves, on the other hand, tended towards being less talkative and wanting to put things behind him.

A training programme I ran for journalists for an international news agency taught me that there are three types of reporter. Print, video and photo. What I learned was that in general, following a traumatic event, the print writer tends to do better than his video and photographic colleagues. Why? My theory is that to tell the story, writers have to use different parts of the brain that allow them to digest and ultimately metabolise the distressing material. They process it. Whereas the video and photo guys often think that the camera somehow insulates them from the trauma. The myth is that they can 'hide' behind the camera, that it puts distance between them and the trauma. It's a mistaken belief but it's an intuitively appealing one that is hard to shift.

Aid workers fall into the same trap.

I once gave a talk to a symposium of various aid organisations. Oxfam, Red Cross and several other NGOs were represented. The other security experts and I tried very hard to disabuse the NGOs of the now completely discredited idea of 'safety through engagement' with the communities they worked alongside. The basic premise is that if a gang or terrorist target an aid worker, that worker will be protected by the local community because they are there to help that community. My personal view is that, if it ever worked in the past, safety through engagement is defunct in today's world. With the likes of al-Qaeda changing the rules, all bets are off. No one is off limits any more. It used to be, for example, that journalists had some limited immunity from being targeted or kidnapped because they were the terrorists' means of communication with the outside world. Cases like Daniel Pearl prove otherwise.

I know of a case where a large, well-known NGO dispatched a twenty-two-year-old blonde girl directly to Darfur, Sudan, straight from her safe, comfortable home in Alabama. Safety through engagement is not going to protect her any more than a cloak of invisibility will. I am all for helping others in any way we can and fortunately, she's okay, but today's terrorism means that war is no longer about soldiers shooting soldiers. Terrorism is about civilians killing civilians. No one is immune.

20

THE CYCLE

At any given time there are hundreds of hostages in captivity all over the world.

This is a snapshot of a typical month in the world of K&R.

In Nigeria's Niger Delta, nineteen people, including two Americans, two Frenchmen and a Canadian, were taken hostage by militants. They were subsequently rescued by security forces in a land, sea and air assault on the stronghold – the first time a rescue attempt had been executed in Nigeria without any losses among those held captive and one of the few examples of a successful hostage rescue operation. A week earlier in South Africa, a local woman on honeymoon with her British husband was killed after being abducted by an armed gang. Around the same time, three Latvian helicopter crewmen working in Sudan were kidnapped and later freed. The Darfur region is one of the current hotspots for K&R and has made it virtually impossible to conduct aid operations in the area as foreign aid workers retreat from the countryside to the main towns to make themselves less vulnerable to abduction. It's funny how people often seem to change their mind about things like safety through engagement once they're on the ground.

Three thousand miles away, kidnappers took a four-year-old Chinese girl hostage after her parents left her at home while at work. They broke into the apartment and snatched the girl along with a bank card. The kidnappers then contacted the parents and threatened to kill the girl unless they gave up the PIN number for the bank card. They gave up the number but the girl's body was later found in a creek near her home.

In the Philippines, a businesswoman was abducted by a gang at gunpoint. Her husband was shot and wounded as he tried to rescue her and another man was killed by stray gunfire. Five days later the woman was released in a village in another province after a joint rescue operation.

In Europe, Austrian police arrested a seventy-year-old man after he spoke to a friend in Los Angeles about his plan to kidnap a California-based jeweller. The friend happened to be an FBI informant. Two Hungarians and an American arms dealer were detained as part of the plot. The gang planned to abduct the jeweller and demand a $5 million ransom.

America was witness to a number of kidnap attempts in the same period. A gang posing as cops abducted a local businessman in San Jose. They demanded $1 million for his release. He was subsequently rescued, although it's unclear if any ransom was eventually paid. Across in St Louis, four men abducted two teenage girls. It transpired that a relative of the girls had been involved in a hold-up at an ATM company some months previously. They were rescued by the FBI the following day.

At least they had been unharmed. In Ecuador two armed men kidnapped a sports reporter while he was on a bus returning from Muisne up the coast to Esmeraldas in the north-west of the country. The men hauled him off the bus and forced him into their getaway vehicle. The kidnappers beat the crap out of him and threatened to kill him and his relatives if he published an investigation he had been carrying out into identity theft by a football player of an evangelic pastor. Seven hours later he was released, the men having trashed his video camera, tape recorder and mobile phone. And in Guatemala, a pro soccer player was killed and chopped into pieces after being abducted on his way to a restaurant. A note found with the body – dumped in five plastic bags under a bridge – suggested the man had been murdered for messing with the woman of another man.

These are just the cases that are reported. Putting an accurate number on the total kidnaps per year globally is impossible because the vast majority of relatives will never contact the police.

We can't prevent kidnappings. But it is possible to equip people with the knowledge necessary to better deal with being abducted. I am often asked to brief people on what to expect if they're kidnapped. Which is a little tricky, since nothing in the average person's psyche and life experience prepares them for the sheer terror of being snatched away at gunpoint. How do you explain to someone that they'll experience probably the most frightening, violent action of their lives? That there will be a lot of screaming and shouting and there's a good chance that guns will be fired? That people might be shot, even killed? That they will be bundled into a getaway vehicle, ears ringing with the sound of discharged assault rifles, the smell of cordite burning their nose, the metallic taste of blood and fear on their tongues? That their heart will be beating so fast it'll feel like it's about to explode?

Answer: you can't.

But you can prepare them for what happens next.

You tell them, they will probably be blindfolded or have a

hood pulled over their head. They might also be handcuffed or tied up with rope or parachute cord. They will be living in cramped conditions, sometimes in a cell-like space no bigger than a closet, the kind of place where you have to leave the room just to change your mind. Sometimes it's a hole in the ground. They will be dirty and have to endure poor hygiene, disgusting food and if they are in a tropical environment, illness is likely to occur, for which they are unlikely to receive treatment. Depending on their captors, they might be beaten up and tortured. If they're a woman, they might be raped. Or they might not but the kidnappers will threaten them all the same.

Then you tell them that it's vital they try to stay calm.

You tell them, don't attempt to escape unless you're 100-per-cent-guaranteed for sure that it'll work and that you have the means to survive outside the stronghold. Escaping from your kidnappers only to find yourself in the middle of the desert without a drop of water to hand does *not* constitute a solid escape plan.

Nor should you ever play the hero. Far better to assume the role of the 'grey man'. Be obedient. Do as your captors say. Defying them might look good on the silver screen but in real life it's liable to result in the gang kicking the crap out of you or worse. Wear a slightly depressed expression. In a group situation, try to avoid standing out. Make yourself inconspicuous. Kidnappers will often single out one person from the group of hostages to be the scapegoat – the whipping boy. Don't let that person be you.

Hostages shouldn't look their captors in the eye. Unless there's a good reason to. Making eye contact can be a good idea, as I've said. Look them in the eye and you begin the ancient human process of becoming a person, not a piece of merchandise. I tell people to trust their instincts on this one. Millions of years of evolution can't be wrong. Everyone alive on planet Earth today has something in common: every single one of our ancestors lived long enough to reproduce. So it stands to reason that there's got to be something in our make-up that tells us how to operate in order to survive.

If the circumstances of their incarceration permit, ideally, the hostage should try to establish a rapport with their captors. It's a lot harder to kill John the family man who's a United fan and watches *Top Gear* than it is to kill the forty-year-old fat bourgeois guy in the corner with no name.

It's also very important to look after yourself both mentally and physically. Exercise religiously. Push-ups, squats, pacing around your cell – anything to keep your body limber. More importantly, you've got to keep your mind limber too. Tend to your psychological well-being. Mind games are a great way of staying mentally alert. Think positively about the future. And never, ever attempt to negotiate for your own ransom with the kidnappers. You will only be undermining the good work of the negotiators. Remember that they're working tirelessly for your release and they're the professionals. You will be going home.

No hostage should expect a rescue attempt. One, they're very rare. Two, successful ones where no one is injured are rarer still. And three, it's the time when a hostage is most likely to get killed. That being said, hostages should identify the safest place to be in the event of a rescue attempt and lie down there if one starts. They should stay on the ground until the authorities physically pick or order them to get up. One of the reasons for this is that the human eye is attracted to movement. If you suddenly jump up you might get shot. It's also because kidnappers have been known to disguise themselves as hostages to try to get away.

The kidnap industry – and it is an industry – is in a growth phase that has been exacerbated by the global recession. In a world where resources are becoming ever scarcer, the people on the fringes of society who may have had a job before, now don't have a job. Or they have less of a job and less money. So they turn to other means of survival. In Africa we are seeing the rapid acceleration of Nigerian piracy. As in Somalia, the pirates carry out their attacks under the banner of political resentment at greedy foreign nationals. Somali pirates have previously defended their activity by claiming that foreign vessels have polluted their coastline and put their fishermen out of business. Their Nigerian counterparts argue that foreign companies operating in and along the Niger Delta are siphoning wealth out of their country. Easy access to firearms in places like Lagos means that the pirates are armed and dangerous.

K&R is like a cancer. When it emerges in a country, it spreads. It takes root. It bleeds the country dry of wealth. It sows terror in the minds of the one class of people – ordinary, decent, hardworking citizens – capable of lifting the nation out of the mire, and it undermines lucrative industries like tourism and investment. When the lid comes off a country and all the systems and political machinery and law enforcement that keep people's behaviour in check melt away, kidnapping tends to flourish. Almost everyone has antisocial tendencies of some kind. But we're fortunate enough to live in societies of plenty, where we can choose to work or go on welfare or steal stuff. If you find yourself in a desperate situation, in a country where there's no alternative means of making money, kidnapping might appear to be a viable option. And once the seed of it has taken root, it's hard to wipe out.

And like a cancer, kidnapping is always evolving and adapting to its environment. Organised crime operates outside the law. It has to adapt to a rapidly changing world, and kidnapping has always thrived on the principles of emotional exploitation, fear and control. The financial reward outweighs the risk of apprehension. The more kidnapping prospers in a country, the harder it becomes for law enforcement to lance the boil. Profits from ransom then fund a new crimewave and enable the gangs to corrupt the justice system through bribery.

The cycle repeats itself.

In May 2010 I was giving a lecture at the London Business School in Regent's Park. LBS is an international school and my audience came from all over the world. One of the students told me a story. He was from Bolivia. He said his cousin had been the victim of an express kidnapping. They seized him at eleven o'clock on a Friday night, took him to an ATM machine and forced him to withdraw as much cash as the ATM allowed. The machines reset the daily limit at precisely midnight. At one minute past midnight the kidnappers hit another ATM and the cousin had to make a fresh withdrawal. He was gone for the weekend. When the student contacted the police, they suggested the cousin had gone to the beach for the weekend or was shacked up with his girlfriend, or his mobile phone had broken or run out of juice. Forty-eight hours is perfect for an express kidnap. After three days, relatives begin to worry. The police might look into it. If the criminals time the withdrawals right, they can make up to £2000 in a single weekend. Along with virtual kidnappings, I think we are likely to see a huge increase in express kidnappings like these in the near future. You can make a lot of money in a short period of time and you don't need the resources associated with a traditional kidnapping. There's no real need for a stronghold. You don't have to pay guards for weeks on end or burn cash feeding the victim.

At the end of the lecture, an Asian woman in her twenties approached me and stole my attention with the line, 'Have you heard about how the government in my country is carrying out kidnaps?'

The local municipal government in the north-west region of this emergent country is run by a minority coalition partner in the central government. The region is rich in sugar plantations.

In this backwater area, the government will kidnap the manager of a plantation, take him across the border to a neighbouring country and demand a ransom from the plantation company. Up in the central government nobody bats an eyelid at this. The coalition holding the country together is fragile and government ministers can't afford to upset the apple cart in case the coalition breaks up and they find themselves ousted from power.

There are signs, too, that Yemen is becoming a dangerous place for Westerners. Tourists have been kidnapped by rebel groups looking to force concessions from the government. It will come as no surprise to learn that Yemen is also the poorest country in the Middle East and is earning a reputation internationally as a focal point of Islamic militant unrest and the home of an al-Qaeda training base.

There's more wealth in the world today than there has ever been at any point in human history. That means there is also more potential for making money illicitly now than at any other point in human history. Criminals will continue to extort money from families and companies by taking people hostage. What concerns me more, as a negotiator, is the propagation of religious fundamentalism, and from every religion. Fundamentalism in the twenty-first century has mostly been an Islamic problem. Developments in the Yemen and unrest elsewhere suggest it will continue to be. But there is a new group of fervent religious movements including the new wave of Christian fundamentalism in America, which has deeply political undertones, and foreign dogmatic organisations. You only have to look back at the surge in Christian militia movements in the nineties to understand the threat that such groups can pose to a country at large.

In the wake of 9/11, the Manchester Metropolitan Police Force located a training manual during the search of a suspected al-Qaeda member's home. Describing itself as 'the military series' of the 'Declaration of Jihad', the manual listed the 'Missions

Required of the Military Organization'. Number two on this list read, 'Kidnaping [*sic*] enemy personnel, documents, secrets and arms.' We've already seen these orders carried out in Afghanistan and Iraq to deadly effect. I have no doubt that religiously motivated kidnappings will crop up in many other countries in the coming days, months and years. The challenge for hostage negotiators will be to devise strategies for countering the kidnappers' tactics and to look for ways of securing the release of hostages other than paying a ransom, which in any case will be redundant.

As I described earlier, politico-religious kidnappings are volatile and have a greater chance of ending in bloodshed. The negotiator has fewer bargaining chips with the kidnapper. If the criminal believes God is on his side, he's not going to listen to anything I have to say. I liken it to reasoning with that drunk. You just can't do it.

Bottom line, trying to stop kidnapping is like trying to stop oxygen. You can be against it but it's everywhere. It's all about money. It manipulates the emotional bond that exists between two people – and it works. What kind of parent wouldn't pay any amount of money in the world to free their child? What husband or wife wouldn't do anything to free their spouse? Until human beings stop caring about each other, kidnap will be a part of our lives.

But what kind of world would that be?

A worse one than we have now, I think.

Other bestselling titles available by mail

☐ Seal Team Six   Howard E. Wasdin and Stephen Templin   £7.99

The prices shown above are correct at time of going to press. However, the publishers reserve the right to increase prices on covers from those previously advertised, without further notice.

sphere

Please allow for postage and packing: **Free UK delivery.**
Europe: add 25% of retail price; Rest of World: 45% of retail price.

To order any of the above or any other Sphere titles, please call our credit card orderline or fill in this coupon and send/fax it to:

Sphere, PO Box 121, Kettering, Northants NN14 4ZQ
Fax: 01832 733076   Tel: 01832 737526
Email: aspenhouse@FSBDial.co.uk

☐ I enclose a UK bank cheque made payable to Sphere for £ . .
☐ Please charge £ . . . . to my Visa/Delta/Maestro

Expiry Date ☐☐☐☐   Maestro Issue No. ☐☐

NAME (BLOCK LETTERS please) . . . .
ADDRESS . . . .
. . . .
. . . .
Postcode . . . . Telephone . . . .
Signature . . . .

Please allow 28 days for delivery within the UK. Offer subject to price and availability.